Twice Upon a Court

Erlinda Dominguez

Book design and printing by Falcon Books

San Ramon, California

Library of Congress Control Number: 2010903479
Paperback edition ISBN: 978-0-615-35919-9
Hard cover edition ISBN: 978-0-615-40813-2

Published by
Advance New York Publisher
244 Fifth Ave Suite # H233
New York, NY, 10001
212-252-2336

www.ErlindaDominguezAttorney.com

This is a documentary of what truly happened in my successful law practice in Hawaii, U.S.A. I made every effort to clearly and fairly set forth the events that I personally experienced, aware that word for word accounting in a book is impossible. But there are verbatim quotes from the court records, and records don't lie. I fight alone, and my opponents are many. They include high-ranking political figures in the Hawaiian State. They would necessarily have a different perspective- this is freedom of thought and speech in America. My style of narration is for the reader to better understand my personal experiences in the technical world of "law practice." There is only one truth and I hope to find that in the readers of this book. This is my true story.

"The world of books is the most remarkable creation of man. Nothing else that he builds ever lasts. Monuments fall, nations perish, civilizations grow old and die out, and after an era, new races build others. But in the world of books are volumes that have seen this happen again and again and yet live on, still young, still as fresh as the day they were written, still telling men's hearts of the heart of men centuries dead."

—Clarence Day

♦ to all the clients of "The Dominguez Law Offices" in Honolulu, Hawaii;

♦ to all my friends and clients in the Philippines decades ago;

♦ to all who gave me moral support and human compassion;

♦ to all who don't have the logistics or the courage to speak, to fight for their rights;

Finally, but not the least:

♦ to the Philippine Hero, the late Jose Rizal, who taught Filipinos to respect others without being subservient, to speak for their rights without taking arms—and he was executed by the adversaries facing the bullets.

—I love you all, The Author

Foreword

Twice Upon a Court is the compelling saga of one woman's journey from a village on a mountaintop in the Philippines, to a Law Professorship in a University and finally to a thriving law practice in the Island Paradise, Hawaii.

In a modest and unassuming manner, Erlinda Dominguez tells step by step the harrowing story of how she came to be attacked and very nearly destroyed, personally and professionally, by members of the Legal Community, who had every reason to be biased and judgmental against her success, yet allowed their biases to influence their judgment.

Ms. Dominguez worked hard for the interests of her law clients, who were trying to obtain justice in personal injury cases, and she helped many people gain their rights under the law. When she herself was placed in jeopardy, she had great faith in the American Legal System, an institution that her father had always told her was the finest in the world. Sad but true, a system is only as fine as those who administer it, and they are unfortunately only human after all.

The author found herself virtually penniless, deprived of her law office and practice that she had built up from scratch, and beset on every side by unfair and questionable tactics from those who seemed determined to ruin her. She is now telling her story as a testament to truth, and also as a fascinating and in many

ways horrifying cautionary tale to those who may be too inclined
to trust that people mean what they say.

Her first book, *Twice Upon a Court,* is a deeply revealing look
behind the scenes of American Jurisprudence, from the point of
view of an intelligent and warm-hearted woman who rises to a
position of trust from which she is able to win justice for her clients, only to be denied justice for herself.

—Roberta Tennant
Editor
Falcon Books

Chapter One

It was in the mid 90s, hurriedly reaching into the year 2000, the turn of the century. My Law Office was conspicuously located in front of the Ala Moana Shopping Center in Honolulu, Hawaii. Nobody would miss it during Christmas. Neon lights draped the Commerce Tower. A huge sign, *Maligayang Pasko*, wished passersby a Merry Christmas in Tagalog, a Filipino dialect.

The back door made it convenient for me to get in and out. I would not be in leg traffic with my clients. By the elevator, I could see the waiting room through clear expanded glass. That would prepare me for what to expect shortly.

This day was typical. I returned from my quick lunch at the mall to find seven adults and a child in the waiting room.

My receptionist, Youme Glanry, was assisting a woman in filling out a questionnaire. Two other women were reading the award plaques for my office. They decorated the waiting room.

Four men were seated on the couch looking at the wall-to-wall murals of Philippine scenes. One stood up to peer through his glasses and read the inscription in brass—Especially Commissioned for the Law Offices of Erlinda Dominguez. A five-year-old boy slept beneath the sign.

The mural was a tribal ceremony of men wearing loin cloths and women with bare breasts. Colorful festivity. The tribe was giving thanks to the heavens for a bountiful harvest.

Mila Cubero, my manager, was talking to the man reading the inscription. She always explained in Tagalog, "It depicts the birthplace of the attorney in the Mountain Province, a remote place in the Philippines. A gift from her mother."

The visitors were all Filipino, except two White men in military uniform. I was to see these officers in half an hour. Both were calmly seated. One was reading the *Honolulu Bulletin*, a daily newspaper.

Sinbad, the office parrot, was perched atop the tall aquarium. He was out of his cage and free to fly around.

Nobody truly knew if the parrot was a boy or a girl. We called him a he and my legal assistant, Dawn Blazet, named him. He seemed entranced with the color of the fresh water fish.

Sinbad was taught to say policy limits. This referred to the highest amount an insurance company could pay the client. He would scream the words repeatedly when he sensed the presence of an attorney, a court reporter, or an insurance adjuster. They were amused.

At that time, he was docile. That was the scene.

The office had the makings of a zoo. But our clients were entertained and they were happy.

* * *

My Law practice was very active. I focused on personal injury. I was a solo practitioner.

I handled varied cases: Dog bites, car accidents, medical malpractice, slips and falls, product liability.

My clients knew they could depend on me. I was a lawyer in the Philippines and in Hawaii. I was an adjuster for Allstate, then for First Insurance Company. The combination of my experiences paid well.

"Erlinda, you have cornered the Filipino market, cases are coming out of your ears."

Kind compliments. And they were from doctors, practicing attorneys, insurance adjusters, and even court employees.

And they may not have known that I had a countless number of clients of other races. I was driven to help injury victims. My color was not important to them. Their color was not important to me.

My employees were also of various races. They came from all over: Asia, Micronesia, California. Everyone wanted to live and work in Hawaii, a paradise island.

None was racist. Even if they were, it did not show. After all, I was Asian and had an accent that I could never completely discard. Not that I would aspire to, anyway.

There was no gender discrimination either. My associate attorneys were all male. This was not planned. Men happened to outnumber female personal injury lawyers in the State.

Most Hawaii female attorneys would rather be State judges or in other areas of the law.

I intensely trained my staff. They were sectioned into manager, associate attorneys, paralegals, legal assistants, secretaries, and receptionists.

We all had to work physically, intelligently, even emotionally. A soothing difference in this robotized age.

Honest and quality work was essential, or I would fire and hire. Frequently, the turn-over was quick. I sought practical and simple resolutions.

It worked. A normal office day started with a cup of coffee and progressed into meetings, calls, and trips to the courthouses.

Pleasant exasperation. Most of the time, this seemed true for everybody.

I labored for the clients and for my employees. They enjoyed their fair pay, extended holidays, and catered food at office expense. They thanked me for spoiling them—sometimes!

My legal assistants, Janet Souza, Wanda Paresa, and Chris Dique, loved to attend the Filipino functions. I always had representatives. Our office name was printed on the back page of every magazine in the Filipino celebrations.

The functions were musical, colorful, and fun. But they always fell on impossible dates. I never attended. Nor could I attend awards ceremonies in the Philippines.

My mother knew I could not leave my office for great lengths of time, and she was all too excited to accept awards on my behalf. Although she was over seventy, she had the strength to travel back and forth to the Philippines.

Clients learned to express their gratitude with food. The results showed in some of us.

"We wish your ladies to be sexy and heavy," joked Joe, Bernie, and Ernie of the Filipino radio stations. Their co-host, Maggie, loved the song, "*Igorota*," meaning a mountain woman in Filipino. Her listeners had our office in their mind.

Our hundreds of clients rapidly grew in number. Their presence in the office was always welcome. Often, a simple answer for their claim status was all they needed.

Many came with cervical collars, casts, or canes. To chase the gloom away, my paralegal, Linda Huang, played the huge music box in the reception area.

The grateful amazement on the faces of the clients was most rewarding when we handed them their fat checks.

I was extremely lucky to practice law in the United States of America—even more lucky to be practicing in the beautiful tourist attraction of Hawaii.

My father used to say, "America has the greatest and the fairest court system in the whole wide world."

His education stopped at fifth grade. He read the local magazines in his *sari-sari* store on the mountain of a small Philippine town. He sold all sorts of things: Dried fish, pots and pans, sardines, loin-cloths for men and tapis skirts for women, even trinkets to decorate their bodies.

My father never saw my large office in Honolulu. Only my tiny room in Chinatown when I was struggling and where I accepted any case, from simple divorces to murder defense. It paid the rent.

I called it general practice. That was before it prospered to personal injury.

In my large office, I implemented an office motto: "Life is too short, let's do the right thing now; Sinbad and tomorrow may not be here!"

Another office motto also took root: "Politicking is despicable and ugly in this office. You lose focus on the merits of your work. Don't do it!"

None of us was really into politics. I never took advantage of the personally signed invitations from the White House. I thought they were flyers. My employees said they were not. The U.S. president and a few senators requested my presence at their exclusive dinners. What an extreme honor—no matter what the purpose was.

"A big opportunity for politicians to grab, some salivate for that," my staff would say. They teased me to travel to Washington and shake hands with President Bush, Sr.

It would have been exciting, but politics was not in me. I never went. Our work was enough.

As the day ended, I could hear footsteps going out the door. One voice after another greeted the office parrot, "Goodnight, Sinbad, guard the office well. We will bring you more nuts tomorrow."

I could see Sinbad from where I sat. The door to my room was always open. He never learned to say goodnight. He was melancholy at day's end. As if he wondered, "Will you really bring me my nuts tomorrow? Will you really come see me again?"

Then, lights were turned off and all were gone.

* * *

It was past 8:30 a.m. one Monday morning. Everyone was in the conference room for our monthly general meeting.

"I'm sorry I'm late. Heavy traffic. An accident happened."

"Yeah, it takes time to scatter your business cards on the street."

"Someone did that last night on same spot," I said. I knew they were just joking.

We all had a copy of the calendar for the next three months. We had to prepare for things to come.

"What happened here?" I pointed to one particular page of the office calendar. It was an extra large book that we paid a tailor to customize. It housed all our office schedules. It was ugly but it served our purpose better than a dozen computers.

"There are four cases scheduled for trial back to back, almost on the same dates," I said. My worry showed.

I directed my comment to Mila. She had a spectacular memory and could be depended on for a ready response.

Instead, Mila looked concerned and a bit fearful. She was this way when she should have done better—in this case, to realize the problem and call it to my attention earlier.

"I entered the dates that Tom Walsh gave me," she apologized.

She used the full name to distinguish him from Tom Kaster. Both were my associate attorneys. As a matter of habit and clarity, we often called each Tom by his full name.

Tom Walsh handled the status conferences. At these conferences, the judge and attorneys worked together to schedule the trial and all pre-trial events and deadlines. The system generally served to avoid postponements.

I invited Tom into my office. I didn't want to have this discussion in front of the others. When I was annoyed, it showed. But he would make excuses, like he had a bad weekend.

Tom's face was flushed and his eyes were red like he had no sleep. I knew he had problems as did everyone else.

"What's the problem, Tom?"

"Nothing, nothing."

"Don't you bring your calendar to the court? You know I have to be at these trials and each one could last a week."

"That's what the judge gave, and that's it," he explained as if it did not matter what the predicament was. I could not believe what he was saying.

Things did not happen that way and I ended the conversation.

I walked to my manager's room.

"Mila, you have to tell me the problems you observe in the office."

I sat myself so that her desk was between us.

"Do you think Tom brings his problems to the office?" Mila glanced at her partly opened door. She was apprehensive that Tom was within earshot.

"Yes. And girls at the front desk notice, too."

"And why was I not informed?"

"I was going to tell you, but you're always in arbitration or court."

Then, she looked more concerned. "Dr. Cel Guerrero also called. She was testifying in a deposition for a client's case. She said Tom Walsh attended, was wearing dark glasses and almost fell off his chair. He left her clinic and never returned."

"Is that true? And did he hurt himself?"

"I read the deposition transcript and the doctor was telling the truth. I marked the pages," said Mila.

My mind was reeling. There were problems in the office. An outsider had to tell us.

"Are there any other problems in this office that I should be aware of?"

"Linda Huang and Byron Hu don't get along. There is a severe personality clash."

After he resigned as deputy prosecutor, I hired Byron as an associate attorney. Linda was my head paralegal, a former Taiwanese beauty queen.

"And as the office manager, what else do you know that you keep to yourself, Mila?" I was mildly sarcastic.

"Some lady employees dislike the dress protocol imposed by their supervisor, Ray Ozaki. They want to bare their upper thighs and cleavage. They say it helps them function in humid weather even with the air-conditioner on full blast!"

Mila was not trying to be funny. She was dead serious.

After our conversation, I met with my employees and tried to patch up differences. Our conferences distracted us from real work. But everybody agreed to cooperate.

Those were expected intervals. Soon, the office would be back to its hectic pace—and all at reasonable peace.

* * *

Late in the week, I called up the clerk of Judge Patrick Yim. He was the Administrative Judge. He took charge of scheduling trials in the First Circuit. This included the County of Honolulu, Island of Oahu, in the State of Hawaii.

I asked for an appointment with the judge. Pursuant to rules, I promised not to discuss the merits of any case. The clerk called back.

"The judge said, come tomorrow afternoon. He will see you in chambers when he is free."

I dressed up formally. I hoped that Judge Yim would remember my first criminal jury trial. I defended the accused in a case of kidnapping, rape, and assault. It was in his court and lasted for several days.

If he remembered me, I would have credibility. After that trial, he complimented my performance. His court reporter nodded and agreed.

That was off the record.

My Filipino accent was stronger then but my English was good. There is no reason the judge could not understand me now even if I become distraught, I thought to myself.

The clerk offered me a seat outside of Judge Yim's chambers. Then, the judge walked to my seat.

"What's up, Ms. Dominguez?"

"I am sorry if this is inappropriate, Judge."

"Go ahead, I'm listening."

"Sir, I have four cases that are unfortunately scheduled simultaneously in different courtrooms. I always attend and I have only one body."

I did not know why I said it that way. It almost sounded lewd. It must have been my anxiety at appearing before him on such short notice.

"Sir, I wonder if I could prepare the motions to postpone without aggravating Your Honor." I was clearly nervous.

The judge pulled up a chair and sat in front of me.

"Erlinda, how did this happen?"

He called me by my first name. Perhaps, he noticed I was mustering all my strength. I managed to blame myself and some confusion in the office.

The judge seemed to size me up as I spoke. He was in deep thought.

"I'm sorry, Ms. Dominguez, I can't do anything. It would be unfair to the others. Their witnesses are from out of State. You may be wasting your time filing motions."

Judge Yim started a bit of socializing. Obviously, to ease my tension.

"I commend you for your practicing law here when you were born in the Philippines. Do you have a partner?"

"No, Sir. I have associate attorneys."

He shook his head mildly. I knew that he was about to suggest something.

"I empathize with you. Perhaps, you should seek another law firm to help in the scheduled trials. But I won't tell you how to run your business. You're very successful."

I went back to the office. I started to prepare the cases that were going to trial. I still had time.

Mila followed me to my room. I could sense she wanted to discuss other problems.

"There are many settlement checks that have to be cleared." She laid them down on my desk.

"Good, the clients will be happy."

Mila's forehead folded.

"Not really. The checks are no good."

"What exactly do you mean?" I mildly raised my voice.

"The medical providers, the no-fault, and TDI people are slow with their liens. Now, they are putting their names on the checks where we can't endorse."

Could this be happening?

My voice showed my anxiety from talking to the administrative judge.

"What do you think, should we stop accepting new cases? Should we farm out some cases? Should we just close our office and work on the hundreds we have?" I asked.

I never said those words to anyone before. I wondered what I was really thinking.

Mila murmured almost in a whisper as her gaze dropped, "We will fail the community, we will disappoint the clients. Please, E.D., don't."

Everyone called me by my first name. Many times, they called me E.D., initials for Erlinda Dominguez. This was normal in the office, calling each other by initials. It was as frequent as calling everyone with full names.

Several options were in my mind. One evening, I handed a list to Mila. It was short.

She glanced at it then removed and cleaned her glasses. Her mood dropped. She did not speak a word.

"Please assess our options on the list. I wish the two of us to discuss them next week. Don't tell the others. I don't want them to worry. Don't even mention it to anyone," I pleaded.

Work in the office continued as usual. Mila and I did not discuss the list. She stayed at work until almost midnight each evening, even on the weekends.

She did the work of others when they were sick or on vacation, as if to say, "There is no need for your options, E.D., everything is alright, we can take care of hundreds more cases at anytime."

Mila did not know what I was thinking and seemed afraid to ask. I didn't open up a discussion.

The employees appeared to suspect. The meetings had become shorter. I was available for all their questions, but they seemed to shy away.

* * *

Brian Oyadomari met with me in a downtown restaurant. He owned an active arbitration office in Honolulu. Trial attorneys, even judges, were on his list of arbitrators.

Brian was not an attorney but he knew the intricacies of personal injury practice. Much more so than many attorneys. He had been an insurance supervisor in personal injury claims.

We were acquaintances, not even close friends, but we could speak at a professional level. I started to talk about the office and my options.

"Erlinda, what a waste if you stop accepting new cases just like that. You are of tremendous help to your clients and to the community—especially the Filipinos. Where will they go? They'll feel abandoned."

The topic actually shocked him. He did not wish to listen. He changed the subject to superficial social conversation.

I went back to the office. My paralegal, Linda, was eager to talk to me.

"The girls were asking me what you have in mind."

"About what?"

"They saw Mr. Price talking to you in your room. It seems that you are out of the office more than usual."

Warren Price was the highly profiled Attorney General for the State of Hawaii. He joined the law firm of his spouse, Sharon Himeno, after he left that government high position. His firm had either been my opponent or co-counsel in a few cases.

"Didn't they think we were discussing a mutual claim?"

"It is obvious you were not, E.D."

I had become quite transparent to my staff. And I worried over their pay, their benefits, and well-being.

The office would still be extremely solvent even if I farmed out cases. It would hurt my clients emotionally, but they would understand. Clients referred their ancestors, descendants, all relatives, and friends to me. We did not need the yellow pages or the internet.

I wanted to confide in Linda, but chose to do so at a later time.

* * *

Days thereafter, Brian and I again met for breakfast. I told him of the office and my possible options. He knew I was serious. He was intently listening.

"I intend to refer new clients to other law firms. Many lawyers have been calling, even writing me. I wonder how they know," I said.

"They have the crumbs and you have the cake," remarked Brian with a chuckle. "Who are those lawyers contacting you anyway?"

I mentioned a few including Agena, Graulty, Martin, Griffith, and Kidani. I knew them to be successful attorneys.

"The word is around that cases are coming out of your ears and clients line up to see you. The legal community likes to gossip when it comes to news like that. Even Hisaka, Agard, or Chung may be interested, who knows," said Brian.

"They have stable and decent law firms, as far as I know. It may be nice to meet with them."

"If I were you, I would choose Price, Okamoto, Himeno and Lum."

That law firm was better known for its initials, POHL. "Why do you prefer them?" I was curious.

"Well, it's actually none of my business, but everyone knows the Himeno family is extremely rich. Mr. Price is the recent State Attorney General, highly profiled and always in the news...their firm must really be very, very powerful, that's public knowledge, oh, yeah."

"I heard that said by many, but I don't really know Mr. Price and his office." And I stared at Brian's face feeling somewhat scared at our topic and the words we were saying. "I don't understand what power has to do with anything. I'm just in legal practice, and I certainly don't need their money," I said.

Brian raised his eyebrow. I may have looked like a simpleton.

"I'm not implying anything, Erlinda. It's completely up to you. You asked and I answered. I don't know more than what the public knows of them. They are always in the papers."

Breakfast was over. I grabbed for the check but Brian had already paid. As usual.

Chapter Two

I met with two partners of the Pohl firm. My only other experience with them was when I faced Warren Price and Sharon Himeno in a civil jury trial, before they were married. That was years ago, must have been in the late 80s.

"What can you offer?" I asked meekly.

"We will pay all expenses and co-counsel with you in all of your claims and cases. We want a blanket take-over," said Sharon Himeno.

Her statement sent shivers to my spine.

"And in return, what do I get?" I was scared, but it did not show.

"You will have freedom and lots of money," said Ken Okamoto. He was married to Sharon's sister, Sandy.

"There are two parts to what you said, Ken. Please explain the freedom part, then the lots of money. How will either of these benefit my clients?"

"Our accountants reviewed your tax returns, Erlinda, and here are the figures."

Ken had writing on every inch of his notepad.

"We pay all the overhead and we keep eighty-five percent of the profits. You keep fifteen percent, which is still a lot of money."

"How about the freedom part?" I asked.

"You will be relieved of work and do what you want."

"You mean I will stop being a lawyer?"

"No, you will be like a queen bee gathering nectar into the door and we will do all the work."

Obviously, we had become comfortable in our discussions. Even metaphorical.

"I don't want to be a queen. I will still have to work...clients depend on me. Without me, they will stop coming. The money isn't as important as my relationship with my clients."

"That's why we intend to hire your own employees and add new employees."

My concern and timidity couldn't be masked.

"Erlinda, we are hoping that the flow of your clients will continue. You are a real rainmaker," said Sharon.

"We will do all the work while you socialize with the clients, wine and dine them, attend all their functions and celebrations," said Ken.

"That's not my style, Ken. Besides, what will we talk about except their claims and cases anyway? We'll just be transferring my conference room to the restaurants or to their celebrations."

Sharon took the notepad in her hand. She was reviewing the figures. She turned up the pages and her eyes widened.

"Wow! Is this over a thousand? How did you manage to get hundreds of clients as a solo practitioner?"

"Lots of know-how and, of course, hard work," I said as if I wanted to confirm that I was competent in my private practice.

"We assure you, nothing will change. Your clients will be coming to your office, meeting with your employees. Your office will only improve with good management and we will add more employees."

I was a bit offended.

"I trained my staff, Sharon. They are extremely competent and know what they are doing. We work hard. I've been told they are the best trained staff in town!"

"Erlinda, you'll be liberated from the stress of management. And I can see it now—there will even be more clients," said Sharon.

Their good intent was clear and I felt some relief. "Will you really promise to keep all my employees?"

"Of course."

"And always keep my office place for the convenience of the clients?"

"Sure. That's part of your appeal to the clients."

* * *

I had time to think things out. The future was promising. Clients would be happier. There would be more cases. There would be less stress on myself and my staff.

But something still didn't feel right. I knew they were highly political, but what could people mean about Pohl's power? I quickly shrugged off this concern. I shouldn't be questioning if it could help my clients and my office.

Prior to closing the deal, subtle fear of signing the contract crept over me. I was all by my puny self. But I had no reason to over-think. A good opportunity should be welcome.

Within days, I accepted what Pohl offered. A partnership was born. We called our relation co-counseling or liaison, still bearing the Law Offices of Erlinda Dominguez on our letterhead. This would avoid confusion with their partnership called Pohl.

It was early in the day. I asked Mila to gather all the members of my office staff. The front door was locked, with a note pasted to it, informing incoming visitors of our late opening. Everyone had to attend.

I was seated at the head of the conference table. Some employees remained standing. Normally, they would drag in extra chairs. They just stood, looking apprehensive and suspicious.

"I thank all of you for being a part of my office," I said softly but clearly. I did not want them to think I was choking on my own words.

"Very soon, this office will be owned by the law firm of Mr. Warren Price—you all know him, the famous recent Attorney General. You will be proud to be part of their group," I explained.

The employees had many questions. Many were concerned about their job security, their pay, their benefits. Some had concerns for me.

"What will happen to you, E.D.?"

"I will be here, I will be with you. I will still be working, but from what I was told, it won't be as much." They were quiet.

"Don't forget what you learned in this office—show your respect to all of them. Things will turn out for the best."

We reminisced about the office. It was our office. It was actually well known. And the employees were generally very loved and pampered by the clients and vice versa.

Things would even improve. I just knew it.

I stood up. They wanted some time to talk among themselves. I heard their kindness while I left the room. "Good luck, E.D."

The Pohl partners were introduced to the staff. Letters were sent to all the clients, or delivered to them when they came. The Dominguez and Pohl liaison was explained. We asked if anybody objected or was uncomfortable.

The Filipino clients hardly said anything. But they knew nationalities from the last names. They asked if the Pohl partners could speak their language. Some made subtle remarks such as, "Our color is different, we are worried."

"Don't ever put that in your heads. They are trustworthy, honest, and fair, even if we don't speak the same language, even if their color is different. This is America."

The clients absorbed what I said. Soon, they would see the partners in person, not just read of them in the news or see them on television.

* * *

I asked Linda to list all claims pending settlement. The two of us were extremely successful in settlement negotiations.

After the list was finalized, I turned to Mila.

"Tell the staff to prepare the files. Let's settle as much as possible. Pohl will be pleased with their profit."

Pohl was not a relative or a political ally. I had never been in that kind of contract before. But I knew our relationship was a respectable business venture.

"It's just over two weeks from your liaison and nearing a quarter of a million dollars in our office income—and in such a short time, too!" exclaimed Mila. "Will the profits all go to them?" she asked, showing concern and some regrets.

"Yes, all of that money will go to them. But they will pay the overhead including our rent for our beautiful office overlooking the ocean. I will have peanuts." I was smiling.

"But Erlinda, we did all the work!"

"That's alright, money isn't everything. Besides, Pohl will help us avoid problems."

Avoid problems? I said it without really thinking of the words. But I was right. There would be more staff, more lawyers to help me provide the quality service my office was already known for—and there would be many more clients as Pohl wanted.

Even if clients were already coming out of my ears, as described by many!

I was proud of Pohl and that my name was now associated with them. One noontime, Ken dropped by the office and came into my room. He closed the door. I suspected it must be a sensitive topic.

"Erlinda, do you mind writing an endorsement letter for Sharon? If she gets the appointment, she will be the first lady Justice of the Hawaii Supreme Court."

"I'd be honored, Ken. That's such a prestigious, moral, responsible and powerful job. I hope she makes it and will be called 'The Most Honorable Sharon Himeno.' What does anyone have against her?"

"Well, you know...political opponents think she severely lacks experience, and that Warren will do all the thinking and deciding appealed cases if she gets the job."

"Nothing may be wrong with that, Ken. Warren had great skills as the recent Attorney General and is Sharon's husband. She assisted Warren in the defense of one of my civil jury trials. Was that the only jury trial she had?" I asked.

Ken just smiled and said, "Our opponents are also attacking her family, allegedly involved in some questionable transactions when Warren was the Attorney General."

"They are crucifying her with rumors. She should exercise her due process, explain the truth," I said, without showing my total lack of experience in political talk.

Ken must have known that whatever he said was in the newspapers and he suspected I already knew.

Our conversation was short. He thanked me and said, "Sharon will get there. If not, there is someone else who will get that position."

"Who? Me?" I was obviously kidding around, hoping that Ken would give me a hint if he knew.

He returned the joke. It was embarrassing. "Do you really want to?"

"No, no—never!" I would never deserve such a sacred position, the ultimate guardian of law and justice.

"You should be in politics. You would easily be elected."

"Not in my wildest nightmares, Ken."

"Can you have one of your girls type your endorsement ASAP, Erlinda?"

"But of course."

I felt sorry for Sharon. She appeared as if she was fighting for her life on TV as her lack of experience was hurled at her. She came a fragment too close, but did not make it.

In a selfish way, I thought that was good for the office. Sharon would be there to help me invite more clients. She was always expensively dressed with designer clothes, and we could certainly use her tremendous appeal for the business.

* * *

In a few weeks, there was an urgent message on my desk. It was from Warren Price.

"Have you heard about the China Airlines disaster in Japan?" he asked.

"Yes, it's all over in the news, but I'm not familiar with the details."

"We should sign up all the Filipino clients." My mind was racing. They want me to be the bait.

"Warren, the clients are Filipino. They never set foot in Hawaii. The accident happened in Japan, the Airline is foreign. How in the world can we get U.S. federal jurisdiction here?"

I could hear his subtle laugh. It seemed he was on the loudspeaker and had people in his room.

"Don't worry, kiddo. We will do all the work."

That's real power, and I still don't know how and what it means, I thought to myself.

Ken Okamoto of Pohl and my manager, Mila, traveled to the Philippines. Flor Martinez went with them. He was my close friend who worked at the Philippine Consulate in Hawaii.

I provided them with the names and numbers of my friends in high esteem in the Philippine government who might be of help.

They brought a bunch of my business cards and the Philippine magazines where my Honolulu office was profiled.

One week in Manila—with first class hotels and accommodations—was expensive. But it paid off. They were one hundred percent successful.

Ken signed up each and every possible client, from serious injuries to wrongful deaths, all Filipinos, right in their hometown—in the Philippines.

I, a Hawaii lawyer, was actually retained as an attorney for people I never met. They just heard of me and saw my face in the Philippine magazines.

"Is this really ethical, Ken?" I asked upon their arrival in Honolulu.

"Of course, it is. We are only helping the unfortunate."

* * *

One evening, I dropped by the office to see my bookkeeper, Richard Gertz. He prepared some papers for me to sign. I depended on Richard to review and correct my financial statements done by an outside accountant.

"Why are all the lights still on this late in the evening, Richard?"

"People from Pohl were entering the files and data into the computers. They have been here many nights."

I thought that Pohl was wasting its time. The staff would best know their notes and many claims were ready for closure.

"Do you know why?"

"No, I am not privy to your plans. How much more could they improve your system anyway?" he said. "Your employees are organized, trained, and well functioning under the circumstances of your loads of clientele."

I decided to stay a bit longer and have a short talk. Richard looked at me like he was wondering if I had second thoughts. Then, he continued. "I'm a believer that if nothing is wrong, don't fix it," he said.

My worry began to show.

"Seems like they are burning all the files away. Do you suppose they will just depend on machines?"

"What exactly did you agree on?" he asked.

"That they will manage the office, nothing said about burning the files. Am I supposed to fear something?"

"Too late for that."

Richard's words scared me. What did he mean too late?

"I always wondered why you stopped going solo when your office was doing so great anyway," he said, looking as if he had concerns with the changes.

"Do you think something bad will happen to my office?"

"I hope not."

* * *

I arrived extremely early one Monday morning. I knew I would see Mila in the office. It was still dark.

"I'm worried. I'm actually terrified looking at these machines. And too many people going around in circles. We almost need traffic lights. I feel we are detached from the clients and from reality. Where are the files in shelf number twelve?" I asked, as I looked around.

"They were transported to Pohl's main office downtown. They are reviewing all the files. The employees wouldn't give out lists until I discuss it with the Pohl partners."

"You don't mean that!"

"I mean it. Such a waste of time for simple stuff. Permission there, permission here. It's hard to move forward. The pace has reached a stumbling block!" Mila complained.

"Be patient, all will stabilize. Pohl means well!"

Frustration and helplessness were shared by the staff. I discreetly gathered my old employees in my office one lunch break and realized that fear was building up.

"I apologize for the inconvenience. Please give us time to adjust. Show Pohl and their employees your respect. Everything will be alright."

It was in the middle of the week. A client walked in to find out when his claim would be settled. Confusion was apparent.

"Where's the file, Linda?" I asked my paralegal.

"It's with Pohl's manager." Linda was referring to Wendy Inouye, the new manager hired by Pohl. "She is computerizing the statutes of limitations," Linda said, referring to the last day the law allowed suit to be filed in the claim.

The file was located in one of the piles of papers on the floor next to Wendy's desk.

"The deadline is not in the computer and the time to file has already lapsed," I said in distress, making sure that the client could not hear us and did not suspect. I asked Linda to file the suit immediately and said, "Don't tell the insurance company the day of filing if asked."

In days, Linda successfully settled the claim. We told Wendy and expected that she would be pleased—we salvaged a claim where Pohl and I could be in a great deal of trouble.

Instead, Wendy seemed indifferent. She was too busy, going to each desk looking at what every employee was doing, including the associate attorneys—just looking and staring at their screens.

I felt I was the only one worrying. Pohl did not encourage my talking to them directly. Wendy had become a conduit of my messages to Pohl and vice versa.

A week later, five clients gathered in the waiting room. They wanted to know the status of their claims. I suspected they talked to other clients.

The employees were at a loss. Manual files were missing. Data in the computers were lacking. We had to reconstruct events. Luckily, my employees were trained to recall.

We thanked our memory. Job well done.

The front desk buzzed me. "There is a call for you from Warren Price, it seems urgent."

"Hi, Warren!"

"Erlinda, you have to do the arguments in the Ninth Circuit Appellate Court in about three days."

"You or your partners could take care of that, Warren, I have appointments to see clients throughout the week in addition to court and arbitration events I have to take care of."

"Erlinda, you sued the United States of America."

"That's just in form, Warren. The injuries of our client are very serious, and the defendant is an esteemed federal employee, I don't want him personally embarrassed."

"My point is, we are all busy, and the associates would not know where to begin," he said. "You may face malpractice if you don't go."

"You had control of the files for many months," Warren.

"Look for a local attorney who will assist you and we will pay what he wants," he said, sounding so alarmed.

I ended up doing the arguments with a hired attorney who did nothing but help me carry my files. I wondered why Warren talked of my possible malpractice, not theirs. But I did not give it a second thought and life in the office went on as usual.

* * *

"Erlinda, is there some way to back out from your contract with Pohl?" asked Linda with deep concern.

"Why do you ask?"

"They want us to follow their system and talk to the computers the whole day. We're having conflicts with their manager. When clients are disappointed, you're the front line—none of the Pohl partners are around. We are worried for you."

I knew exactly what she meant. Linda's concerns were appreciated. "Erlinda, they don't want our clients coming in the office, they prefer scheduled telephone calls," she said.

That part really bothered me. I called up Sharon and Ken. They devoted their time attending to their own cases at their Pohl firm in the downtown area. They did not call back.

Ken was in one day and I took the opportunity to express my concern. "We will lose our clients if there is no personal touch. The clients are not robots and many of them don't like telephone explanations," I said.

"I understand, I'll talk to Sharon and Wendy."

Mila was right. Permission there, permission here.

I invited Linda into my room, I did not want to lose her. She was well versed in legal documents and in settlements. Our office would be incapacitated if she left.

"Give us all a chance, Linda, and tell this to the rest of my employees. Pohl is doing its best to build, rather than wreck the office. Look at the computers they added and a few new employees. Everyone is struggling to adjust."

My old staff members were frequently called my employees. This distinguished them from the new ones hired by Pohl or those who came from their downtown office.

My employees were afraid to talk when a Pohl employee was around.

That was no way to function in an office, but I knew things would get better, sooner if not later.

But politicking had started to rear its ugly head, and I did not know how to stop it.

The Pohl partners, perhaps, were not even aware of what was happening.

Wendy had to pass on my concerns to either Ken or Sharon, then, to all the Pohl partners in their downtown office. I preferred not to speak too much. My employees understood and were quick to rectify the errors of others.

"E.D., we are instructed by Pohl not to bother you at all with questions. But their associate attorneys are unavailable or have no answers," said Chris, a legal assistant, with a bundle of files in her hands.

I read the list of questions Chris and Janet wrote down.

"The Pohl partners and any of their bunch of attorneys can answer those. They are simple TDI, No-Fault and lien issues," I assured them.

"E.D., our questions have piled up on their desks and we are told they are being researched."

"Researched? There is no need for these day-to-day issues. Bring me all those files and I will answer your questions this very minute. Otherwise, everyone will be buried in files, files, files."

"We discuss among ourselves so we don't bother you with questions, but their manager demands that we pick up the paper clips and sort out used papers to be recycled. It pulls away from our time to fight for thousands of dollars in each case. We lost the comforts of your office, Erlinda," said Linda.

Truly unbelievable...East is east, west is west.

My employees were relieved. They eagerly anticipated each time I was available. They tried to be discreet like kids anticipating a scolding if they deviated from Pohl's orders.

Everyone knew what Pohl expected of me—spend time socializing with people like a queen bee, gathering more and more nectar, and not be distracted from that task.

Only a glamorized legal entertainer which I felt it was immoral to be. I had to work!

Claims of clients hardly moved. And I was expected to continue the flow of hundreds of clients? How? And it was my name on the front line. I knew something wrong was quickly happening, but I did not even have the luxury of time to assess that.

Chapter Three

Early one afternoon, Ken dropped by the office. He had to pass by my room to get to his own. My door was open as usual.

"Hey, Erlinda, I thought you are in the mainland vacationing. What are you doing here?"

He meant what he said. He didn't even know I was around.

"Ken, the reason I am tied to my chair is that there is really no trial attorney assigned to help me. I have been spending hours in arbitrations, courts, talking to clients. There are only twenty-four hours in a day."

He walked into my room and sat down, looking at my desk. It was L-shaped, extremely large and full of files, one on top of the other.

"I can hardly see you, Erlinda. Are you there? The files are so tall," he joked.

"I'm here, Ken, try to peep underneath the desk and avoid staring at my extremely high heels."

Ken sat down and faced me.

"My partners and I have been discussing and decided to have Roy Chang, Ray Tam, Walter Kirimitsu, Peter Carlisle, and Robert Browning handle the depositions, arbitrations and trials," he said.

I had heard of Mr. Tam and Mr. Carlisle. They were known as good civil trial attorneys. I also had appeared before Mr. Kirimitsu, an experienced civil arbitrator. Mr. Browning was the prosecutor in a criminal jury trial I defended.

"Who is Roy Chang?" I asked. "I never heard of him."

"He handles personal injury. He will really get into extensive advertising in the yellow pages."

"Never mind the ad, but does he have experience?"

"Of course, we are friends."

The attorneys Ken mentioned were brought to the office. They were dignified, sociable, and were of great help.

Later, Mr. Tam would become an Executive Legal Consultant, Mr. Kirimitsu a Justice of the Court of Appeals, Mr. Carlisle the State Prosecutor, Mr. Browning a Judge at the Family Court, and Mr. Chang never showed up either.

They left as quickly as they had appeared. A few weeks later, things were back to the chaotic mess we had before. I asked Sharon what else we could do.

"Well, we have a falling out with Roy Chang. He complains that it would take him days to review one file."

"Days?"

My questions annoyed her. She did not wish to discuss it any further. She stayed a few minutes in the office before hurriedly leaving.

Weeks came and went. I began to call and write short memos to Sharon and Ken.

I was working more than I ever did before our liaison. I was also worrying more—a queen bee doing the work of the soldiers.

They had to know.

"Your associates are intelligent but most do not know personal injury, nor could they try a case alone. I have to be assisted.

The insurance companies will not give us what we want if they know we are unable to try the case," I said.

No response.

I asked if Ken would do something. I hoped he had ready solutions. Instead, he said, "I have to discuss this with my partners, I will tell them of your concerns."

* * *

One mid-morning, Sharon suddenly walked into my room. It was a pleasant surprise. I had not seen her in weeks.

"Erlinda, this office is like a ship. There can only be one captain of the ship."

She never looked so serious before.

"You mean the captain should be you, Sharon?"

"Yes." She was not angry. Or it did not show.

"But, Sharon, you are hardly around. I haven't heard from you in weeks. That's why you can see me here every day even on weekends."

Her response was quick.

"We think all our associates know what they are doing. Did it ever occur to you, Erlinda, that you may be demanding too much?" She asked it so softly, it was difficult to react.

Our discussion was not getting anywhere. Understanding this, she stood up and walked away.

I followed her to her room. I did not wish to be confrontational, but our liaison had to survive.

"Sharon, you can confirm what I tell you. Months ago, Ken traveled to Manila and signed up all the clients in the China Airlines disaster. He used my name."

"Oh?"

"Ken has not returned the Manila clients' calls. I don't think he had time to read their letters. Your downtown office is working on the claims. What do you want me to do? The Philippine clients think I'm their lawyer."

Sharon was clearly recalling.

"I am not involved in those cases. I'll talk to Ken," she said as she started to leave. "Have a nice day, Erlinda."

I went back to my room with the stacks of files still on my desk and five more clients waiting to talk to me.

I wrote a note to Ken. I called him. I told him I was pulling my name from the China Airlines claims and would not be a co-counsel with them anymore. They could have all the fees.

He said, "Okay, alright."

I wondered, Is that all he would say?... Is it that simple? Aren't they concerned about any potential malpractice?

Then, I answered my own questions. None of the clients was in the United States. Pohl would probably call them up. Or, Pohl would resolve the claims as if I had not withdrawn.

I never found out what Pohl did.

The associate attorneys continued to settle claims quickly and for small amounts. They were getting their instructions from Pohl. They were not accountable to me. They had been told that I was not their employer and Pohl was their boss.

I tried to settle as many as I could even if my involvement was discouraged. There would be less clients to pacify. And I did not wish to lose the rest.

Some clients had transferred to other attorneys. I feared a domino effect. What would happen to our Dominguez-Pohl liaison? What would happen to the office and the employees?

Mr. Flores, my old loyal client, had referred his friends and relatives through the years. He called me up on a Sunday.

"I'm sorry to call you, Attorney," he said. "But there were three of us who came to see you. The new manager sent us home because we had no appointment. You did not know."

I could sense the hurt in Flores' voice. I quickly apologized. I asked him to come during my office hours.

"Thank you for telling me and for not seeking another attorney," I said to all three men as I addressed their claims in my office.

Flores was referring to Wendy, the manager hired by Pohl. She had no law degree but she even managed the work of associate attorneys. I wondered how. I felt that was part of Pohl's privacy and I had no business inquiring.

The saying was making complete sense to me. East is east, west is west and never shall the twain meet.

Wendy's presence put Mila's position in peril. Mila was my manager and her pay was high. She knew the proper court filing procedures. And she spoke the Filipino language—a great help in sustaining business.

Stress was showing on her face. I sounded apologetic. "I can't hire, I can't fire, I can't increase your wages. I have no say. I hope you realize that."

Mila did not say a word. I could almost read her mind, What did you do to the office, Erlinda, what did you do to us? Why did you ever bring strangers into the office? I could entertain clients and would not drive them away!

"If you are thinking of it, don't resign. Let them just fire you. It's not the end of the world. The situation should not get any worse," I was imploring.

My employees were not happy. What if I lost my most competent employees who were in the grinder every single working day—Linda, Mila, Youme, Chris, Janet and others? What would happen to the clients, the office, and my contract with Pohl?

* * *

One morning, I noticed that Lei Santana and Mary Faller were not in. Lei was a paralegal and Mary was my part-time secretary. She was an older lady and I allowed her to choose her time of work.

"Where are they?"

"I don't know," was everyone's answer. They either really did not know or did not want to get involved.

"I have to know, Wendy, did they resign?"

"Yes."

That was all she said.

They did not even say goodbye…was it something I said? In a couple of days, I got a call from Mary.

"Erlinda, Pohl had drastically cut my hours. How can I survive? They have terminated my benefits."

"I don't know what to say, Mary. I am not your employer anymore."

"Lei and I have been to the Department of Labor. The department said, you will be responsible for our unemployment benefits. We're sorry to do this, Erlinda."

"Mary, tell Lei I'll do what I can. What has happened to you is wrong!"

I tried to discuss Mary's urgent situation with Wendy. As usual, her response was to talk to the Pohl partners. I spoke with Sharon a few days later.

"It's not our fault if they don't like their hours. Technically, they resigned. They should not be complaining," she said.

"Sharon, there is already a complaint against me at the Department of Labor. Won't you do anything to help? Especially Mary—She has been sickly and she urgently needs her employee medical benefits, please, Sharon."

"They were your employees. It's your duty to pay their unemployment benefits. We are not here to reward people for what we don't need." She was stern. But otherwise, very polite.

"You fired them, Sharon. We can solve the problem. I will hire them back and you pay them their wages as our contract says."

I picked up the phone to call Mary and Lei to re-hire them.

"Don't, Erlinda. I'll discuss the situation with my partners. You don't need to make that call."

I did not hear from Sharon again. Neither did I hear from Mary or Lei. Pohl must have taken care of the problem.

* * *

John Yuen was hired by Pohl as an associate attorney. But he looked to me for answers in the cases assigned to him. One evening, he walked into my room.

"Erlinda, I have learned so much from you, but I am leaving your office."

I was frightened by what he had just said. He was a great help. He worked long hours with no complaints. Mike Kaneshiro and Steve Brittain had left. The office will be handicapped. It appeared John wanted to confide in me.

"I'm sure that Pohl wants me to go, but would not fire me." He had difficulty saying the words. "When they want something, they make it clear in many ways and they get whatever they desire," he continued. His voice was breaking.

"John, what are you talking about?" I was hoping to prolong the conversation.

I asked him to please have a seat. He did.

"Erlinda, your old employees who are not lawyers are getting paid higher than me because you gave them that. And here I am, an overworked lawyer. I discussed my wages with Pohl's manager. Since then, I was treated differently. It's unhealthy. I can't live this way."

"Please don't say that. Your mind may be playing tricks. I never saw the partners screaming at you."

"Not the partners. None of them is ever around in your office anyway."

"For example, what did someone do to you?"

"It's unprofessional to say. I just wanted to tell you, Pohl will get all their hearts' desire."

"Don't scare me, John, you're a big help to me."

"Forget what I said, Erlinda, I did not mean it. I am just in need of a vacation—and you really should have one too. You deserve it more than any of us. My apologies for bothering you."

I felt so sorry for John. It was late in the evening. He was vague and emotions had become volatile in the office.

"Can't you wait until next year, John?"

His answer would have been the same even if I begged. John resigned and he was gone.

I gave some thought to what had happened. I had become the only one in the office who was working as both a rainmaker and a more than a double-time worker.

It had been that way since my written contract with Pohl, and soon, another year would be over. The Pohl partners had almost completely vanished from the office.

An unpleasant thought crept through my mind. I wonder what Pohl would do to me when they don't need me anymore? When clients stop coming?

John was right. I deserved a vacation more than anyone else. I was beginning to think ugly thoughts.

* * *

Christmas time again. Our neon lights sign, *Maligayang Pasko*, was a clear sight at the mall. It made the Filipino community happy.

Each late afternoon, Linda and I switched on the neon lights, ablaze in the night sky.

The day before Christmas, the Catholic nuns at Ewa Beach called the office. They were family friends and referred clients to us.

"We did not see your neon lights when we went to the cathedral store at the mall last night. Don't you hang them up anymore? We could see only three letters remained, '*gay*'…what is happening?" they asked with obvious concern.

"That's impossible."

I walked to the desk of Rick Moad. He was the brother-in-law of Ken and he did varied work in the office.

"What's the story on the neon sign, Rick?" I asked. "Linda and I switch it on in the afternoon and it is off at night."

"E.D., it is Pohl's instruction that I unplug your greeting. They think it's a fire hazard."

"Can't Pohl extend the courtesy of telling me their concerns instead of doing things behind our back? It seems childish with distasteful repercussions. Do they respect me? They don't even do it right when they unplug. They're putting our office in trouble."

"I'm sorry, E.D., please don't blame them, but I was told not to say anything to avoid confrontation."

"Confrontation about what, Rick? The language of the greeting sign which is Filipino?"

Rick was silent.

I turned away. They unplug the greeting and turn it off every evening when nobody else is in the office—They do that hoping I'd never find out.

I wanted to deny what I was thinking. They just take matters into their hands? How can one defend oneself when things are discreetly done? And they are never around to discuss it? Nobody should live this way. It is inhumane.

I called up Sharon. "The sign is a tradition, I've hung the lights for many years. It makes my Filipino friends happy. They have extended families into various races and we have them also for clients. The sign is really my goodwill to the community."

"It's risky. It could burn the building," she said.

"I wish you were more candid with me, Sharon. That's all I ask. I would not do that to you for a million bucks, for sure!"

* * *

"You have to take a cruise, you may be stressed out," said a friend, Dr. Nick Joaquin. He was the primary physician of many of my clients.

It was strange that the subject of a cruise was brought up by Dr. Thomas Sakoda in the same week. He was the neurosurgeon for many of my clients.

I wondered what would happen if I was not in the office. I decided to stay away for a few days and made myself available just in case they needed me.

No calls.

The staff appeared happy to see me back.

Then, Wendy came into my room with two huge files for a husband and wife. Early into my liaison with Pohl, we managed a compromise. Dozens of computers were okay, but we wanted to save the hard files and office forms that were regularly used.

Mila had long since resigned. Wendy was the only manager instead of two.

"There's a complaint against you in the ODC." She used initials to abbreviate the Office of Disciplinary Counsel Board. This office oversees the conduct of attorneys.

Wendy handed me the complaint.

Something happened when I was gone. The subject matter had always been confidential with the Board. My previous instructions for the clients were still clipped to the records which were ignored by the staff.

Pohl was not included in the complaint.

I had to file my answer in the limited time allowed. Rick was to immediately mail my written response, which I prepared and signed. I entrusted the matter to him.

One early morning, I was in the coffee room. Through the glass windows, I saw my letter to the ODC on Rick's desk, unmailed. I did not know what to think.

"Rick, my time to respond may be too late. Why didn't you mail the letter?"

His answer was slow. He looked almost sorry to tell me.

"Sharon has to read your letter before it gets out. I'm sorry, Erlinda, I'm just doing my job. She will prepare your answer. You should not be involved."

I could not believe what I was hearing. How can I not be involved when the complaint is against me?

They just use my name—they don't care if I perish or sink or that my law license is affected...all my actions have to be approved by the partners?

"Something has to be done, Wendy," I told the manager. "There has to be a procedure of checks and balances from the front desk to me. We should protect each other. The Pohl partners are never here to see what's going on."

"I'll discuss it with Pohl," said Wendy.

Finally, Wendy and I managed to agree on a new procedure. It was geared to prevent disasters like ODC complaints. She had to be informed of everything before it reached me. Even a simple call from a client.

I wondered why. Did Pohl think I was hiding clients and taking away from their profits? But I did not want any discussion. I knew that Pohl would call it confrontation, and they hated that. Besides, there was too little time for extra discussions.

Instead, I wrote Pohl a letter. "Please spare some of your time to really see what is happening...I made a commitment to protect every term of our contract to the best of my ability."

My plea was falling on deaf ears.

All my employees worked harder. And so did I.

* * *

One afternoon, Luisa Rigney approached me. She was a file clerk and assisted in calls and organizing papers. In her hand was a letter clipped to its envelope. The envelope looked familiar even from a distance.

"There's another ODC complaint against you."

Luisa was waiting for what I had to say while I read the document.

"The file reflects that the client called numerous times to talk to me. You took the calls. Why didn't you tell me, Luisa?"

No response.

Luisa turned the files toward her. She had placed them on my desk. She flipped through the pink message slips attached to the file.

I repeated what I asked.

"You took the calls, you wrote these messages, you never said a thing to me. I see you every day. Why, Luisa?" Her response had a tone of defiance.

"I was just doing what I was told. Blame Wendy, not me," she said, then hurriedly walked back to the front desk where the phones were ringing. Youme was alone and needed help.

I looked at the pink slips of the calls from the client, then the complaint.

"Please, God, no sabotage!"

That Sunday, I saw Dr. Cel Guerrero at the Kahala Shopping Mall. She was a psychiatrist for some of our clients with head injuries. She invited me for a snack.

"Erlinda, don't mind my saying so...many of your clients are displeased. Their questions are not answered and their calls are not returned."

"Well, Doc, you and the community know that my office has been absorbed by the Price Okamoto Himeno & Lum firm. Even our letters to your clinic state their name. There have been changes in management. Everyone has difficulty adjusting."

"Try to do something before it's too late and you lose all your clients. Worse still, you may be in bigger trouble."

"I'm doing all I can. Let's talk of nicer things."

Every day brought me closer to the end of the Pohl-Dominguez five year contract. The second year had barely passed. Does this mean I will be working in fright for the next three years? The thought lingered in my mind.

It was affecting my well-being. But my employees did not have to know. I did not show them.

The Catholic nuns at Ewa Beach dropped by. They had no appointment, but I asked Youme to bring them all into my room. Every visitor was welcome, with or without an appointment.

Their arrival was in the middle of another hectic day. As they walked into my room through the long hallway, they carried cakes they baked for me and my employees.

They noticed that the office looked dismal. The parrot was not chirping. Garfield, the fish, was fading away. The music box was never played.

I thought that was the reason the nuns came. They were family friends and referred clients to me.

"It's a difference of day and night," they exclaimed. All they could say was pray for peace.

How true. That was what the office needed most!

Chapter Four

More months passed. Many of our clients left and sought refuge with other attorneys. Financial problems had begun.

"Erlinda, what do you say if we downsized the personnel and the office space, and transported some employees to our downtown office?" asked Sharon in her unexpected visit to the office.

"It would not work, Sharon. As you know, the clients are used to this office and we can't afford to lose any more employees. Who will do the job? We should really sit down and discuss this."

I wondered how Sharon could even ask the question. She just mumbled, "Oh, okay. I just wanted to know. See you later."

A few weeks had gone by and I did not hear from Sharon.

One morning, files were piled in rows on the floor reaching to the hallway. The shelves were being emptied.

Something was happening and I did not know what it was.

"What's happening, Janet?"

Janet quickly stood up from her chair. She was busy computing the medical bills of a client and did not expect to see me by her desk.

"We were told by the manager that all files will be transported to the Pohl office downtown and nothing will be left here. Didn't she tell you, Erlinda?"

I was embarrassed. I did not respond. Nobody told me and those were my files from my office! Those were my clients, their referrals, our extended families.

Janet watched me as I proceeded to my room.

Later that week, there was a call from the Wagner Rental Agency.

"Ms. Dominguez, why are you ending the lease of your office?"

I was shocked.

"I am not ending the lease. This has been my office for many years."

The caller seemed confused.

"Well, Mr. Price's firm says that you have no involvement in this matter, and that we are no longer your agent. You have to vacate the premises as soon as possible. I'm surprised that they did not explain things to you."

Pohl did not have to spell out anything to me anymore. I suddenly remembered what happened to John, Mary, Lei, Mila, and the others. Especially John's parting words.

But I'm not just an employee. I own the entire office, we have a signed written contract.

The office was not earning millions anymore. In fact, it was struggling to survive. Pohl's multiple computers and complex networking did not really help. The personal touch to clients dwindled. Now, it came to this!

I called up Ken.

"Ken, you transported the files to your downtown office. You ended the lease. Am I out of your life in the middle of our contract?"

His response was quick and seemed rehearsed. He had discussed it with his partners and my call was anticipated.

"No, Erlinda, we have a room for you in our downtown office where everyone will be stationed. Sharon can explain this more to you."

I could not speak what I wished to say. What gives you the right to make my entire practice disappear and replace it with a very barren room in your office?

* * *

My mother was arriving from the Philippines. It was her annual school break trip to visit me. She traveled with my eight-year-old niece, Michelle.

They had lots of luggage.

"You lost weight, I can feel your bones. Are you not eating?" my mom asked in her nurturing tone as she hugged me.

"My muumuu dress is just two sizes bigger," I said, knowing she would not believe me.

"Yes, Auntie, you look like a toothpick. You look like a scarecrow. The Philippine barong dress we brought for you is five times your size," said Michelle, giggling.

I knew that my mom would ask me lots of questions. I worried for her and not for me.

Soon after dinner, she had my assurance that it was not personal. It did not involve my family. It concerned my profession, my business, my office, my livelihood, my license, my self-respect.

"I made a mistake, *Mamang*," I said, using the affectionate term many Filipinos call their mother. "I made a terrible mistake of giving up my office to the Pohl people."

"Are those the very nice people you introduced to me in your office before?" she asked.

"Some of them," I said, knowing that not all the Pohl partners set foot in the office.

My mother was very intuitive and analytical although she only reached grade school. She was listening intently. I chose the words to say.

But everything was hurting her.

I explained how it appeared so positive in the beginning. Then, how the office income was literally draining from millions to zero. Many employees who found her cute were gone.

I described how my letters would not get out without Pohl's supervision. How the Christmas neon lights were turned off without my knowledge. How the files were transported from the office without my knowledge. How the lease of my elegant office space was suddenly ended without my knowledge!

My mother cried so much.

"You never did harm to anyone. You never stole or concealed a client. I know you would rather starve than cheat. Why have they done this to you?"

She did not sleep a wink that night and looked so tired and lonely the day after.

In a few days, my mother went back to the Philippines with a heavy heart.

I felt so guilty.

Some time ago, I heard people in the legal profession call Pohl powerful. Even my employees said so. I should have insisted that they explained what the word meant to them.

Does power include taking the law in your hands? You can be the judge, the jury, the witness, the executioner all at one time?

Just a lawyer's soliloquy. There is just no due process, is there? A contract means nothing?

I was past confusion. It should now be easier for me to talk.

Sharon and Ken had been the spokespersons of Pohl. I left messages for them to call me and wrote them short notes, saying we ought to discuss everything that was going on.

Finally, all three of us were in the conference room of the office. They knew the reason for our urgent meeting, or they would not have responded on short notice.

"Thank you for meeting with me, but I must now respectfully ask that we sever the contract. We can't wait for the five years to end. My office is gone. I cannot work in a room in your downtown office."

I had hardly finished talking when Sharon said without hesitation, "Okay, okay. You have a choice, Erlinda," she said, looking at me straight in the face. "You can have all the claims and cases and pay all the overhead."

Ken was nodding his head. He was observing my reaction.

"If you mean I take back my office, that's impossible. Many of my trained employees are gone, I think my office has been ruined...I don't mean to blame anybody. My reputation in the community is no longer the same."

I could read their minds.

"Yes, you can have all the clients. I will always be available to help if there will be problems, but I will not be in your way," I said.

They wanted to hear that.

"We will check our records and pay what is owed to you," said Sharon.

"Thanks, that's very nice of you."

"What will you be doing?" Ken asked curiously.

"I will not compete with anyone's practice. I will go on a sabbatical leave."

It pleased them and our discussion was over. I was hoping it would be our very last.

We parted and as they walked out of the office, I recalled the sadness on the face of John Yuen when, one evening, he said goodbye. And something else that I had heard people say, "Pohl will get their hearts' desire."

I came to grips with what that had meant.

I gathered the employees, my own and those hired by Pohl. They were all uneasy and did not really know what I was going to say.

"The office will be completely closed. I will not open a new one. You will all be with the Pohl law firm in their downtown office."

Linda, Youme, Janet, and Chris, even Mary Nacpuy who was hired by Pohl and spoke Filipino, were almost in tears. The rest were quietly staring at me like they had long expected what was happening.

Attorneys Lawrence Cohen and Bob Kohn were sad to let me go, and were curious to know if I would open my office very soon. I wished them luck and said, "I will not have an office. The two of you will be great in your lawyer profession."

All the employees pitched in for a luncheon for me. They signed the biggest card I had ever seen.

"Thank you, E.D., for all that we have learned from you and what you have been to us."

"Pohl will take care of you. I wish you all the best in your life!" I said, and we all looked at each other with unspoken feelings of regret and sadness.

Soon, my entire office would disappear. I had to act quickly.

The clients had to be informed. We sent out letters. We scheduled calls and meetings. We gave them a choice of transferring to other attorneys.

Wanda adopted Sinbad, the parrot, and took him home. Garfield, the fish, who entertained guests with his colors for over a decade was still alive and active. Everybody wanted him.

Office equipment was sold by Pohl. But the murals were folded. They were mine.

Clients called to say goodbye or sent us cards. Some came in to purchase what was available. A small chair, a tiny desk.

An end table would do. Their reason was touching. In memory of the Law Offices of E.D. It was the end of the year 1996.

* * *

I did not feel I was on leave from the practice of law. I worried for the clients. Occasionally, I would call up Pohl's office, or my old employees would call me.

They asked me legal questions and procedures. They missed my ready responses. It was the blood of our Ala Moana office, they said. A quick pace for clients' receipt of their benefits, productive results for all those we could help.

My employees remembered.

People called. I referred them to social security, unemployment, and so on. They were grateful.

New personal injury clients looked for me. I directed them to the law firm of Pohl. Many of my old employees were still there and they knew what they were doing.

I encountered old clients in restaurants and in stores where they worked. They had a common question I never clearly answered.

"When will you open your office again, Attorney?"

Adversaries in the legal community started a rumor that my license was suspended. None of that was true. But I did not have an office where I could explain.

Occasionally, I attended small social groups. I had more time to spare.

Brian Oyadomari became a close friend, not just an acquaintance. He encouraged me to get back to active practice. I thought that would be disastrous.

All the clients taken by Pohl might return to me in a deluge! I did not have the facilities. Nor the employees to accommodate them.

"You will dispel the rumor about your license when you open your office," said Brian.

But it was too recent. My liaison with Pohl had just ended.

Visits to the Philippines were more convenient. My mother was not as strong. She had difficulties with long trips.

In some sense, that was good. She did not have to know that my office she was so proud of was completely gone.

I took trips to California for a feel of the personal injury legal practice. Nationwide, procedures and the laws are virtually the same.

Practice in the mainland could be very rewarding. I might find ways to help using my profession. Those were just my wishful thoughts.

* * *

Year 1997. I received a letter from a local law firm of Trecker & Fritz. Their name was not familiar. From their letterhead, it seemed to be a small office of two attorneys.

The letter asked for the files of a couple—Barnedo and Barnedo. I remembered the case. Two and a half fingers of Mrs. Barnedo were severed by the Japanese-made noodle machine at her place of employment. That was almost ten years ago.

Pohl and I recovered about $200,000 in worker's compensation. There were a few dollars short of $485,000 default judgment rendered by the Hawaii federal court that we earned against the Japanese manufacturer.

The Japanese company did not contest the case. They did not even bother to respond.

I had asked Pohl about the current status. They retained a Japanese law firm to collect. Basically, that was all Ken would say.

The manufacturing company had no assets located in the United States or they were successfully hidden. It was incorporated in Japan.

Trecker & Fritz could send their representatives to Japan. But if they collected, they might refuse to pay our share of the fees and expenses.

That would be the problem of Pohl.

I contacted Linda Huang. She was still a paralegal for Pohl. She had always been resourceful and competent. She also had a good memory for clients. Pohl could not get rid of her.

"Linda, please prepare the files of Mr. and Mrs. Barnedo for delivery to the new attorneys...you know what the procedure is. Remind your manager, I have already called her."

Lawyers cannot refuse to part with the files of a client. That's ethics. I had no intention of doing that. I was sure neither did Pohl.

In a few days, Linda had photocopied vital portions of the files for Pohl's safe-keeping. She called me.

Delivery to the messenger of the new attorneys had been complete. A receipt was signed in the presence of Pohl's receptionist.

Everything Linda did was standard procedure.

* * *

Year 1999. I was back to the practice of law. Life on sabbatical was boring. My new office was beside the downtown office of Pohl. Nothing intentional.

I shared an office with Brian. No employees.

If I needed anything, it was contractual. For instance, messengers, researchers.

"Feels great to be back in action, Brian."

"Your enemies had a holiday during your sabbatical."

"That's okay, I'll start all over again!"

Word spread in the community. I began to see familiar faces.

My previous clients dropped by. It was to say Hi or bring in a new claim.

My office was small but kept me busy. The clients knew I had no associates or partners.

Roy Chang had his law office in the same building. He once was hired by Pohl to do work in my Ala Moana office. Roy needed more cases. I referred some to him. Occasionally, I used his small staff of three women. It was mutually convenient.

Roy had one other attorney in his office, Harvey Demetrakopoulus. If he was a silent partner or an associate, I did not know.

Harvey seemed respectful to the clients. He hardly ever spoke. Or if he did, it was on basics. Nothing complicated.

They called their firm Shim & Chang. I never saw Mr. Shim in that office. I assumed he retired while his name continued in perpetuity. Many law firms had the same style. Surely, to gain more clients—use the prestige earned by the predecessor.

One morning, I got a call. He called himself Steve Lane. I did not know him. Never heard of him. But he sounded like he had known me for years.

I sensed he had a small-time investigation practice. He said his office was named after him and his associates. But he did not have a single associate. I was concerned if he was legitimate.

"Ms. Dominguez, I work sometimes for the Honolulu law firm of Trecker & Fritz. I can show you my ID if you wish."

I was trying to recall this man. But I really never met him nor heard of him.

"They asked me to get the files of the couple, Barnedo and Barnedo, from you. Your client there was hurt by a noodle machine...her hand, remember? The U.S. District Court Case?" he said.

It was clear he was asking for the files surrendered by Linda Huang of the Pohl office to his bosses.

"The files were delivered a long time ago to the firm you say hired you," I said.

He seemed unaware of this.

"They don't have the files," he said.

"That's not my problem, I don't have them," I said mildly.

"Ms. Dominguez, can you provide me with whatever you have?"

"What happened to the files? Talk to the Trecker & Fritz employee who received them, Mr. Lane."

"I don't know. This project is new for me."

Linda had saved copies of portions of the files before delivery. She was still with the Pohl firm. Surely, she would remember.

"Someone might call your office, Linda. Do you recall the Barnedo files you delivered to the messenger of the new attorneys?"

"Yes. That must have been well over a year ago. Why are they just asking now?"

"Please make sure to show the receipt signed by that messenger if they persist."

* * *

Weeks went by. Nothing happened.

"You have lots of mail today," said Brian.

One envelope came from a lawyer, Francis O'Brien. I recalled his name as one mentioned by my ex-employee, Ana Buenaflor.

Ana worked for the law firm of David Schutter, a criminal attorney. O'Brien worked in that office. His name was also mentioned by a few of my clients whom he represented in their divorce cases.

I read his letter.

He wanted me to refer the Barnedo case to my malpractice insurance company. He claimed he was a new co-counsel of the clients.

My suspicion was probably right. Trecker & Fritz or their messenger lost the files Linda Huang delivered. They needed a buffer. A protector for their misfeasance.

The letter accused me of failing to collect the federal default judgment of almost $485,000 in Japan.

Where's the malpractice? Why doesn't he go to Japan to collect and find out?

But the matter merited serious consideration. Very serious. I called the Pohl office. I had provided them with a copy of the letter.

Sharon asked that we discuss the matter in person.

I walked over to Pohl's office, just steps away from my own. The receptionist brought me into the conference room, which was adjacent to their waiting room.

Their office was large. The partners and the employees were inside. They were not visible. How I wished I could see my old employees and talk to them again!

But there was no way that they would know I was around unless Sharon told them, which she did not.

I explained the case to Sharon. My vivid memory was my great ally in my profession.

Sharon was listening. She hardly talked. At times, she would nod her head like she agreed with all I said.

She asked to be excused then came back with Ken.

"Hey, you look great, Erlinda...I hear you are back in practice."

"You look good, too, Ken. And yes, I have a very small office right beside your building."

I again began to narrate.

Ken was observing me. He recalled some events—perhaps as told to him by Sharon.

"Isn't that the federal case where the Japanese company was incorporated in Japan?"

"Yes, Ken. You never told me what happened."

"Nothing. A Japanese law firm has been helping us."

"Nothing happened?" I asked softly.

I was expecting a practical answer like, "Well, they are in Japan, it's like collecting in Iraq, and their assets are well hidden."

But Ken did not respond. He instead turned to Sharon as if he wanted to know more of the case. Sharon did not react.

I did the talking. "There was no other company liable in Hawaii. The client's employer traveled to Japan to choose the noodle machine."

Sharon was listening and Ken was trying to recall.

"All the files were delivered to the new attorneys. Linda saved copies of some portions. Perhaps they're in your shelves?" I asked.

"Don't worry, Erlinda, they can travel to Japan. They can continue to try to locate the company's assets in the United States. Nobody is stopping them. Sue for malpractice? That does not make sense!" said Ken mildly, showing no worry or aggravation.

"Too bad, there are not enough cases to go around," said Sharon. "It's not like you, Erlinda. Clients come to you. They wait for you. You never ever beg. You don't need to beg."

Ken would soon leave for the day. I was told he always played golf with other attorneys, sometimes, with judges—and there was nothing wrong with that.

Sharon appeared ready to leave. She would meet her girl-friends at the Neiman Marcus cafeteria—their hangout.

What an easy life, but not the kind I wished for myself, especially in the legal profession. I gathered my stuff to leave.

I walked back to my office. Clients were patiently waiting for me.

* * *

There were more letters from O'Brien. He requested a face-to-face conference, no doubt to know more about Pohl's involvement.

Sharon agreed. We were to meet O'Brien in Pohl's office. Certainly not anywhere else.

Sharon and I talked behind closed doors. I repeated what she already knew. Again, she hardly said a word.

Pens and papers were available. Sharon was not writing. I couldn't be paranoid. Surely, Pohl had no invisible recording going on. We were in this together. We were not opponents.

The receptionist knocked at the door. "Mr. O'Brien and Mr. Fritz are both here."

The duo sat themselves side-by-side in front of me. They were huge men, early seniors, but I did not recall ever seeing either of them in the courthouse—or anywhere else for that matter.

They began to empty their briefcases. Many papers came out. Those were portions of what were delivered to their messenger by Linda Huang over a year ago.

They had pockets on their shirts and pants. They could have carried a dozen tape recorders running at the same time. I wouldn't know.

Isn't that supposed to be illegal? I discarded the thought.

If the conference was to be productive, I had to give as much information as possible. We did nothing wrong anyway. All I had was a purse, pad, and pen visibly resting on the table.

Ken was not there. But his voice was still clear. Erlinda, legal malpractice for not collecting in Japan? Don't worry...they can travel to Japan if they want.

The conference was not courteous. It was confrontational. It was one-sided. O'Brien was interrogating me. It seemed he did not care about Sharon's or Pohl's involvement.

Fritz would whisper something to him. Then, the questioning would continue.

I concluded that they did not do their homework, they were fishing and taxing my memory for events of a long time ago.

They did not know how Mrs. Barnedo's accident happened. Why so ignorant? She was now their client. They should know.

I thought their questions were just intimidation as many attorneys do when talking to any opponent.

The duo, O'Brien and Fritz, said the files that were delivered by Linda Huang were incomplete. "Was their messenger fired or is she still in their office?" They evaded the topic.

"Please tell me why you waited so long to complain of these missing files," I said.

They just looked at each other and refused to explain. They said it was their work product—an attorney's privilege—their right to be silent.

Sharon was quiet and observing. Once in a while, she scratched notes on her pad. I was hoping she would say a word in my defense, we were partners. But she did not.

She would look at me when I talked. She would look at them when they talked. Then, she called it a day.

O'Brien and Fritz put their papers in their briefcases, thanked Sharon for the meeting, then left.

Sharon wanted me to stay a bit longer. We left the conference room and moved to her office. She began to speak in a very serious tone.

"Erlinda, the problem will not go away. Perhaps, you should consider settlement."

"Sharon, we all agreed there is no malpractice."

"Erlinda, you have no malpractice insurance. It will be hard on you. Your name will appear in the *Business Pacific News*. Your name and reputation will be ruined."

She said name and reputation. She knew I valued those more than all the power and money in the world. But she seemed to assume that Pohl would be immune from the *Business Pacific News*.

"We worked on the case together. There's no conflict between us, is there?" I asked.

"No, but it would be best if you hire your own attorney. We have our own. We will work together. Do you have someone worthy of consideration?"

My mind was going around in circles. I was not really prepared for her question. But I managed to respond.

"I might hire Roy Chang. He is in the same building as I am. You know him, in fact. You introduced me to him when he worked on some files in my office."

"Very good, Erlinda. I think Roy is competent and yes, we will work together. You should not worry. Tell him to call me."

I thought about the conference. I knew that Sharon was right. With or without an iota of malpractice, we were in for a suit. That was almost understood in the legal profession.

Roy Chang was in the elevator as I returned to my office. He was with Harvey. Whether they had a motion in court or were having snacks at the coffee shop, they were always together.

They discussed cases anywhere—while walking, while eating, while driving.

"Hi, Erlinda!"

"Can I come to your office now? I have something personal I need to speak with you about."

They had nothing immediately scheduled. We proceeded to their office. I explained the potential malpractice suit and told them of my meeting with Sharon and the opposing attorneys.

Would they accept me as their client just in case? Roy readily agreed. No second thoughts. I did not think Harvey had a say in the matter.

"Roy, if...a very remote if...if there would be a conflict between me and Pohl, would you continue to defend me?"

"Of course. You are our client, not them."

"Forgive my asking, it's just that you had been friends in business. You were hired by them to work on my cases some time ago, remember?"

"That was years ago. And why do you think I stopped doing work for them? Erlinda, our loyalty is to you. They are not our client. You are! Besides, I don't see an iota of conflict between you and Pohl. They can be your main witness."

I was a bit embarrassed as though I was investigating their integrity. But I had to know—just in case.

Harvey asked what I would do if the situation was reversed—If I was defending them as my clients.

"Without a shadow of a doubt, I will defend you all the way. This goes true for any client I accept."

Roy opened the Bar Book for the list of attorneys. They were unfamiliar with our opponents. Their faces were there.

The legal profession in Honolulu had many lawyers. Some were successful. Some were struggling. Our opponents hadn't quite made a name for themselves in the legal community.

I was now a client of Roy and Harvey. They were confident. We parted with their similar conclusion. "Don't worry, Erlinda. Their malpractice claim appears like a bluff for the mighty dollar. You know how our profession is sometimes."

Roy was soft spoken—just like Ken and Sharon. But they did not have to be loud to convince me of whatever they said.

Chapter Five

Within days, an envelope arrived from O'Brien. There was an unfiled complaint. His cover letter came as a threat: Settle now or an embarrassing complaint will be filed against you.

He claimed that the injuries of Mrs. Barnedo were severe. Her fingers were deformed. I thought, So what, she could have died, but if we are not liable, we are not liable.

The unfiled complaint named me and Pohl as defendants.

We were being sued. It must have been obvious in my opponents' minds that Pohl was as involved as I was.

The opponents were extorting settlement from me, from Pohl, or from both of us. That was our combined conclusion.

I contacted Sharon. I left message after message. My calls were not returned. Perhaps, she was on a short vacation or she was ill. I was just told she was not in her office.

Then, she finally called. She explained that she was no longer involved. The matter was in the hands of her husband, Warren Price, the lead partner of the Pohl firm.

Sharon promised to send me a copy of Warren's letter to the opposing attorneys. That was the only thing that happened, she said, as if to stop me from doubting or inquiring more.

But I wondered if Warren was angry at O'Brien and what his letter said. Warren could not be more familiar with the case than I was. He was never around in my office.

A copy of Warren's letter arrived. It was on my desk. It was hand-delivered with a big mark of confidential on the envelope. Warren's letter was addressed to O'Brien.

In his letter, Warren called O'Brien by his first name, Francis. He reminded him of their long term friendship. His first paragraph was social and intimate as if they were the best of friends. Was it all political courtesy?

How would I know? I was not in politics.

I was impressed with Warren's letter. His skills as the recent Attorney General were obvious. He analyzed the situation. Nobody was stopping O'Brien from collecting from the Japan company. And if they couldn't, they would know if it was due to any malpractice. Speculation, theory, or guesswork was obviously not evidence.

Warren was defending me, but as the letter went on, he denied involvement in the case. He said that I had my own cases and they had theirs. He did not seem to even know me.

Warren's denial may have been quite innocent. It was still early in the game. He did not check their records. After all, we had hundreds of clients together.

I sought an audience with my attorneys, Roy Chang and Harvey Demetrakopoulos.

They were waiting. Again, both made it clear that together, they were my attorneys, and would defend me one hundred percent. They read the unfiled complaint against me and Pohl.

I observed my attorneys to see if they showed any sign of discomfort. Instead, Roy's words were soothing and very assuring.

"We will sue Pohl on your behalf if we have to. We will do what is necessary to protect you. We assure you that, and we only ask that you put all your trust in us," he said.

I was in safe hands. I had found attorneys who were thinking the way I did. All loyalty goes to the client!

"There is nothing much to do right now. Just bring us the filed complaint when you are served," they said.

"I authorize your office to accept service for me," I said. It was just for an emotional buffer.

Through my years of practice, I had been subpoenaed. I had been summoned. I had been sued—all in line with my profession. But nobody, in my twenty years as a practitioner, had claimed I committed malpractice.

* * *

Days after, Nikki from my attorneys' office called. The sheriff had just left their office. The filed malpractice complaint was served on Roy and Harvey just as we agreed.

They were waiting in their conference room. They had the complaint ready for me to read. I sat in front of them. My worry showed as I read the document.

"Why am I sued alone? Pohl has been completely dropped! They are not mentioned anywhere in the filed complaint!"

"Pohl may have signed a tolling agreement," said Roy.

I knew what a tolling agreement does. It would toll and suspend the time for the opponents to sue Pohl. Meanwhile, they wanted me to fight the battle alone, to test the water?

Roy must have talked to the Pohl partners. In a sense, that was alright. As Sharon said, we were to work things out together even if I was on the front line.

But my serious concerns had to be addressed.

"But Roy, I had been reporting everything to Pohl. Why did they keep the tolling agreement from me?"

"They did not. They mentioned this to us. We are now your attorneys and your spokespersons. Besides, you cannot object if they want to sign that."

"You're right, but I prefer that they also talk to me even if you are representing me. We are not enemies."

* * *

Days quickly passed.

I was again discussing the case with Roy and Harvey as their office hours were closing. We agreed that I would be their co-counsel in the case against me.

As my own co-counsel, I could sign documents or appear in court if they were unavailable. I could even conduct the depositions if needed and save on my attorneys' time and fees.

We had twenty days to answer the malpractice complaint.

I hired legal researchers. I did not expect that Roy or Harvey would spend much time in research.

Ronald Federizo was an associate attorney of Pohl who had recently resigned. I contacted him.

His response was quick. "Ms. Dominguez, yes, I'm looking for work. Any work will do, even a messenger or an interpreter."

He would be reasonable, even cheap, in his fees. He was looking for any work. I was delighted.

Ron was his name to his friends and family. He asked me to call him that. I asked him to always call me by my first name.

We agreed to meet at a neutral place, McDonald's. We secured our conversation at a corner table. There were few customers. It was safe to talk about an embarrassing topic.

That was the first time I saw Ron. He looked neat and he was eager to work.

"I heard great things about you, Erlinda. I wish I had gotten to know you much earlier."

He was referring to my heydays—the pre-Pohl season.

Ron did not mind my asking personal questions. It was important to me. He did not know my opponents or any of my previous associate attorneys. He did not know Roy or Harvey. There was no conflict.

"Ron, if I may ask, why did you resign from Pohl?"

"The way I was treated. They would send me to places without more than a day's preparation," he said meekly.

"Really, like what?"

"For instance, to go to the traffic court for a ticket."

Just how many days does it take to prepare for a traffic ticket? I thought, but did not ask him. This was the first time we were meeting. My purpose was for research, not to try a case.

Ron was continually writing. Almost like reviewing for the Bar Examinations. I worried that the issues were more complicated to him than they seemed to be.

Ron's price was more than what Jennifer Smith was charging me. Jennifer was my researcher for years. She was not a Hawaii lawyer, but her resume said she was a California attorney. But Ron had a family to feed. He even called me generous.

Moments before we parted, he said, "Erlinda, I ask of you...in fact, I beg you not to mention to Pohl that I am doing work for you—not yet anyway."

"Why not?"

"I'm just a small fry in this community."

"But they will not do anything to you! I just don't see the connection."

"Well, they are involved in the issues.... Oh, okay...but don't volunteer the information," he said smiling.

"I don't gossip. I don't socialize with them. I hardly stepped in their office. You never saw me there, did you?"

He appeared content with my response.

Then I teased, "Will you be a politician someday? You can do anything—messengering, interpreting, lawyering—everything."

"Nah..."

"How about a State judge?" I was still teasing.

"Possibly, Erlinda. In a few years. I never handled a court trial, bench or jury. I want to learn from you."

I observed his face. He looked serious. He must really dream of becoming a judge.

"What judgeship are you aiming for?"

"The circuit trial court, but I need adequate experience to be worthy of the position."

"Do you need jury trial experience for that?"

"I don't think so, but of course, it will help."

"Will you open your own office soon?"

"It's almost impossible to make it in private practice."

I went home pondering my social conversation with Ron. I forgot to ask him to be discreet about the malpractice research. But he did not wish Pohl to know. I felt everything was alright.

Then, I wondered what kind of hold Pohl had on Ron. He did not want them to know he was helping me. Will he ask their help, and can they help, when he applies for a State judgeship in a few years?

I should not waste my time conjecturing about other people's lives. I didn't see any conflict. And that was important.

* * *

Roy and Harvey were in the parking lot as I parked my car. Roy said the malpractice case was assigned to Judge Dexter Del Rosario. "Do you know him, Erlinda?"

"Not really. He has his roots in the Philippines. I hear he also worked in a litigation firm before his appointment. We have to be careful with our arguments. He could be very judicious."

"How do they assign judges anyway?" asked Harvey.

"Seems like they just flip a coin," said Roy jokingly.

We had very few days left to file my answer. Harvey was preparing the draft.

The three of us had to review the final document. That's how we agreed to do things.

They were to join Pohl in the suit to fully protect me.

Finally, they called. It was the last day to file. They wanted me to be at their office to discuss the case. Again, we were in their conference room.

The door was closed. Nobody else could hear us.

Harvey handed me the answer he prepared. He shared a copy with Roy. We read it paragraph by paragraph.

"I don't see Pohl included here, I thought you would include them as a third party defendant to protect me, even if it's just on paper, since we are friends," I said, surprised.

"It will just complicate matters," said Roy.

"I don't wish to lose my right to sue them. They were as involved as I was, probably even more so."

I insisted that Pohl be included. Harvey stood up to pull the Rules of Court book from a shelf.

"The court might close soon," I said as I looked at the clock. I was worried.

Roy was finally persuaded. He instructed his paralegal, Nikki, to prepare the third party complaint against Pohl. In minutes, the draft was ready.

Nikki handed the papers to Roy. He didn't even read them. Then, he shook his head. "I'm sorry, Erlinda. We really can't sign this. You are a co-counsel. You should sign it."

"I don't understand, Roy. It would look funny that I sign one document and you sign the rest."

"It's just a matter of courtesy. I worked for Pohl. My belief is it's too premature to include them until things sort of clear up and we have enough basis, but you are insistent."

"You know me, too. And I am your client. But that's okay. We are running out of time. The courts are closing in minutes. I'll sign."

Harvey readily handed me a pen. Both of them looked at me intently, making sure I signed in all the designated spots.

The phone was ringing.

Nikki knocked while she opened the door. "There is a call for you, Roy, from Sharon Himeno."

"Excuse me," said Roy, and he politely stood up. He proceeded to his room. I heard his door close.

"Harvey, there is a telephone right in the conference room. He could have taken the call here."

Harvey said nothing. We were silent. I knew the courts would soon close.

"Is the call so urgent that it can't wait?"

"I don't know," was Harvey's response as he, too, looked at the clock.

Roy came back.

"Roy, what did Sharon have to say?"

"I'm sorry, Erlinda. We should not file the third-party complaint against Pohl even if you sign it. We just can't do this at this time."

"What's my choice, Roy? You are asking me to find someone else to represent me at the last minute. How about my rights?"

"Erlinda, we already said we can always include Pohl later when things are clearer. You are just not used to being a client. You have to cooperate with us," said Roy.

"That may be too late if Pohl is not included now."

"No. It will never be too late. I researched that part. I agree with Roy, you are just complicating matters," Harvey said.

"Are you sure, Harvey? You really researched?"

"Yes, yes, and yes! You saw me read through what I marked in the Rules of Court. It's getting late, we better file your answer right now and don't blame us if we miss."

Nikki was asked to walk over to the court to file. Pohl was not named. "Don't forget to mail the copies for the others," reminded Roy as his paralegal walked out of the room.

I did not have time to reflect on what just occurred. Clients were waiting for me to get back to my office.

Everything should be alright. A nonsense malpractice suit as all of us agreed. Nothing to worry about.

And Roy's promise was clear—You are our client, not Pohl.

One afternoon, Harvey called. "Our opponents are including your former associate attorneys. They are now sued with you."

I left my office, took the elevator and went up to my attorneys' office. I read the complaint. Five of my previous associate attorneys had been included as defendants in the suit in an amended complaint.

"Look at this," I said. "They did not include the most involved associate attorney, Stewart Merdian. His name is all over the records of that case. You know why he was not included?"

"No," said Harvey, looking ignorant and confused.

"Merdian became an adjuster for American Insurance Company after he was fired from my office. My opponents could be settling personal injury claims with the insurance company as we speak."

"Politics!"

"I agree."

"Why was he fired?"

"He overqualified himself in his written credentials. He lasted only a few weeks before I let him go."

We discussed what my former associates would do when they were served with the complaint. They could hire their own attorneys. That's normal procedure. Of course, if they have insurance, the company will pay for their lawyers.

"They might also blame you, Erlinda. You will be facing suits by your previous clients and your previous employees."

"Wouldn't that be a shame! After all the things I had done for them—even if I ended up firing some."

"Now, you know how politicking works, Erlinda."

* * *

The case was admitted into the Court Annexed Arbitration Program. It was called CAAP for short. There would be an arbitrator with sufficient skills and experience appointed by the administrative judge.

The rules needed two trials: the first, for the product defect personal injury case, as if it was contested. If there was a product defect that caused the client's injury, the second trial is for the malpractice—what did the attorney do wrong?

The arbitrator would hear the case and his or her decision could be appealed to the court.

Someone with a conflict could not be appointed to arbitrate. For instance, blood or affinity relationship, or very close friendship with a party could be serious grounds to disqualify. Even strong feelings for or against a party are most improper.

The screening was for due process, fairness, integrity of the court system, and obviously, to preserve public trust and confidence in judicial and administrative proceedings. That is the ultimate dream of America—the Rule of Law.

We worried that the case would be removed from the arbitration program. That can happen if there were great delays. Arbitration could minimize expenses and embarrassment.

"Let's just wait and see," said Roy.

"The arbitrator should only be someone with sufficient litigation skills to hear the case, otherwise, there will be severe injustice," added Harvey.

"And of course, without any conflict, or that would be the worst injustice of all injustices," I said.

"It will not be too difficult if the nominated arbitrator will immediately disclose any potential conflicts."

"You're so right, Roy."

The three of us were busy. They had other cases to take care of. So did I. We had to meet face-to-face again when all the other defendants who were my former associate attorneys were served with the summons.

I advanced payment for fees and expenses to my attorneys in lump sums. I did not need their hourly breakdown nor did I have to wait for their billing statements. They were very pleased.

* * *

Another conference. My former associate attorneys had been served and filed their own answers.

"William Copulos is represented by Calvin Young and Steven Goto, and he has a cross-claim against you," said Roy.

"I expected that. I fired him. He was so inexperienced in court trials. With the hectic pace of my office, we could not wait for him to learn. He threatened to badmouth me in the community. Now is his chance for revenge."

"Thomas Walsh is representing himself and has also a cross-claim against you."

"I also fired him for his conduct. He hired an attorney to claim unemployment benefits from me and failed. Now, he is getting even."

"How about Ron Ashlock, he is represented by David Chee, did you fire him, too?"

"He hated any kind of court appearances. My office could not afford to pay for his research. His quitting and my firing were sort of simultaneous, I was ahead by a split second—he was gone. They will try to get even," I said.

Roy and Harvey began to laugh.

"You have no friends, Erlinda. You fired everybody. They will spit venom all over you."

"I did not fire David Kuwahara. He relocated to Maui. I endorsed his application to be a circuit trial judge. He learned a lot in my office. I don't know if he pursued the judgeship."

"Well, he is represented by Christopher Bouslog and has a cross-claim against you."

"His attorney had a personal injury practice and I recall some of his clients transferred to me."

"How about Thomas Kaster?"

"I did not fire him. He relocated to California. He joined the office of the famed attorney, Melvin Belli. Someone from that office was contacting me for Tom's credentials. He has no cross-claim against me, does he?"

"No."

"He always admired my law practice. Tom worked for me twice, in my old office downtown, then, in my Ala Moana office."

"Many are just envious of you, Erlinda. You are not from here and yet, you have tons of clients."

"Their envy is unfair. I just want to help people through my profession, especially the injured and the underdogs. We worked hard in my office to produce really quality work."

The malpractice case began to generate heavy paperwork. Fees and expenses were escalating. I paid them all, and more. My finances were draining into the case.

I was not running out of legal help. I paid legal researchers. They researched and assisted in briefs.

But they had a common message once they were told of the involvement of Pohl. "Erlinda, you don't have to say that I am working for you in this case."

I had made a conclusion that each one shared the same feeling about themselves...a small fry in the community. Just like what Federizo said some time ago.

Too much apprehension in a small part of America—Hawaii—and it was happening to me. Something I never personally experienced in all the years of my legal private practice.

* * *

"Nothing is going on in the court of Judge Del Rosario at this time, is there?" I asked.

"Erlinda, your malpractice case has already been reassigned and transferred to Judge Marks," was Roy's response.

"What's his first name?"

"It is a she, not a he."

"I must have been too long on sabbatical. I'm no longer familiar with judges' names."

"So are we. It's not every day that we go to court," said Roy.

"Not even every week," added Harvey.

"Is she alright? I mean, her experience and that sort of thing...more than Judge Del Rosario?"

"We heard she was a family court judge for divorces and adoptions. She could have been an associate of a solo practitioner at some point. Don't worry, judges go through a screening process before they get appointed," said Harvey.

"Who does the screening?"

"We don't really know, we think, by the judicial commission based on written recommendations by anybody."

"How long has she been at the trial court?" I asked.

"At least many months, and this should not be the first case she will try if it gets that far," said Roy.

"I heard that the candidates for judgeship don't have to show experience of handling a court trial. I heard that judges could be appointed if they hardly stepped in a trial courtroom. I have the right to worry, if you don't mind."

"Erlinda, your worry is our worry, but judges learn right on the bench while they are doing their function. They have a vow to keep," said Roy. "With our successful Hawaii arbitration program, a miniscule percentage goes to civil jury trial. I could almost predict that your case will stop at arbitration."

"I'm just curious why my case was transferred to another court. That does not happen often."

"We have no idea. Perhaps, Del Rosario was overloaded."

"Why was my case chosen and not another? And we weren't even informed."

"Erlinda, stop! You are asking too much. Even questions we can't answer. Courts have their own system," said Roy.

"Well, the arbitrator will hear the case, but the judge will still rule on motions, and if trial is needed, she will preside and make the rulings. I am the defendant. I have to be really concerned."

"You are over-worrying. No arbitrator has been appointed yet. You might win and the case could end in arbitration."

"I don't mean any disrespect, but is there a quick way to find out about judges? Their personal lives should not be secret if their roles are public. My profession is under attack."

"The public has really no business poking their noses into judges' affairs and lives."

We have no business? I was always curious about the judge for every case I handled. A matter of habit. The legal articles could not be wrong. Know your judge. Am I over-worrying for nothing?

I thought I was—as Roy and Harvey said.

Chapter Six

One afternoon. "You will finally get to see Judge Victoria Marks," said Harvey. "Her clerk called. The first conference in her chambers has been scheduled."

Although there was no need, I wanted to attend. This would be the first time I would see the judge.

Such a conference was normal for status and scheduling. That's where the judge discovered what was going on with the case. Some problems could be discussed, such as witnesses' depositions, complexity of the case, and so on.

Roy, Harvey, and I were present. Our opponents, O'Brien and Fritz, came with their assistant female counsel. I never saw her before. The chambers of the judge was packed with attorneys.

The plaintiffs, Mr. and Mrs. Barnedo, were not in the judge's chambers. Their presence was not necessary.

I was seated beside my lawyers. I intently listened to all that transpired. Scheduling of events was discussed. And the judge was informed of the status of the arbitration process.

The court clerk was doing the Court Minutes, paying close attention to what everyone was saying. The judge wrote her notes on her pad. Roy and Harvey and the other attorneys were also taking notes. No need for a court reporter.

The conference was over within an hour or so, and we returned to our offices.

"Judge Marks is very nice. She hardly said anything. That's why the conference was quick, even with that crowd," I said.

"See? She is actually the right judge to preside in your case. Now you believe us," said Roy.

"Really very nice," added Harvey.

There were delays in the appointment of an arbitrator to hear the case. Each time the administrative judge nominated one, there was an objection, or the appointee would decline.

All the participants in the case had to be informed. It would give them time to assess the qualifications and any conflicts.

The slightest appearance of impropriety was abhorred by the program. This made the CAAP successful. It made the malpractice case drag somewhat, but that was acceptable, as everyone involved preferred arbitration.

Although simple enough, the case was very serious and sensitive and there were multiple participants.

The CAAP had probably never seen a case with such a magnitude of lawyers, whether a party, a witness, and so on, especially a malpractice case, as they were hardly ever filed.

The hope was that an arbitrator would soon be appointed so that the arbitration process could begin. Surely, each one involved had better things to do.

* * *

Months had passed by and an arbitrator could not be located to hear the malpractice case. The problem continued—it was difficult to find one well versed in civil litigation and with no conflicts.

Finally, there was a letter from the Barnedos' attorney, O'Brien. He realized the extreme difficulty and suggested that everyone should agree or stipulate to Attorney Walter Davis to arbitrate, a lawyer who had extensive trial skills and experience.

I met with Roy and Harvey. We concluded that Mr. Davis was indeed well qualified and highly respected in the legal community. And we knew he was a civil litigator who owned and led his law office, with numerous associate attorneys.

"Let's hope everybody agrees to his appointment and that he has no conflicts! It's so difficult to find one who is capable with impeccable credentials," said Roy looking relieved.

We signed the confirmation papers. There were no problems with the rest of the attorneys. Everyone had investigated and agreed to Mr. Davis as a capable and impartial arbitrator.

"It's such a great feeling," said Harvey. "It would be worth everyone's time to knock this nonsense case into oblivion so that they all can get on with their lives—wherever they are!"

How true. Not all my associate attorneys who were sued with me were still in Honolulu. The case was a disturbance.

Then, one day, I frantically called Roy. He preferred that my calls were first screened by Harvey.

"Harvey, I got mail from Ed Aoki from CAAP and confirmed it with Frances Yamada. They're removing the case from the program. I will be losing my opportunity for an arbitrator."

"I'll find out why."

"The CAAP did not even inquire from us. Are they going by any written procedures, or can someone just call them up to quickly remove the case from the program?"

"We don't know, we have no idea of their internal procedures."

Later that day, Harvey said my opponents could not find Mr. Walter Davis to arbitrate.

They nominated Mr. Davis, now they could not find him?

I knew that Mr. Davis was in semi-retirement, but he was active in arbitrations and mediations. He had closed his litigation office.

I contacted the Hawaii State Bar Association, HSBA for short. The clerk provided me with a number to call. I gave the number to Harvey and he shared it with O'Brien.

It took just a couple of days to track down Mr. Davis. He had no conflicts. He agreed to arbitrate. We informed Judge Karen Blondin, the judicial administrator for the CAAP program. The case was back in the arbitration track.

My opponents may have had second thoughts about their choice of a competent and skilled arbitrator. They seemed to wish to skip arbitration and go straight to trial with Judge Marks.

"Do you know why?" I asked my attorneys.

"We have no idea, no idea at all."

* * *

Start of another week. "Here's a copy of the Interrogatories they want you to answer," said Roy.

"There are questions here of who was involved. I have to mention Pohl. They handled the case to the end," I said.

"Erlinda, Pohl can testify for or against you. Be careful. You should discuss your answers with Sharon," said Roy.

I did not think much of what Roy said. I knew I would win in arbitration anyway. That would be the end of it. And Pohl and I were together—I had their support.

Sharon called. I did not have to call her.

"Erlinda, your answer to the interrogatory should be that you and Pohl had a different understanding. You thought we were involved in the Barnedo case and we thought we were not."

"But Sharon, you were really involved. Pohl is on the contract papers the clients signed, and they were on the list of our joint clients. I will not commit perjury. Your office had the files before delivering them to the new attorneys."

"They don't know of our involvement. But if you tell them, it will complicate your defense. It will prolong your case and may never go away. We are not lying and neither are you. Despite the papers, our understanding may be different," said Sharon. "Besides, you should have talked to me instead of the manager before surrendering the files to their attorneys."

For some reason, I heard that as a mild threat but did not think much of it. Perhaps, she was right. Mention of the extent of their involvement might only complicate a senseless case.

* * *

One afternoon, I waited for Roy and Harvey in their office. When they arrived, they looked exhausted. They must have come from the courthouse for a different case.

"Hi, Erlinda." They paused to talk to me.

"As you both know, I talked to Sharon. I still think I should clearly state their involvement."

They were suddenly formal.

"Just because you and Pohl shared an office does not mean they were involved," said Harvey.

"Huh? What did you say?"

"We are wasting our time dwelling on 'he said, she said,'" said Roy.

I did not expect their remarks. That was the first time my attorneys talked to me that way. They must have been talking about my case before they came in. Did they encounter one of the Pohl partners on the way? Their offices were footsteps apart.

"Did something happen to provoke this?" I asked.

They just proceeded to their respective rooms with their files and papers in tow.

Their secretaries, Rondie and Glenda, were a few feet away. "They are tired. They had heavy motions in another case. Discuss it with them some other time," said Glenda.

I went back to my office a few floors below.

There were many other things I had to do. I couldn't dwell on what had happened.

* * *

An early call from Harvey. "They want to take your oral deposition in their office."

My opponents wanted to question me under oath before a court reporter. Their clients would carefully work around my testimony when it was their turn to be deposed…a lawyer's gimmick.

I asked Harvey to insist that the Barnedos testify first. They were the plaintiffs who sued. Our request was months ago.

Harvey did not readily grasp my intent. But his lack of experience didn't bother me. He followed Roy's orders and Roy was already a veteran attorney.

There were too many letters, calls, and discussions regarding deposition schedules. Finally, it was arranged that the Barnedos would be deposed first.

The plaintiffs had relocated to Chicago. That was where they would come from. The last time I saw them was in 1996. It was now 2001. I wondered how we would react when we saw each other.

It was arranged that I do the questioning. I knew the events that transpired and could help dispel the accusations.

There were two of them, Mr. and Mrs. Barnedo. Their depositions would definitely take more than a day. It would be unfair to rush them to recall events of years ago.

There was no need for a Filipino interpreter. It helped. Mr. Barnedo was a licensed dentist in the Philippines. Mrs. Barnedo had an undergraduate course in nursing. Their English was good.

It was 8:00 a.m. The conference room of my attorneys was used. I walked in and greeted everyone.

Seated beside O'Brien were his clients, the Barnedos. They appeared calm. They must have been relaxing in the room before my arrival. The court reporter was ready. I was right on time.

Mr. Barnedo looked the same, just heavier. Mrs. Barnedo had hardly changed, just a bit older. Nothing alarming in their middle age.

I automatically glanced at Mrs. Barnedo's right hand where she lost two and a half fingers. She had it folded resting on the table. I did not have a good view.

Mr. Barnedo was to testify first. The court reporter did her job...Do you solemnly swear...nothing but the truth?

I began to speak. I asked Mr. Barnedo to answer what he knew and not to guess. I asked him to have me clarify a question if it was unclear. I tried to make him as comfortable as any questioning attorney should do.

Just minutes into the deposition, O'Brien asked for a recess. He went out the door with Mr. Barnedo. They talked at the end of the hallway. Then, they were back.

I continued to question him. Again, O'Brien asked for a recess to talk to his client. I agreed. Again, he went out to the hallway followed by Mr. Barnedo.

There were many more such interruptions. It was best that I was generous. Intervention by the court would cause delays. I was concerned that the couple had to get back to Chicago to their jobs and their family.

Two days were not enough. I worried that the week would soon be over and the depositions were incomplete. There were too many recesses and time that I allowed for recollection.

My co-defendants, who were my former associate attorneys, did not have to attend. Intermittently, they sent their own counsel to watch the proceedings. They were ordering the transcripts.

After all, I was still responsible for their actions in my office. What the law calls *respondeat superior*. Command responsibility! It would be unfair that their pockets be involved.

Mrs. Barnedo testified next. I prepared her the way I did with her husband. Her responses were easier and shorter.

She was in the room the entire time that her husband testified. Under the rules, she had the right to be present.

Finally, the depositions were completed. I politely thanked both husband and wife. They would soon leave Hawaii. I was sure they had enjoyed their visit with their friends and relatives.

They looked at me as if they wanted to say something. Not hostile, not adversarial, rather something friendly.

Perhaps to say, "We know you did a lot of work for us, we don't understand all that is going on."

But I did not wish to get close to them. And O'Brien would not leave them alone. They were no longer my clients. They were my legal enemies.

* * *

I dropped by the office of my attorneys one morning. They were eager to hear what happened. I had ordered rush transcripts. Some were prepared as depositions were happening.

"Can you believe their testimonies?" I said, as Roy and Harvey flipped through the records. "Read the dozens of pages of their 'I don't remembers.' I highlighted the portions for your convenience."

"Wow, Mr. Barnedo did not recall anything, not even the hearing of their case in the federal court where he was present. As if it never happened," said Roy, showing his amazement.

"They forgot their $200,000 worker's settlement even if they signed every sheet of the document? That's unreal. And you asked the department for less than $5,000 for your office fees," exclaimed Harvey.

"We had tons of clients, Harvey. Some were *pro bono*—our contribution to the community. We were hardly paid for pampering Mrs. Barnedo with her long disability benefits and fighting the insurance company for many years."

Roy was nodding. "Your law firm was commendable, Erlinda."

"I owed my success to my hard-working employees who showed their respect to all my clients, no matter who they were."

"But, Roy, how could they prove their case with 'I don't know and I don't remember'?" added Harvey, still in amazement.

"It would be impossible," said Roy. "All the transcripts must be purchased immediately. They will be our ammunition during the arbitration," he added.

My oral deposition was scheduled. It was my opponents' turn to ask me questions.

I discussed my testimony with my attorneys. I told them I had to testify that Pohl was involved if I was asked. As I spoke, I observed the facial expressions of Roy and Harvey.

"You mean, you shared the same office space with Pohl at one time?" asked Harvey.

"Harvey, that's a bit degrading. I was in partnership with them. What you call 'sharing office space' sounds somewhat insulting."

"You worked in some cases together, not all," said Roy, and his tone was very formal.

I realized that Roy and Harvey had not read the records, not even the affidavits of my previous employees, Linda Huang, Mila Cubero, Chris Dique, and Luisa Rigney.

"What...where?" they asked looking for my contract with Pohl and the affidavits as they flipped through the pages of records on their desk.

"Pohl is named all over your records. The Pohl-Dominguez contract listed the claims of Mr. and Mrs. Barnedo. These people were our joint clients."

"That's just a list. Do you have other proof? And as far as affidavits, their bias could be brought out when they testify," said Roy.

"Bias of who?"

"We don't know yet, Erlinda. It's best you have evidence other than 'he says, she says.'"

"Are you my attorneys or what?" I asked. My annoyance showed.

They looked at each other, then at me.

They began to laugh, like they were just kidding around. I managed to say, "Why do I feel like I am the enemy and Pohl is your client?"

"Erlinda, we are protecting you. We don't want any surprise evidence to be sprung at you later."

Harvey knew where my thoughts were going. "If Pohl is sued now, it will complicate matters. Do you wish this case to drag on for years?" he asked.

"We are all attorneys. We know the law. I'll be under oath. I will try to keep Pohl out of the picture. But I will not place myself in perjury," I said, hoping that another confrontation would not occur.

Our discussion was over. I was not sure what we had accomplished. Just aggravating each other. Yet, I had no time to even begin to really distrust them.

Pohl was on my side, they said so. We are in the same boat, if we sink, we all sink—one of Roy's metaphors. And it was a nonsense malpractice suit as both my attorneys agreed.

I should not waste so much time reading between the lines.

* * *

The day of my deposition to testify before a court reporter arrived. I proceeded to my attorneys' office early in the morning. I didn't know who would be with me, Roy or Harvey.

They were talking in their conference room when I arrived.

"Erlinda, it would be better if we were not with you. You're a lawyer and our presence is unnecessary."

"You mean, I will have a dual role. I will be answering and I will be objecting at the same time?"

"Nothing wrong with that."

I could represent myself alone. But I preferred if at least one of them could be there as moral support.

"I know you are busy. But Harvey, can you please come?"

Harvey looked at Roy, as if to ask, "Should I go?" Then, he opened his briefcase beside him, took out some papers and said, "Let's go, or we'll be late."

"Thanks, Harvey."

We walked toward the courthouse. Along the way was the office of my opponents, where I would be deposed. We made small talk. We hardly mentioned the case. We were both relaxed.

The receptionist directed us to a small conference room. O'Brien and Fritz were seated side-by-side. Papers were inside their unopened folders on the table.

The court reporter was ready. She was not the same person I hired to interrogate Mr. and Mrs. Barnedo.

My assigned chair was in front of O'Brien. I asked Harvey to sit on my left side, but he remained standing.

Then, he said, "I got to go now, Erlinda. Good luck." He said goodbye to O'Brien and Fritz and walked out the door.

I did not act surprised or humiliated. I was in the territory and presence of my opponents. It was planned that way. That was what I made it look like.

"Alright, Harvey, see you later," and I waved my hand at him as he was on his way out the door.

My testimony was about to begin. O'Brien had a call on his cell phone. He stood up, walked a couple of feet away to the open door in front of me.

It must have been intended. I heard everything he said. His tone was social and jovial. "Wil? Hi! Okay, Wil, don't worry, everything will be taken care of…okay, Wil!"

I was sure that the caller was my former associate attorney, William Copulos. O'Brien had sued him with me. Who would be calling O'Brien now anyway?

I felt I was fighting this battle alone! It was worse because my opponents knew it. But I convinced myself that Roy, Harvey and Pohl were with me all the way.

O'Brien did the questioning. My answers came out easily. I did not have to make up my responses as we went along.

I told him I passed the Bar Exams in the Philippines with flying colors. The same thing happened for the Hawaii Bar Exams. I handled jury trials by myself, civil and criminal.

How I wished I could do the questioning of O'Brien and confirm my suspicion that his qualifications were inferior to mine. But I was the witness! He knew almost nothing of me, born atop the mountains where births, marriages and deaths were hardly recorded, and I was already a Professor of Law in the two Philippine Universities and the Attorney of a municipality, wearing my super mini-skirts! Decades ago.

O'Brien asked about my associate attorneys. Yes, they did work for me. I was their employer and I was responsible for their actions, something I had always made clear.

Pohl's involvement came out.

O'Brien was visibly upset each time I mentioned Pohl's participation in the Barnedo matters. I thought he would be delighted. That was a huge reason for my testimony.

The day was almost over and he was running out of questions. Fritz was seated beside him and made notes for him to read. Then, he would repeat the same question.

Each time that his assistant counsel, Mrs. Sunderland, acting as a paralegal, handed him some notes, he would go over them for a long time. My deposition had become long and boring. And I realized how alone I was without Roy and Harvey, literally facing the multitude of opponents and attacked in the enemy camp—me, rolled into one: the client, the attorney, and the witness!

Finally, on the second day, O'Brien ran out of points and words to say and my testimony was over.

Thereafter was a long weekend.

* * *

In a few days, my attorneys wanted to see me. I brought the transcripts of my deposition.

"How did it go, Erlinda?" asked Roy.

"It was okay. But Pohl's name came out as my partner in the Barnedo claims. I was under oath."

"Oh?" was Harvey's reaction.

"You have to show real proof that Pohl was involved or you will appear a liar or a fool," said Roy, rather softly.

He was not joking. I observed his face. He looked serious.

"How can you even say that? You are supposed to be my lawyers. I am not a liar and I am not a fool. I never called my clients that...one reason I had flocks of them."

Mild anger may have been present in my tone.

"Come on, Erlinda, don't be sensitive. Attorneys are supposed to have no emotions."

"I'm not a robot, Roy. I am a human being as you are. To be honest with you, I testified that Pohl probably had bigger fish to fry, that's why activities have stopped. You taught me that expression for Pohl, remember?"

Roy did not respond. Instead, he said, "You should not have said that. It's so wrong."

"Your metaphor is so wrong? How?"

"Sensitive, sensitive," Harvey said smiling and almost teasing. He was trying to diffuse the tension.

We pulled away from the mention of Pohl. We were getting off topic. After all, Pohl was not sued.

I turned toward the elevator to get back to my office. "You both have a nice day."

Roy answered my greeting with advice. "Erlinda, don't rock the boat, that's all we're saying."

I wondered what he meant.

Everyone prepared for the arbitration hearing before Mr. Davis. It was fast approaching.

My attorneys named all the lead partners of Pohl as witnesses, Warren Price, Sharon Himeno, Kenneth Okamoto, Bettina Lum. I had no doubt that they would testify in my favor.

A liar? A fool? I found Roy's words a bit disturbing. But surely, he did not intend to hurt me.

I contacted Pohl's manager, Wendy. "May I have the Barnedo records kept in your office? Your paralegal Linda made some copies before delivery to the opponents."

"I don't know, Erlinda, I'll tell Sharon you called."

Sharon called. "The girls did not find any records. They may have been discarded. That was a long time ago."

"Sharon, there was a receipt signed by the messenger of my opponents when she picked up all the files from your office. I need the receipt. It's important."

"We only found a crumpled draft of the receipt from Linda's trash can. That's all."

"Please send that to me. At least, I have proof that we gave the opponents all the files, should that come up."

"It's just a draft in Linda's handwriting. It was not signed. It will not be of any help to you," said Sharon.

Linda had been gone from the Pohl firm for almost a year. It was not possible that the cleaners had not entered her room during that time. I did not speak my mind.

"How about the data in the computer, Sharon? Surely, those have not been discarded."

"I'm as computer illiterate as you are, Erlinda. I'll have the girls get to that."

In a few days, Julie Tam, their senior manager called. I was always comfortable talking to her, she was professional.

"The computers have all been donated, Erlinda."

"Donated to whom, Julie?"

"I don't know. We don't keep track. Maybe the Salvation Army or the Goodwill, or even Big Brothers."

"I may not be using the proper description, but you know what I mean—the brains of the computers—the data—the information for each case. Pohl spent nights computerizing my hundreds of files when we were together—to save data. Please!"

"We have none of those, Erlinda. They must have been destroyed then trashed."

"How? Can we trace them right away?"

"I don't know how. Even so, Sharon says that's all the information we have. Nothing more."

My calls thereafter were no longer returned.

Chapter Seven

One afternoon, I saw a piece of paper by my fax machine. It looked blemished, dirty, and crumpled. It was Linda's draft of the receipt that Sharon said was found in the trash can.

That was all that was available according to Pohl—crumpled paper in a wastebasket!

My office had always photocopied clients' records. Mila, my previous manager, kept some. These records helped her phenomenal memory when we discussed cases.

Her departure was sudden when Pohl took over. She asked my bookkeeper to store her stuff in our Sand Island storage. I imagined she hoped to be back to work for me someday.

I located Mila's sister in a Honolulu produce store. Mila had been working as a ticket checker for the airlines in Washington State. I called her up later that day.

"Please tell me that there is hope some copies of the Barnedo records are in your stuff at Sand Island?"

I could hardly wait for her answer.

Mila was recalling. Then, she said, "That case involved Japan. Ken Okamoto sometimes called me about the case. The couple always dropped by the office for their disability checks."

There was some hope.

A handyman was of great help while part of my weekend was spent sifting through boxes. There were papers everywhere. Some pertained to my bookkeeping. Some were for Mila—her personal papers, and a few for past clients she had kept for her use.

Finally!

There were about ten sheets of paper that referred to Mr. and Mrs. Barnedo. I would try to make sense of them. Anything beyond the wastebasket paper was an improvement.

What I found was paperwork from Pohl in 1993. The notes were scant. The originals were portions of what was delivered by Linda Huang to my opponents' attorneys before I was sued.

There was a memorandum of Sharon supervising her paralegal. Two attorneys in Pohl's firm were assigned to the case. I wished I could figure out their names, but the papers were unclear.

The retainers and authorizations signed by Mr. and Mrs. Barnedo for Pohl were also there, along with a written report done by a Japanese lawyer addressed to Ken Okamoto of Pohl's office.

A legal bomb was in my favor. Roy would be pleased. I was their client fighting for my rights. And I was not an enemy of Pohl—I should not be called a liar or a fool by my lawyers.

The week was just beginning. I no longer felt free to talk to my attorneys on short notice.

But they wanted to see me immediately. I told their staff that I had located some interesting papers.

Roy read what I found. He shared them with Harvey. As they turned the page, one after another, I made quick explanations. Their eyes widened.

"Why did you not give these to us earlier?" asked Roy.

"You asked me for more proof of Pohl's involvement. You don't know what I went through to find these. You may not like what you see, but those are the facts."

"Someone dropped the ball!" Roy looked at Harvey, then looked back at the papers.

"I don't understand your slang, Roy."

"Erlinda, don't pretend. You're not naive. I am not saying that the someone is you. I will have to investigate this."

"What is there to investigate?"

"Is it alright if I talk to Sharon about these?"

"You don't need my permission. Pohl and I are in this together, remember? I know you have been talking to them. I will not stop you now. I did not manufacture those papers."

I left their room. They were still reading. I could hear them talking. "Now, we have to provide copies to the other side!"

"You should!" I murmured. I did not know if they heard me.

* * *

Days after, the courthouse was full. We were there for different cases, not mine. Nobody was in much of a hurry. We stopped to talk a bit.

"No offense intended, but did you find out who dropped the ball?" I asked Roy.

"It's not that important. It could have been you, it could have been them."

"I know it was not me. Why did they do that?"

"Well, you know them. They always have bigger fish to fry!"

"Wow, your slang is making me hungry, Roy. That's all it's doing," I said as I looked toward the cafeteria.

"You are Americanized, Erlinda. You're playing games?" He was not angry. In fact, he chuckled a bit.

"See you later."

* * *

Neiman Marcus in the Ala Moana Shopping Center was having a big sale. I decided to shop. I expected to see Sharon and her sister, Sandy, at the Cafeteria, their favorite spot.

They were always friendly. They waved their hands when they saw me anywhere. I saw them sipping their tea.

They were with Bettina Lum, a named partner of their Pohl firm. The store was full of shoppers with small Neiman Marcus drinks—to encourage buying sprees.

I went around the various departments in the store.

In half an hour, I had finished my shopping. I went down the escalator and Sharon was looking at some perfume. I approached her. "Hi, Sharon, you're out shopping today!"

Without a word, she turned her back.

She must not have noticed. The crowd was thick and confusing. I went around her. I raised my right hand and moved it side to side in front of her eyes.

"Hi, Sharon, how are you?"

She turned away.

I could see her join her sister in the crowd. I eventually lost them.

In a few minutes, I saw Sharon again and she glanced at me from a few feet away—that was all.

Very odd. Very odd indeed!

* * *

The following morning, I dropped by my attorneys' office to bring research materials. I had no intention of staying. But Roy came out of his room and said, "Hi, there." He seemed to be in a good mood.

"May I see you in your room, Roy? Just one minute of your time, please?"

"Of course. Come in. What's up?"

He pressed his intercom and called for Harvey to join us. It was no longer strange. Both had to be present when I was their audience. I convinced myself it was for their convenience, so that one did not have to repeat to the other what was discussed.

A question crossed my mind. "Is this the kind of news that my attorneys should know?"

I preferred to be safe than sorry.

It was rather embarrassing. Neiman Marcus, store sales, shopping sprees, perfume and so on, could hardly be the topics in a serious case. But I had to tell them. They had to know.

I explained what happened. I was hoping their answer would put my mind at ease.

"You see...Sharon did not wish to speak to me in Neiman Marcus. I'm positive she saw and heard me. Did anything happen that I should know about?"

"The problem, Erlinda, is you ruffle feathers," said Roy.

"I'm not totally sure of what you mean. I don't speak your language with precision," I said.

"What Roy means is you irritate people," said Harvey. I could not tell if he was smiling or sneering.

"I irritate people?"

"Pohl is upset."

"Oh, you mean Pohl, not people. What about?"

"About your discovered hidden treasures," said Roy.

I knew that they had shown the records that I found to Sharon. They must have hand-carried them to Pohl's office. It was in the next building, just a few steps away.

"I discovered proof of their involvement, Roy. Who would expect a problem like this after a decade?"

Roy was silent.

"Will Pohl now testify against me? What will they say?" I asked with worry in my voice.

"Erlinda, you are killing your own case. You're intentionally destroying your chances, even if they are more than excellent. If I were you, I would make amends."

I asked Roy to explain what he just said. He claimed there was nothing to explain. Then in jest, he said, "Our one minute session is over."

"Goodbye!" I said and left.

The quick talk with my attorneys bothered me. I felt that I made Pohl my enemy.

How can an enemy testify for an enemy?

Roy had said, make amends.

I immediately wrote a letter to Sharon. My letter sounded like a global confession of sins to Pohl. I apologized for any misunderstanding. I assured them I took responsibility for my mistakes before their time. I knew, however, I had none.

As I was writing, I remembered the word used by many to describe Pohl—powerful! It showed in Roy and Harvey, and it was now showing in me. Yet, it was hard to explain.

My letter was mailed. A copy was transmitted by fax for quicker receipt by Pohl. I could not stand any more cold shoulders by my main witnesses. At least, I was learning a lot of Roy's slangs and metaphors.

A copy of my letter was delivered to Roy and Harvey. They were pleased. Their tone when we talked became lighter. All seemed well.

* * *

Arbitration day was fast approaching. So much had happened. This time, my case would be heard. Finally, my due process! Everything would soon be over. Much ado about nothing.

I contacted Harvey. I wanted to be sure we were ready for the arbitration. It would happen in their office.

"Is your conference room large enough for everyone?" I asked.

"Your former associates will be on standby. They know you will not testify against them," said Harvey.

"Will the Pohl partners and employees be there?" I asked.

"They are witnesses. They are also on standby. They are in the next building if there is a need for them," Harvey answered.

"How about Mr. and Mrs. Barnedo? Have they arrived from Chicago?"

"We don't know."

It was early in the morning. The arbitration would take place at 9:00.

Harvey was in the conference room. There were extra arbitration briefs, for Mr. Davis' ready reference, laid out at the head of the table. That was where he would sit.

The briefs contained organized events of what happened in federal court where my opponents said the malpractice occurred.

Mr. Davis must have received all the briefs and exhibits from every party days earlier. He had the legal role of the judge and the jury at the same time.

The briefs described the Hawaii federal lawsuit against Marukiku, the Japanese company, for the injuries to Mrs. Barnedo's fingers, the orders of the federal court to serve the summons by certified mail and newspaper publication, the uncollected federal default judgment for almost $485,000, and the counter lawsuit in a Japanese court against Mr. Barnedo.

Roy explained that in Japan, the head of the household is always the husband. The non-inclusion of Mrs. Barnedo in the paper summons must have been intentional, more cultural than legal, and the Japan summons was not even served.

"Harvey, I don't see copies of the deposition transcripts for the arbitrator to read."

"There's no need, Erlinda, you are here and the Barnedos will be here to testify."

"What if they don't come?"

"They signed affidavits. We agreed that Mr. Davis can consider those records."

"Their affidavits are very bad for me. They claimed I never returned their calls and did not care. Remember all their 'I don't know and I don't remember'? What was the point of my taking their oral depositions? And why did you agree to what could damage me?" I worriedly asked.

For the first time, Harvey looked very concerned. He stood up to talk to Roy. I followed him. They were searching for the deposition transcripts. They did not know where they were.

"If you don't mind, Mr. Davis can have my copies," I said. My disappointment showed.

"Okay."

Nikki approached us. "O'Brien is here."

"Is he with somebody?" asked Roy.

"He is alone. He says his clients are not here."

"Bring him to the conference room."

We were all waiting for the arbitrator. I had not seen him since I was on sabbatical leave three years earlier.

Mr. Davis walked in. He recognized me. I had appeared in proceedings that he arbitrated. We stood up and each said, "Good morning."

"Good morning also to you all, Mr. O'Brien, Ms. Dominguez, and Mr.?"

"I am Roy Chang and he is Harvey Demetrakopoulus. We represent Ms. Dominguez," said Roy.

Roy and Harvey could be identified by their last names and looks, but there were other attorneys involved. Mr. Davis did not want to make a mistake.

Mr. Davis was a litigation attorney, but did not know my attorneys. Roy and Harvey must not be that well known in the legal community even if they had been in practice for many, many years.

But there was no cause for worry. They seemed to know what they were doing.

"Where are the other attorneys?" asked Mr. Davis.

"They are on standby," said O'Brien.

"Where are the plaintiffs?"

"The presence of my clients is waived. They are in Chicago but have testified in depositions," added O'Brien.

"Oh, here they are, the deposition transcripts," said Mr. Davis. He flipped through the pages that I highlighted. He was reading. Then, he began the proceedings.

"You are all attorneys," he said. "But I will still adhere to the rules of arbitration. Even if we relax formality, I will follow procedure and apply the law to the facts proven by the evidence."

Mr. Davis continued. "This is a very serious matter. I will use logic and common sense. This is not really a complex case."

He turned to O'Brien. "You are representing the plaintiffs who brought this suit. I'll hear you first."

O'Brien began his case. He explained that he had three counts against me and my office.

"The first?" asked Mr. Davis.

"My first count is that Ms. Dominguez and her office earned an uncollectible default judgment against the Japanese company in the U.S. District Court."

"Why uncollectible?"

"She did not comply with the Hague Treaty."

"She did not what?"

O'Brien was almost mumbling some words and was hardly audible. We did not know why. Harvey was straining to hear him as he took down some notes. I quickly scribbled, "He has nothing to say."

"No compliance with the Treaty of the Hague Convention," O'Brien said loudly. "Ms. Dominguez only served the complaint by certified mail and by newspaper publication. She should have gone through the central agency."

"Who is the central agency?"

O'Brien did not respond.

"What is the central agency? The post office? The consulate? Is it defined in the Hague Treaty?"

"It's not defined, but the Japanese Consulate would do."

"That's your definition?"

"Well, yes."

"She did as she was so ordered by the federal court?" asked Mr. Davis. "Wasn't it by certified mail and by publication?"

"Yes, that's true."

"And the Japanese company obviously received the mail. They did, after all, counter-sue?"

"Well..."

"What does the Hague Treaty mean to you as to service?" asked Mr. Davis as he turned the pages of the treaty.

O'Brien pointed to portions of his brief.

"There are theories on what the Hague means, but does the Hawaii Supreme Court have an interpretation?" Mr. Davis addressed his question to both O'Brien and Roy.

"There's none," said Roy.

"Did the U.S. Supreme Court interpret the Treaty?"

"Not that I am aware of," said O'Brien.

"No," said Roy and Harvey. Roy added, "But nationwide, courts in other states have interpreted it in the same method adopted by Ms. Dominguez and the federal court in Hawaii: by certified mail. She did more than that by also publishing the summons to find out if the Japanese company had a representative in Hawaii who would appear in court."

Mr. Davis was seriously listening, then spoke.

"Did you try to collect in Japan?" he asked O'Brien.

"No. We believe it will not do us any good because of the defective service."

"That's not evidence, that's a guess," Mr. Davis remarked politely. "You might succeed in getting paid the default judgment Ms. Dominguez earned against the Japanese company. In judicial proceedings such as this, you cannot assume," said Mr. Davis. "What's your second count?"

"The Japanese company sued Mr. and Mrs. Barnedo in a Japanese court and Ms. Dominguez failed to defend them."

"Is there a law that obligates Ms. Dominguez to appear or send someone to appear before the Japanese Court?"

"Well...none, but if we were the attorneys, we would have gone to Japan," said O'Brien.

Then, Mr. Davis turned to me.

"Do you have a license to practice in Japan?"

"None whatsoever."

"Were you retained as the clients' attorney in Japan?"

"No."

"Did you tell the clients that you would hire a Japanese attorney to defend them in their court?"

"No, sir."

He looked back at O'Brien.

"What happened in that countersuit? Did the court in Japan decide against your clients?"

"We don't know, neither does Attorney Dominguez."

"Well, it's your case. You have no evidence of the result in the Japanese Court that would show whether or not your clients were damaged in that case for having no lawyer?"

No response.

"Even if there is an adverse Japan judgment presented to me, I don't see how it would have any impact in the U.S. But was there really any Japanese judgment?"

"We don't have that."

"How is that relevant if you don't know?" asked Mr. Davis softly but sternly.

"Just as I explained," said O'Brien.

"What is your third count?"

"Ms. Dominguez failed to sue the Hawaiian company. If she did, we would not be here today. That company is now defunct."

"The Hawaiian company is called Royal Trading?" asked Mr. Davis. "What kind of business did it do?"

"It was selling saimin, noodles, food supplies...it had insurance. Lots of insurance."

I thought Mr. Davis would laugh. He did not.

"Insurance is not relevant. I don't care about the noodles. Did it sell the machine?" he asked O'Brien.

"Not really. We theorize that it was somewhat a seller because..."

"Theory is not evidence. How was it involved?"

"It seems like the owner accompanied Mrs. Barnedo's employer to buy the machine in Japan…they were together…so…"

"That does not make him a seller," said Mr. Davis. "That makes him a travel companion," and I saw him smile.

"I have read your brief and your exhibits, and asked you to expound. Do you have any more counts?" Mr. Davis asked O'Brien.

"No, sir, I'm resting my case."

"Mr. Davis is really so skilled, logical and professional, it clearly shows from his questions!" whispered Harvey who was obviously pleased.

"He made it appear that O'Brien's case is pure nuisance," I scribbled, and Harvey smiled.

"Alright, let me hear from you." Mr. Davis turned to Roy and Harvey. "Who will present the defense?"

Roy stood up and walked to a huge chart resting against the board. It was a diagram. He began arguing the apparent absence of an office of the Japanese Company in the United States.

"Did anyone fully investigate the Japan Company's assets in the U.S.?" asked Mr. Davis.

I thought Roy would say that the Warren Price firm did, but he just said, "The case is now with the new attorneys and they should do that."

But he was alright. He argued as if he were in court. He was confirming all the material points that Mr. Davis brought up.

Then, Roy exclaimed in a much louder tone, "The only factual issue here for the jury, if this case is tried, would be the involvement of the Hawaiian company. But selling noodles is not the same as selling the machine. It was not in the chain of distribution."

I was reading Mr. Davis' mind—I know, I know, common sense. The arbitrator had decided. I could sense it. He was just allowing Roy to finish his speech as a matter of courtesy. Then, Mr. Davis analyzed the case.

"If the Hawaiian company did not sell the machine, it was not in the chain of distribution, it had no liability—a purely legal issue. The suit would have been frivolous if Ms. Dominguez sued the company.

"As for the manner of service on the Japanese company, obviously, the Hague Convention Treaty is for the courts to construe what it means and how it would apply in this case. Ms. Dominguez had the right to her judgment call and was approved by the federal court. Mr. O'Brien, you may not agree but that does not make malpractice.

"As for the Japanese suit against the clients, Ms. Dominguez had no legal duty to hire an attorney for the Japanese court. There is also nothing presented about the result of the Japanese countersuit against your clients."

Listening to Mr. Davis speak, I was sure that his decision would be for me.

Arbitrator Davis turned to all of us and said, "I will decide this case based on the evidence, not on guesses or assumptions. If appealed, the trial will need live witnesses."

He continued, "This is a serious matter involving the legal profession of defendants and the injury of plaintiffs. Nobody wants to be in either position."

Then, Mr. Davis' tone became more formal as he made his closing remark.

"I was appointed to decide. I have no conflict. I have a vow to keep. I will do the legal and moral thing or I have no business sitting here. Mr. O'Brien, I'm sorry, you have no case. My decision is for the defendants. You will all receive my written decision in a few days."

We stood up for Mr. Davis' departure. O'Brien extended his hand to shake Roy's. I could not hear what he said. He must have congratulated Roy for winning.

"Thanks," said Roy.

I stayed behind.

The excitement of Roy and Harvey was immediate and apparent. I was pleased that they were happy for me.

"Thank you so much for your services," I said.

"We have been telling you, Erlinda, there is no malpractice. You just don't listen. You always make a big deal of everything," said Roy.

I did not know when I made a big deal. But Roy's huge chart and Mr. Davis' decision convinced me that they were really on my side. They worked hard. And we won. No need for confrontation.

"Do you think they will appeal?" I asked.

"They would be crazy to do so," said Harvey. "We could hit them hard with attorneys' fees and expenses."

"I hope they don't."

Within a week, I dropped in to see my attorneys. They were in their coffee room.

"I won, but there is still the stigma of being sued for malpractice," I told Roy and Harvey.

"Magistrate Kevin Chang and I were talking at the federal courthouse. He complimented you and said, 'Erlinda? Malpractice? Unbelievable! She would not forget to sue even a witness on the sidewalk if she could!'" said Harvey laughing.

"I respect him, too. We had been adversarial in high civil litigation. He deserves his present position. He seemed to quickly know how to decide the issues without guesses, which is a skill that is critical for his position."

Then, I handed Roy an envelope and he pulled out the content. "Are you sure, Erlinda?" asked Roy and I could see he was pleased. "This is too much!"

"Yes, I'm positive." I had just paid them more fee than agreed on. "I'll prepare my share of the fees for the arbitrator."

"Erlinda, Mr. Davis informed the CAAP, he does not wish to be paid for his services by the parties."

Just like me, Mr. Davis kept on with his pro bono services—his contribution to society—to help impart justice.

Chapter Eight

The rule allowed an appeal to the trial court, filed within twenty days from service of the arbitration decision. I marked the deadline. It was easy to recall. The decision was signed on Valentine's Day, February 14, 2002. On the last day, O'Brien appealed.

Harvey called.

"Roy wants me to tell you there's not much to do. We will just wait and see if they really have the guts to go to trial with nothing."

"Harvey, do you know why they appealed? With their lack of evidence, it almost seems that someone is telling them to keep going with a hit or miss, assume and guess. And please check if they appealed in time. It seems they are late and their appeal document may be insufficient."

"Check mails?" Harvey showed mild annoyance. "Me, check mails?"

Harvey was insulted with my request, but I just let it go. I could do some reconstructing to find out. I wondered what could happen if their client was not an attorney.

Weeks were passing by quickly. I did not wish my opponents to have time to find or create evidence although I was unafraid of the truth.

I requested my attorneys to seek dismissal from the judge using a Motion for Summary Judgment. There could be a quick disposition of the case without a trial.

That should happen as the facts were clear and undisputed, which would result in a legal action of the judge in a summary proceeding.

Roy and Harvey would provide the judge with the same materials presented to the arbitrator. The arguments with the arbitrator and with the judge would be identical. We knew our opponents had not improved on their evidence.

The malpractice case had been pending for three years. Our opponents had guesses and assumptions. By the rules, the court must not wait for evidence to happen in the future.

We prepared for our motions. They would be heard before the judge to whom the case was transferred, Judge Victoria Marks.

One obvious ground or legal basis was the Hague Treaty. The Hawaii State Supreme Court never had the occasion to interpret the portion of that international law regarding service of process in foreign countries or if Japan was a true signatory.

It's not up to the jury to interpret the law. And if there could be several reasonable interpretations undetermined by the court, there was no error. Attorneys had the right to what the legal authorities describe as their judgment calls.

Another ground was there was no law requiring me to hire a licensed attorney, or practice before the Japanese courts—especially since I was not an attorney licensed to practice in Japan. Really a basic argument.

And my opponents had no proof of the result of the countersuit filed by the Japanese company that had caused them damage. They had no Japanese judgment.

Another ground was that the Hawaiian company, Royal Trading, did not sell the noodle machine that injured Mrs. Barnedo. It was not in the chain of distribution of the sale of the machine. I was right not to sue the company.

I remembered the words of Arbitrator Davis. The case was not really complex. But common sense and logic were needed.

Our foremost ground, however, was the statute of limitations. The malpractice suit was filed outside the limited time provided by law. Six years in the State of Hawaii.

In 1989, my office filed the federal suit for Mrs. Barnedo's injuries. She and her husband enjoyed their disability benefits year after year. In 1993, we asked the federal court for the default judgment against the Japanese Company. In 1999, they sued me and my office.

There are statutes or laws that limit the time to file suits. It had been over a decade! Many witnesses had died or disappeared. Laws also protect the person sued—the defendant.

"We have covered all the grounds. This malpractice case sounds so glamorous, but there is nothing to it—all it has is false grandeur!" said Roy. "Nothing should get to the jury."

"Your opponents could make a thousand counts, but if there is no case, there is no case. They are trying to tarnish your name and reputation," said Harvey.

"You're right, Harvey, they only sued me when I came back from sabbatical leave and reopened my legal practice."

It revived my confidence in them when my attorneys talked that way. The arbitration decision must have made a good impact.

"Later, we should claim for all my expenses. I paid you generously, but you deserve it," I said. "I just wish this nuisance would go away."

When the motions were signed, another conference was scheduled in their office.

"There's just no reason that the judge will deny the motions. We will soon be celebrating," commented Harvey.

"You mean that?" I asked, although I believed him.

"Have I ever lied to you, Erlinda? We all know that their case is nothing but fiction. All theories with no evidence."

Roy was nodding. I recalled his big chart and diagram. He had done decent work for me thus far. We won in the arbitration. He must really be protecting me.

* * *

My attorneys were laughing as I entered their conference room one afternoon. They were in one of their better moods. Their office work must have been lighter.

"I was just watching Judge Judy on television," I said. "She yelled at the plaintiff, 'You came to tell me a story not a case, you are wasting my time, get out of my courtroom!' I hope that happens in my case."

"I saw that, too," said Harvey. "Mr. Davis must have felt that way when O'Brien presented his story, not a case. Judge Judy is really quick, so intelligent and funny, rarely soft spoken, but so right."

They had a television set in their office. I knew Roy and Harvey watched programs during their breaks.

"One more thing before I go," I said. "No State court should be questioning court rulings in the federal case. If the jury trial proceeds, don't you agree it would amount to that?"

"We agree. We should have elevated this malpractice case to the federal court. That's where all the alleged problems originated," said Harvey.

"It's too late for that talk," retorted Roy. He was clearly annoyed at what Harvey just said.

"That was what I asked you to do before. Do you want me to have the researcher work on that?" I asked. "The federal court is a separate and a higher court. We could probably still do something now."

"We know what we are doing, Erlinda," said Harvey. "You are wasting your time and money on research," he added as he redeemed himself to Roy.

"Are you having second thoughts of our representing you?" asked Roy in his usual low tone.

"I'm here to professionally discuss my case with you. I hope I may be of help in my own case."

I convinced myself that nobody was really angry. That was just the way we talked sometimes. In some ways, Roy and Harvey were right—I was not used to being a client.

* * *

Harvey called. "Can you drop by to sign your affidavit for the motions?"

Roy's paralegal was a notary public. It was convenient to sign affidavits.

Finally, our motions were scheduled to be heard.

"You don't have to come, Erlinda," said Roy.

"Will the two of you attend?" I asked.

"Yes."

"I have read the opposition briefs. They just rehash the same things from the arbitration," I said.

"That's true. The judge will see how fictional their case is," said Harvey.

Roy was again silent. He just looked at Harvey as if to say don't use that word again!

"I hope you read the research materials which I hardly had time to do," I said, and I looked at both of them.

"Everything is under control, we know what we are doing. There's too much discussion and too much research. It's overwhelming for nothing," said Roy.

"We're doing our own research. You are wasting time and money," added Harvey as he pointed to volumes of research materials in one corner of their room.

At least, they were concerned about my finances and litigation expenses. And their services were of much help to me. It saved me time to attend to my clients' cases.

My name appeared as co-counsel, but Roy and Harvey were in full control. I thought that was the better way. But I was getting more careful of what and how to say things.

Was my Filipino accent still so strong that it could be misinterpreted? I did not think so. Even then, I was their client and had the right to politely demand. They should know that.

Neither did my color have anything to do with our occasional heated discussions. The spouses who sued me were also Filipino. But they were simply clients, and I was a lawyer-client.

I should not be thinking that way, or I was certainly at an extreme disadvantage.

In the afternoon, Harvey called. "We lost all of the motions, I'm very sorry, Erlinda."

"Why?"

"We presented the same arguments that made Mr. Davis decide in your favor, but Judge Marks did not wish to dismiss the case. She thinks that everything should go to the jury, everything—the factual and the legal issues."

"Did she state her reasons?"

"Not really," said Harvey, as if it would not be productive for him to explain.

"But the motions were heard and there were arguments?"

"Of course. She disagreed with us, that's all. She does not even have to state her reasons. She is a judge," said Roy.

"You mean the judge will ask the jurors, who are lay people, to decide the meaning of the Hague Treaty law and to guess the laws of Japan?"

"It seems to be that way," said Harvey.

"Courts interpret the law and the jury is told to apply the law to the facts in evidence. The jury does not interpret laws ever!" I said automatically and in desperation.

"We know that, Erlinda. You don't have to lecture us. Reserve your arguments. You may want to represent yourself."

Harvey sounded so worried. He was simply making me his sounding board for what all of us felt. Sheer frustration.

"How about the argument that the case was filed late?"

"The judge thinks that the six years limitations began to run from the time the clients were told by their new attorneys that your office made mistakes, under the discovery rule."

"Are you kidding me, Harvey? The new attorneys even lost the records delivered to them. They should be facing the malpractice, not me."

"No time for jokes, Erlinda."

"The client could locate any attorney who would tell him what he wants to hear fifty years from now and resurrect a dead case? There's no such thing as statute of limitations in Hawaii?"

Both Roy and Harvey looked grim. It appeared that we were in for a confusing and long trial.

"I don't mean to be repetitious, but we will soon come face-to-face with the jury. The judge has to decide the meaning of the Hague Treaty as to summons and its applicability. It's really now or never!" I said. "It's no guessing time as the judge admitted she was doing. Everyone's constitutional rights are at stake."

"Erlinda, you better read the transcript. You seem to doubt us. We thought we were clear but we did not seem to be on the same page with the judge. Perhaps, you could have done better."

They were getting irritated. I thought it best to suspend the topic.

I read the transcript when it arrived. Roy and Harvey were not lying. After long debates among the attorneys about the Hague Treaty and the Japanese foreign laws, the judge ruled in a short single paragraph which read verbatim:

THE COURT: "I have to confess. I'm sort of shooting from the hip in trying to respond to your question about when and how do you want the Court to decide on the law, I guess. But I would encourage you to file an early motion *in limine*."

Although I had a good idea, I later asked Harvey what the American slang of shooting from the hip meant exactly, in relation to the serious court proceedings—words I never saw in the law books, or heard in a courtroom.

He explained—it was a cowboy shooting wildly without any target, in this case, the issues.

"Harvey, with all due respect to the court, instead of guessing as she admitted, the judge seemed determined to have the jury interpret the Hague treaty and the Japanese laws, which is not their role to do. She was already talking of motion *in limine*—the procedure to sort out the proper evidence shown to the jury. Why?"

"I have no explanation, Erlinda. We can't force judges to do what we want even with tons of research. Our role is limited."

My worry was overwhelming. I had to bring up my deep concerns with my attorneys.

"Was the judge actually sending us a message that a different judge should take over? It would be too burdensome for her if she never encountered this kind of problem before. Who knows, this had always been what she wanted—to get out of the case. That would be fair to her and to everybody."

"We don't think so. If we said something, it will also be a guess. It will lead us nowhere. We think that you're being repetitious and you are appearing more ridiculous."

As I walked away from their office, I just said softly, "You don't have to raise your voice. Your services are not free. I have been paying you big time!"

But we were all lawyers. I should be used to that kind of talk.

* * *

Roy was on the phone. We had to prepare for a pre-trial settlement session with the judge. I thought it was serious. He did the calling and wanted me to see them immediately.

"Perhaps you should seriously think of settling the case," he said.

"I don't understand. We called the case fictional. I won in arbitration. Now, you're telling me to seriously consider settlement?"

"Well, we have to say something to the judge. Besides, this case should just disappear. You will have no further litigation expenses. There will be no problems for anybody. Done. Kaput!"

"I know everyone is tired, Roy. The judge should have dismissed the case."

"Even if she did, it would not necessarily end there. Your opponents can appeal. They can do other stuff."

"Like what other stuff?"

Roy was annoyed. "It's up to you, Erlinda. At least I told you my thoughts. There are no guarantees at trial."

Why would any judge gamble with my fate in a jury trial if the facts are clear? It's unconstitutional to attempt to make a case. The court would just apply the law to the facts and dismiss the case. As in the arbitration, O'Brien was just telling a story, not presenting a case. Mr. Davis decided in my favor, right there in the arbitration room. Simple, nothing complicated!

"Can't you do something? You represent me," I added, and they knew I was extremely worried."

"Well, we tried and we failed. Your fate will be decided by the jury. You are entitled to your own opinion, as is the judge. This is a free country."

Roy sounded as if he was scolding me, but his tone was already familiar and acceptable, often soft and extremely civilized.

Settle the case? My conscience and self respect would never let me live with that decision. It would be immoral.

* * *

My attorneys required my presence in the settlement conference. We were early. One more time, Roy asked me to consider settlement.

"Alright, Roy. Offer twelve thousand? That ought to make them happy…at the most, perhaps, fifty? Don't lay all our funds on the table. They have no evidence. You, yourselves, agree. I am paying them for tarnishing my name."

"Judge Marks might be insulted with such a paltry amount."

"Roy, the judge is not a party."

"She's trying to help everybody. She's doing her job. She might find your offer offensive and a waste of her time."

I did not believe that my offer was a waste of time. I attended settlement conferences for my own clients. Judges often suggest the outright dismissal of a baseless case even if the conference was called settlement.

The schedule arrived. In a few minutes, we would appear before the judge. We should not be seen arguing among ourselves.

O'Brien and Lane, his investigator, were together. Lane was carrying two briefcases. But he always insisted on being in the judge's chambers although he was not an attorney.

Mr. and Mrs. Barnedo did not travel from Chicago but they were available by telephone. My former associate attorneys were not there. They had been dismissed from the suit by my opponents, and they knew I would never betray them.

It was regular procedure. Judge Marks talked to Roy and Harvey while O'Brien waited for his turn outside the judge's chambers. Roy was the spokesperson. The discussion was semi-confidential. Nobody was around except the court personnel.

The judge asked how much we were offering, a standard procedure in such a conference.

Roy looked fearful to say anything that might offend the judge. This was professionalism to him. All I knew was that the judge was not a party and she should not bring in her feelings.

Roy hardly discussed our defenses. He just mentioned them quickly and in passing. It almost seemed that it was just a matter of how much I was to pay, not whether my opponents had a case.

With Roy's soft voice, and the judge not talking so much, it was difficult to understand exactly what was going on. It was like a silent body communication.

Then, looking almost embarrassed, Roy mentioned an amount we discussed and I authorized.

It was O'Brien's turn to talk to the judge. We had to wait outside the chambers. It was taking longer than we expected. I wondered what they were talking about. My curiosity was normal.

The door opened and O'Brien stepped out. We were called in.

Judge Marks looked at Roy and talked almost inaudibly. I thought I heard her say something that sounded gruesome, "Why don't you split the baby?"

She glanced at me. There were words said before and after that I hardly understood. They became a blur.

It was shocking. The metaphor was graphic, and I would never be used to it. Was I only imagining morbid things?

Harvey looked more shocked as I quickly whispered, "Did I hear her words right? How much? Tell her we won in arbitration."

"Shut up! I think they're asking too much," he whispered. "I can hardly hear what the judge is saying."

The conference was over. There was no settlement. We went back to our offices. The three of us were exhausted.

The day after, I was back in my attorneys' office.

"They have the nerve to ask for half a million? Is that what they are demanding?" I said in disgust. "How they wish! They already lost in arbitration. To today, they have not improved their evidence—they have none."

"There's really nothing specific, Erlinda. They're making known that they are at hundreds of thousands of dollars. They had letters. Nothing new and surprising happened in the conference."

"They threatened to add interest, their fees, and their expenses when they prevail. The judge was in the middle so everyone would be somewhat pleased and the entire problem would disappear forever," added Harvey.

"You mean, splitting over a million when, as the arbitrator said, they have no case? They assume they will win at trial?" I asked in disbelief. "Pohl signed a tolling agreement. My opponents have become brazen. Perhaps, Pohl should now settle so all problems will disappear. They're very, very rich. They don't need the money and they have insurance."

"Let's just move on," said Roy. "We will have to prepare for trial. You keep on mentioning Pohl, we are again sidetracked on the issues."

* * *

I worked more hours in the cases of my clients and kept away from thoughts of my case. I could be tied up in court during the trial. A load of work when I returned would be too burdensome.

One morning, I was in the courthouse for a client's case. I saw John Yuen at the lobby. He had became associated with the Ahuna Law Firm in Kailua since he left Pohl's employment and my office.

He looked different from when he resigned. He was now happier and more relaxed. He had even gained weight.

I still had a list of researchers. Some were licensed attorneys. But I wanted back-up support for eventualities. I was also hoping for more moral support from John.

"I'm glad to see you, John. I may need your help in research. You can do that outside your office hours, yeah?"

"I'd be delighted, Erlinda. How is Judge Del Rosario in your case?" he asked.

"The case has been transferred to Judge Marks."

"The female judge?"

"Yes, there is only one Marks on the bench, I think."

"Erlinda, isn't she the wife of Attorney Marks? Why is she getting involved in your case?"

"Who is Attorney Marks?"

"He works in Pohl's office downtown...maybe a giant partner. He used to be the Attorney General after Warren Price."

"What?"

I knew that John was mistaken. He must be referring to a different man. There were many Marks in the phone books. Hawaii had many attorneys, many residents and many, many tourists. I did not even know the names of my next door neighbors.

We slowly walked to a corner of the courthouse and talked in a low voice.

"John, what are you talking about?" I said in distress. He looked apprehensive. He hurriedly changed the topic to a forthcoming Hawaii Bar Association function.

"The judge is the wife of a partner at Pohl? You worked in my office, John. You know that Pohl and I were the attorneys for the Barnedos who claim my office committed malpractice, even if they were not included in the suit."

"Erlinda, I'm sorry. I think he's a different person and Judge Marks is very new on the trial bench...I can't connect them...I really can't tell. I think I was wrong, I'm sorry."

"You were spontaneous. And Pohl hired you before. Please, John, help me on this."

"Just like you, I was hardly in their office. And people there keep to themselves, within their circle. I don't know more than you do. You and I were both outsiders to them even when we worked together in your office. You know that, Erlinda."

John had urgent things to do and asked to be excused.

Like the rest, he did not want to be really involved. I never blamed him. He had to survive and worked hard for his clients, a good man.

I quickly left the courthouse to make some calls. The Bar Association could not release information. The Judicial Commission was on recording. The Court clerks would not say anything. And I was too ignorant to explore the internet. Besides, personal information about judges was usually deleted.

Roy and Harvey were waiting for me. I had requested an urgent meeting.

"It seems my real nightmares are just beginning," I said.

"Why so?" asked Harvey.

I told them of my trip to the courthouse, my talk with John Yuen, what he said, and what he did not wish to say.

"Who is this John?" asked Harvey.

"He was hired by Pohl to work in my office at Ala Moana shortly after our written contract. I think Roy met him there."

Roy was intently listening. I tried to anticipate what he would say. Then, he spoke in his usual mild way.

"Erlinda, we don't know much about Judge Marks. She was married to Robert Marks, the attorney who is in Pohl's office. That was a long time ago. Their present relationship is vague."

"You should know how things are sometimes...divorce here, divorce there, divorce everywhere," said Harvey, making the topic light and almost forcing a laugh.

"They may now be strangers to each other. We should not be investigating the lives of judges. It's disrespectful and rude. That would be disruptive of their role to hear cases," said Roy.

I said, "This problem has no place in court—if the judge who will try my case is the spouse of someone in the camp of my ultimate legal enemies even if they were not named in the suit. That mocks the entire judicial system, don't you both agree? We should tell her. She may not know the issues."

"The judge, herself, will tell us if she has a reason to step aside. That's what they call recusal."

Roy looked at Harvey as if he should not have said the word.

"Isn't that mandatory? I have clear potential and very serious conflict with Pohl. We should go through the same process we had used to screen the arbitrator, Mr. Davis. Judges are not exempt from the rules of ethics. They might even be held to a much higher standard, don't you think so?"

"Erlinda, the judge must really believe she will be fair and just. That's her call to make. It's not for you to dictate what judges do. None of your business, really!"

"Roy, you are again getting irritated. Did you even find out why the case was transferred to her from Del Rosario? You said you would. All of these happenings may be innocent, but they are scary to me. You are my lawyers. We have to know, it's critical."

Just as I suspected, they suddenly had other things to do. They insisted that I schedule a future appointment to discuss the matter with them at length.

Harvey was still talking as I walked toward the elevator to go down to my office. Both were looking at me. "Erlinda, don't be paranoid. It will only confuse the issues."

I did not know what to feel, but knew that something must be done. I decided to do some research.

There was little doubt that judges had integrity. They had seminars and standards of morality. But I had to confide my concerns with Roy and Harvey. They were paid to defend me.

In a few days, I was back in my attorneys' office.

"Please move for Judge Marks' recusal. I think she is very much married to Attorney Marks in Pohl's office. I can prepare the form for you to sign. For all we know, she's waiting for our motion to let her go."

"Why? I don't think she knows that Pohl was involved in the Barnedo claims. I don't think she knows anything about Pohl taking over your office, your claims and your cases," said Roy.

"The Pohl partners have been identified in the court records, and brought up in conferences with her. Pohl and I had disagreements when we parted ways. I'm your client! Let's remind her if she forgot—please! Her husband is with Pohl and as we speak, may be having a coffee break with Warren Price. I don't mean any disrespect. I'm just scared."

Roy immediately stood up. I thought he would walk out the door. But he was just breathing deeply and looking out the window for a few seconds. Then, he sat down again.

"If we recuse her, there will be grave consequences," he said, looking so worried.

"How?"

"It's too late. The case is ready for trial. You can be sanctioned, and we will not look good to the judge for you."

"But I did not know, Roy. Mr. Davis' qualifications were screened even by those who were out of Honolulu for a fair arbitration. And now this? This is unbelievable!"

"It's not that unbelievable, and she is not bad. You will just antagonize her. And I really think she could be in your corner," Roy said, and he smiled at Harvey.

"I didn't say the judge is bad. You know how the subconscious mind works. I want the law applied for me, not that she is in my corner. I believe in the merits of my defenses."

"One more time, Erlinda. I'm telling you. You're killing your chances with the court."

"You are losing track of the merits of your case. You are getting personal," added Harvey.

"How?"

"Recusals or disqualifications of judges are personal. You will ask her to step aside? That would attack her integrity. Judges know themselves. You can't be choosing your own judge."

My attorneys were putting elements of hypocrisy into our profession. I was deeply hurt and angered.

I was not yelling, but I said, "You are both cowards—afraid to say anything to offend the judge, afraid to defend me, afraid to talk, afraid that your legal practice will be affected. I don't wish to practice law in your style. That's not living. That's existing in glamour, that's all you have! That's all!"

I offended Roy and Harvey and I quickly apologized. "I'm sorry, really so sorry. I must be distraught and confused. Please understand my situation. I take back what I said."

They both seemed to understand and sympathize.

"Let it ride. We should be a team, we have a trial to get through," said Harvey. "You won in arbitration, the judge will clearly see the evidence was the same in arbitration where you prevailed. You are needlessly worrying," said Harvey.

"But when will she see?"

Finally, Roy said, "Let's compromise. When the records are clearer, I'm sure the judge should bring up her relationship. We will then ask her to step aside. Fair enough, Erlinda?"

Harvey looked at me with encouragement. But I just responded softly with, "I don't know. I guess. Whatever you think is best...I can't think anymore. How much clearer can the records be, they are so clear as we speak!"

As I stepped out of their office, many thoughts seemed to follow me ...The judge is the wife of a partner of Pohl. Then, Roy's voice...She could be in your corner, you might antagonize her, there may be nothing to disclose... that's her call, you know the rules.

Lawyers are embarrassed to lose a case. Certainly, Roy and Harvey could not be an exception. Nothing bad will happen, I repeatedly assured myself. Or, I would spend twenty-four hours a day worrying for nothing.

Chapter Nine

Roy was in his lighter mood one afternoon when I dropped by their office. He appeared to have good news. "Be seated, Erlinda," he said as he invited me into his room. He did not bother to call for Harvey. Must be a quick talk.

"Justice Paula Nakayama and Justice James Duffy of the Supreme Court are on my side. I just know their train of thought. I was just talking to Justice Duffy a few days ago."

"Really? How well do you know them, Roy?"

"Oh, we know each other pretty well. It's hush, hush, and I had no reason to tell you this. Paula and I worked together before. Do you know any of the five justices, Erlinda?"

"I practiced before the courts of Justice Simeon Acoba and Justice Ronald Moon before they were appointed to the Supreme Court, that's all."

"How about Justice Steven Levinson?"

"No, I heard he was a partner of David Schutter, the famed criminal attorney, a long time ago. I don't know if that's true. I would prefer that he was not. O'Brien worked in Schutter's office. I'm not implying anything. Hawaii's legal community could be small."

"You did not meet Justice Acoba at a social function? His roots are Filipino, although he was born in Hawaii."

"No. I hardly ever attend functions. And as for Justice Nakayama, the only female justice, I did not have the pleasure of meeting or seeing her. I'm glad that you worked with her before, Roy. Was she your partner?"

Roy did not respond but asked, "You're not social, Erlinda?"

"No."

Roy was likable and sociable. That was a big asset in his practice. I was thinking that way as I returned to my office. I was really in good hands.

* * *

Again, I dropped by the office of my attorneys one early morning. They were kneeling on the floor organizing charts for the trial. Their mood had drastically changed.

"Isn't it tragic?" I said. "You are working long hours. And here I am spending too much money for a case we thought was nonsense from the beginning. A tremendous turn of events!"

"That's our profession. You must know that the public has a poor perception of attorneys and the system sometimes," said Roy as he stuck more labels to his records. But he was smiling.

Roy had blurted out something almost unconnected to what I had said. He was physically and mentally exhausted. It did not look good.

"There must be a reason for everything, a purpose," said Harvey.

"Are you awake, Harvey?" I said. "You sound like you're talking in your sleep."

"Well, things don't add up. It's difficult to change gears and adjust. The trial is coming up in a few days! We never thought it would get this far."

I remembered how Harvey was annoyed at my request that he would check their mails when my opponents appealed. They must really dislike any kind of manual labor even for a client.

My attorneys looked worn out and depressed. I did not want their mood to remain dismal. It might affect my trial.

"Good news," I said. "My previous manager, Mila, will arrive from Washington. She will testify about all the work my office did. There's no truth to the Barnedos' accusations that I did not return their calls for many years."

"They should have dropped you as their attorney if that was true. But years later, we are now made to prove the opposite of what they claim," Harvey said.

"I agree," said Roy without hesitation. "Erlinda is presumed guilty of malpractice until proven otherwise, and we still don't know what their malpractice case really is."

The Pohl partners were on call for the trial and so were their employees. They would testify if we needed them. My former associate attorneys were also on standby for my opponents.

It looked like somehow, Roy, Harvey, and I were finally a more solid team. It added to my confidence while the jury trial of the case against me and my law office was looming over our heads.

* * *

It was early morning. It was not quite 8:00, but my attorneys were in their office, possibly since dawn. I wanted to help if I could.

"They're preparing for the Motions *in Limine*," said Nikki. "Everything is under control."

They would once more appear before Judge Marks and discuss the evidence that could be submitted to the jury. Discard what the rules did not allow.

The procedure is geared to protect constitutional due process, the right to be heard with competent information, to cross-examine and interrogate your accuser.

"Nikki, if I could be of any help, you know where to contact me at any time and at any place."

My attorneys had my cellular and land phone numbers. I asked my friends and relatives not to tie up my lines. They understood. Their moral support was enough.

Clients came to see me as usual. They were unaware that I was facing the worst challenge in my career. There was no need to tell them. I wanted their full trust in me as it had always been.

The revenues of my legal practice helped in the tremendous expenses of my litigation. I had no choice but to continue practicing law.

Important events in my life were on hold. I could not visit my country. My mother was not as active and could not travel from the Philippines to Hawaii. She had been told of my case by my siblings in the kindest way possible. She never wavered in her trust in me and in the U.S. judicial system.

I was behind in other things: my taxes, my dancing lessons, even my jogs in the parks. My relationship with my family was not as intimate either. I seemed to be missing most of my life as everything was out on a chaotic standstill.

My friends told me of Paul Newman playing the role of a lawyer in the classic movie, *The Verdict*. He did everything possible against all odds. The truth prevailed. I hoped the same thing would happen in my case.

But that was fiction and mine was reality.

* * *

"Come immediately, Erlinda, we have to talk. We are dead in the water," Roy cried frantically on the phone.

I hurriedly drove to their office wondering what could possibly be worse than the current situation.

Roy and Harvey were waiting for me. They were seated side by side in their conference room as usual, scanning through records laid out on the table.

Harvey closed the door, then went back to his seat.

I had hardly seated myself comfortably when Roy began to talk. "Erlinda, be prepared for what we are to tell you!"

"Something happened?"

"We filed our Motions *in Limine* early as Judge Marks suggested—to guide her on how to rule on the Hague Treaty and the Japanese laws. But she ruled the same way, all those legal questions will go to the jury," said Roy.

"And the judge has admitted into evidence bulks of papers that will assure the opponents' winning without supporting live witnesses," added Harvey. "She will continue to admit just papers."

"What do you mean bulks of papers?"

"Just papers. Papers that the judge did not screen. They will be the opponents' evidence."

Harvey looked angrier as he continued to explain.

"Just what are those papers?" I asked.

"Affidavits, medical records, transcripts of court proceedings—with the discussions, questions and answers among the magistrate, your associate attorneys, the clients—from when you were fighting for the Barnedos against the Japanese company. Those bulks of papers will come as they are, uncensored!"

"The whole nine yards of papers and papers, without supporting live witnesses!" exclaimed Roy. "We will really be buried in nothing but papers."

"That's not the way cases are tried. I was fighting for the opposite in the federal court, to get the Barnedos something even if my office had just a glimmer of hope that the defaulting Japanese company would have assets in the U.S. ready for its payment."

"We know. You did more than what you were supposed to do."

"The way the judge wants to try the case should not happen in court, not even in law school mock trials. We cannot cross-examine those papers. It's like giving to the jurors textbooks and ready-made cooked evidence of tons of objectionable hearsay for my opponents without my say. You must be joking," I said in a panic.

"That's how the judge ruled. What can we do?"

"I'm entitled to a trial within a trial. This is a malpractice case. The product defect case I filed for the Barnedos in the federal court must be tried like it was contested. Then, another trial for the malpractice to find out what went wrong."

"We argued all of that, we really did," said Roy.

"This procedure is used throughout the entire United States to give practicing attorneys their due process. Law practice is not life insurance, you know that!"

"Erlinda, the judge did not agree with the Hawaii case law in the Greenstein case and the unanimous case laws which set forth the need for two contested trials. She even refuses to bifurcate and separate the malpractice and the product defect trials," said Harvey. "Everything will be a chaotic confusion."

"What will we do now?" I asked in total alarm. "Do what you can. Continue to object, please!"

"Give her a chance, she will come around," said Roy. "She will really come around."

I somewhat understood the American slang, but was not too sure what Roy really meant. I was scared to speculate that the judge was too inexperienced for trial. Roy, Harvey and myself never heard that she personally handled a jury trial in her practice before her appointment. Perhaps, not even a bench trial.

"This is a legal nightmare. I will be tried on papers and everything goes to the jury, including legal questions? This is not an uncontested divorce or adoption case that the judge may have handled."

"Erlinda, we agree with you, but there's no sense that we punish ourselves and agonize over this. Let's do the best we can, and we can always appeal," said Roy, trying to pacify me.

"Do the Barnedos have any live witnesses or will they just haul their piles of records and papers into the jury room?"

"They have Allen Williams as their legal expert. He flunked the Bar Examinations in California, made it the second time around, and now works here as an attorney in a law firm. Those are his expert qualifications," explained Harvey.

"And Williams is supposed to be better than you, me, my associate attorneys, and the Hawaii federal court? Now, I know you were kidding all along and I did not even know it."

"Erlinda, this is a desperate situation. Listen well to everything we're telling you. We don't have much time," said Harvey.

"If he testifies, what exactly will he say?"

"That your office and the federal court were both wrong in the method of service of the summons to the Japanese company."

"Please tell me that everything is just a very sick joke!"

There was no joke.

* * *

My attorneys prepared for trial. They had Nikki, their paralegal, call me when they wished to inform me of anything.

"The Waikiki hotels want your credit card numbers for the hotel expenses of our witnesses," she said.

"And our experts have to be paid in advance," reminded Harvey. "They reserved their hours for your case."

One by one, my witnesses were accounted for. I was resigned to spending too much for something that was not necessary.

The owner of the defunct Royal Trading Company, Roy Ueijo, had been located in Las Vegas. He needed a downtown hotel where his Hawaiian friends could visit him.

Ueijo would testify that he sold noodles to the employer of Mrs. Barnedo and did not sell the machine that injured her. His company was not in the chain of distribution of the product.

Our Engineering expert, Dr. Richard Gill, would arrive from California on the date of his testimony. He would testify that the machine was not defective when Mrs. Barnedo put her fingers on it to wipe the rollers that were clearly rotating. He will perform a common sense demonstration.

Our legal expert in U.S. law, Elton Bain, had his office in Honolulu. He would testify that I did not violate the law of the Hague Treaty by publishing and mailing the summons to the Japanese company, as the federal court ordered. The Hawaii federal default judgment was not defective.

Our legal expert on Japanese law, Professor Mark Levin, scheduled his trip from Japan with members of his family. He would testify that the Barnedos could get nothing in a Japanese Court. Japan had no laws on product defect as in the U.S. It would not make a difference if I pursued the case in Japan.

"How strange and bizarre," said Harvey. "Lay people will decide the validity of what the Federal Court ordered and what Erlinda's office did and did not do in Japan. It seems the U.S. District Court of Hawaii is also on trial in a State Court. What a shame."

My attorneys knew the potential notoriety of the case. Its effect might be far reaching. After all, the market was saturated with foreign-made products.

And here we were—before a Hawaii State court telling the jury lay people to decide everything—involving Japan, and Japan did not even know what we were doing."What is really going on?" I asked in obvious worry. Roy and Harvey did not have any further answer.

We knew that the Barnedos would come from Chicago empty-handed. We concluded that their attorneys would play with the minds of the jury—hoping to confuse them and make them guess.

* * *

I was again back in my attorneys' office.

"I feel I am being pressured to settle. Like an accused in a criminal case being forced to confess to murder he did not commit, merely for a lighter sentence."

"We don't blame you, Erlinda," said Harvey. "But this is just the trial court, as we keep on telling you. We can always appeal if anything bad happens."

We continued to review the charts to be used at trial. Roy and Harvey were seated on the floor organizing each one of them. They were working for me.

They were overwhelmed. I wondered how they would do.

I started to guess about their performance as I watched them on the floor, surrounded by visual aids, charts of the evidence and laws. Pohl introduced me to their firm. I had not known of them before.

How emphatically did they argue for me before the judge? Did they just go along with what the judge said and were afraid to offend her? They never invited me to attend those hearings.

Many times, I would find out something happened in court long after it did.

All three of us seemed afraid to say anything. But I had to talk of my nagging concern.

"I want the judge recused now, Roy. She has to step aside. We will be doing her a favor, unburdening her. There are many more cases where she could preside. Please, please, do not be angry with me. You would do the same if you were in my situation. You once said, judges learn while they hear and try cases. I don't want my case to be a guinea pig."

"Erlinda, if you have a slim chance remaining, you will blow it all away. You have the right to appeal just in case. Recusal is too late. We told you that before. Don't be repetitious."

"Why do you think this is happening to me, Roy?"

"To be honest, the judge asked us to persuade you to settle for your own benefit. I think we brought this up before when you were distraught. The judge said you are hated by the jury."

"How could she say that? She is new in the circuit court. I never tried a case before her. She does not know me except perhaps from Pohl's office where her husband works. But that's not enough to judge me."

"Well, she said the jury gave you a low figure in your recent trial before Judge McKenna. Jurors hate you."

"That's on appeal. How could I be so prejudged?"

"We're just saying what she said."

"Do judges talk to each other about other cases?"

"They are human. Their rooms are side by side. You certainly don't expect them to be reclusive and live in isolation," said Roy.

"See, Erlinda, you don't have to be blunt. It's identifiable because you are a woman and not from here. Other attorneys use the massage technique. The last thing we need is for you to frustrate our efforts as your attorneys."

"What are you talking about, Harvey?"

"I'm saying that we could reach the same point without your being bluntly direct and confrontational."

"I don't understand, I'm sorry. I thought that when we were in court, we had to argue. And if my accent makes me blunt, it is unintended, and in my case, you have done the talking, not me."

"It's not your accent, it's your defiance and insistence on doing things, such as recusing or disqualifying the judge. We don't see each other eye-to-eye on issues."

"I'm sorry, this is America. We are free to insist without having to beg. Other countries use physical violence and we don't. We use our mental skills and moral values. That's what makes this nation great, isn't it?" I asked.

At least we were speaking more freely than before. No longer discussing just laws, but reality, human beings, topics outside the courts, topics not mentioned in the rows of legal books in our offices, things that attorneys do not tell their clients, or are afraid to tell the judges.

"But the judges could have talked about other things. Why me? I am not famous, am I?"

"No, Erlinda, you are infamous!" said Harvey, wanting to crack a joke in a tense situation.

"You made yourself a topic. You're the only one in history who has the guts to sue Pohl. They're very well respected and powerful in the community, made up of high-ranking people in Hawaii," said Roy smiling.

"It will hopefully never come to my having to sue them to vindicate my rights. I don't want to be a public topic. I am not in politics. And, Roy, when I hired you, I thought you had the guts to sue Pohl for me!"

They ignored my last sentence as if they did not hear it. Then, they struggled with their next words. I knew that they were figuring out what I was thinking.

"I feel trapped, and I cannot really explain my feelings to both of you. But I feel there is no way out."

"Now that I think more of it, the judge has really something up her sleeve," said Roy in a tone of optimism.

"You mean she will make a miracle in my favor?"

"We don't know. But very possibly. She has a lot of judicial discretion."

"I'm not hoping for favorable discretion, Roy. I just want the laws equally applied. I ask for no favors."

Everything was again turning into a blur. I did not know what to say, what to suggest, what to do.

Harvey looked at both Roy and me. "I just have this sickening feeling...there is a purpose in what's happening."

"Harvey, whatever your unseen purpose is, I find it totally immoral to settle!"

I left their office, passing by the *feng sui* arrangements and decorations in their waiting room. They were similar to Pohl's *feng sui* arrangements.

* * *

When the court transcript of the hearing on the motions *in limine* arrived, I read them away from my attorneys' presence.

In that hearing, the attorneys were trying to convince the judge of what evidence the laws and rules permit to be shown to the jury for its consideration.

Harvey attempted to exclude any testimony of my former associates that would be a personal attack on me.

A portion of the discussion between Harvey and Judge Marks appears in the transcript of February 26, 2003, verbatim:

MR. DEMETRAKOPOULOS: We don't want, we have had conversations with other people who were unhappily brought into the case and dismissed. They said if I had to testify I am going to talk about Erlinda Dominguez is a bad lady to work for. Slave driver.

THE COURT: I think one of the things would probably come out, and I'm guessing, but that she ran the office in, sort of parceled things out to people, so that the guess is so that they could not steal her coffer.

MR. DEMETRAKOPOULOS: If that is in fact the case, I am not aware of that.

It was hurtful. The judge who was presiding in my case was getting personal, talking about my fear of someone stealing my coffer. And I was not even there to defend myself.

My researchers explained what the comment meant: Silas Marner hoarding his gold! That was never how I ran my legal practice, not even when I contracted with Pohl.

How could the judge guess about my office and my coffer? Why would she even guess at all? Guesswork has no place in courts and my coffer is not the jury's business. She's always guessing and it is completely out of topic.

In my mind, I interpreted what the judge said in the Filipino dialects. In Ilocano, *ti pugtok ket tapno saan da nga matakao daydiay baul ti kinabaknangna.*

In Tagalog, *sa tingin ko, para hindi nila nakawin yong baon nang kayamanan niya.*

In Igorot, *kinwanik, to adida mentakawen san binaul nga kadangyan na.*

I thanked Harvey for making a short statement in defense of my office and told him what others thought the coffer implied.

"Harvey, how can I be so prejudged in a courtroom during a serious and formal judicial proceeding with such a description?"

"Don't dwell on it, Erlinda. You are not at all that way. In fact, you're the opposite. The judge does not know you yet and did not mean anything. She had never mingled with you"

"Does the judge have anything against me, Harvey? As you said, she does not know me yet."

"Of course, nothing, Erlinda."

"Do I have to mingle with her?"

"That's not exactly what I meant," and he looked annoyed.

"I'm sorry to ask, but where does she get her information about me? From the Pohl office where her husband works? She is the assigned judge, making rulings and decisions. It's scary."

"You're paranoid again, Erlinda."

My unfamiliarity with the American slang and metaphor was causing me more distress. We could have been taking her remarks out of context. It would be unfair to the judge. And I left it that way.

Chapter Ten

Trial day had arrived.

I met with Roy and Harvey in front of the courtroom on the fourth floor right after the courthouse opened at 8:00 a.m.

Mr. and Mrs. Barnedo were seated on a bench in the hallway with their attorney, O'Brien. They were casually dressed and wearing light sweaters, ready for the chill in the courtroom.

They did not look at me, but knew I was there. They appeared relaxed. They must have arrived from Chicago two days before.

I dressed up formally, like an attorney should, even though I was the defendant. Roy suggested a subtle color for my suit with no shining objects. Not even a simple pair of earrings.

That seemed so hypocritical, but I advised my clients the same way when they appeared in court.

The potential jurors were on the lower floor being indoctrinated with what to expect. Then, in groups, they stepped out of the elevators and proceeded in our direction to the benches around the lobby.

We decided to get into the courtroom and take our seats. We should not mingle with the jurors. That was only ethical.

O'Brien and his clients used the lawyers' table on the left side of the room facing the judge's bench. It was closest to the jury box.

Roy, Harvey and I had the lawyers' table on the right side.

Roy's chair was next to the aisle that separated us from our opponents. It was arranged that Roy would be the lead counsel and had to be comfortable getting in and out of his seat.

I was on the far right side and Harvey was in between. Harvey helped me adjust my chair, saying, "That's how low the chair will go."

At the risk of angering my attorneys, I said, "Is the judge mentioning her relationship with a Pohl partner? I am about to be tried. And I thought you went into her chambers without me."

"No, Erlinda. We will really be upset if you repeat this one more time," said Roy and his face was very stern.

"I'm sorry, Roy, but I was recalling what you said before, that the judge might have something up her sleeve. My fate will be in the hands of unknown people, guided by her rulings and instructions. I'm so worried."

Again, Roy was irritated. He kept sifting through the records laid on our table. He also checked the many charts that were resting on the bench behind us. He tried to look calm, but I knew he was very tense.

People react to stress differently. I decided not to talk if I could help it. It was no time for confrontation with my attorneys. Trial was upon us!

The bailiff checked the courtroom. The clerk was at her seat next to where the judge's bench was. The court reporter was near the podium and was ready.

We were just waiting for the jurors to come in. That would be the first step.

I thought to myself: So, this is how it feels to be a defendant. I should have known since I sued hundreds of people on my clients' behalf.

From my seat, I visualized how I looked to an audience when I was fighting for my client's right to be heard. It was not an ugly scene. I belonged to a respectable profession.

But this time, I was the defendant. I would not be leading the fight. My attorneys would defend me. My name and my career were in their hands.

The room seemed to get colder. Nobody was talking. Roy and Harvey had their heads down reading the records. I was just staring at the podium, the witness stand, the court reporter, and her machine.

Dead silence!

The judge entered the courtroom and took care of basic matters with the attorneys.

"You have to renew your motions for the case to be dismissed," I whispered to Harvey. "That will preserve my rights if appealed." Harvey did not seem to understand what I meant.

He turned to Roy and they had a quick discussion.

"Erlinda, we will just be repetitious and annoy the judge, mark my word! But I'll do what I can."

We waited for the jurors to get in.

My attorneys' tension was dreadful to watch. Perhaps, they would get used to the courtroom atmosphere on the second day. They knew their business, but I did not know how much jury trial experience they had in their career.

It would have been too disrespectful to ask. Besides, when I retained them, nobody thought it would ever reach trial stage. And I kept thinking, what possible things did I miss?

Then, I no longer cared if I really angered my attorneys. I would just tell them one more time.

"Please move for the recusal and disqualification of Judge Marks. Soon, somebody from the Pohl firm will testify and that is where her husband works," I whispered. "She should really step aside now—that's my opinion of what is fair and moral for both sides regardless of what you think."

They looked at each other and Harvey said, almost inaudibly, "You're too much, you don't even know what Pohl will say."

I knew I had again angered the two people who were supposed to defend me. I couldn't help it, or I would always blame myself for not speaking.

Days before, the court had provided both sides with the jury lists and jurors' cards. Those records included personal information for each juror. Roy, Harvey and I screened them.

We reviewed each name and crossed out those we wanted to graciously dismiss. Dismissal would happen during the jury selection.

By the rules, each side was entitled to three challenges in which we could let a juror go without any reason. Beyond that, it had to be for a valid cause, for instance, if the juror is not a U.S. citizen, is deaf and cannot hear the evidence, or has severe vision difficulties that would disallow viewing the exhibits.

Roy would handle the jury selection, the *voir dire*. He had to be courteous and personable. He would be observing the jurors and they would be observing him. Jurors are human.

"The jurors are coming in," announced the bailiff. We stood up and turned to face and silently greet them. There were many jurors. I worried that the courtroom would not be large enough. There was a good mix of race and gender.

The crowd quietly walked in and was seated by the bailiff. All appeared decent and respectable.

Nobody knew what was going on in their minds except themselves. We did not personally know them.

The bailiff made sure the jurors were comfortable. He asked if they needed anything. There was hardly any response and some just shook their heads. Then, he told the clerk we were ready.

The clerk stood up, left her seat, and walked to the judge.
The judge nodded.

"All rise. The court is in session," announced the clerk.

The Court Calendar was read. My trial was the only one scheduled. It was the civil case of Barnedo and Barnedo versus Erlinda Dominguez, dba The Law Offices of Erlinda Dominguez, and Ron R. Ashlock, Thomas Kaster, William Copulos, David Kuwahara, Thomas Walsh for legal malpractice.

My associates were no longer individually involved. I was fighting for me, for them, and for my entire office.

There was the usual "Good Morning" from everybody—the judge, the attorneys, the parties, the jurors.

Then, the judge made the standard preliminary remarks on what would happen next and what the jurors could expect.

The judge asked them to tell her if they knew any of the participants, whether they were a party or a witness. She identified me as running a law office in Honolulu, Hawaii. She introduced us with our full names.

First, Mr. and Mrs. Barnedo as the plaintiffs and O'Brien as their attorney. They stood up, faced and bowed to the jurors.

Next, myself as the defendant and Roy and Harvey as my attorneys. We did the same. No juror claimed to know any of us.

One by one, the judge read the names of all the potential witnesses and asked the jurors if they knew anyone. A few had heard of some witnesses, but their familiarity was insufficient for them to be excused from the courtroom.

The trial witnesses list was long. It had the names of my former associate attorneys. It also had the names of the Pohl partners and their employees, and a swarm of doctors and medical providers.

I scribbled the names of the Pohl partners and passed it to Harvey. Price Okamoto Himeno & Lum.... They should be the ones on my hot seat.

Harvey glanced quickly at my notepad and looked back at the judge. He was not irritated, just uneasy. He was assisting Roy and was expected to be quick with anything that was needed.

The judge read the standard initial jury instructions. Then, it was time for selection. The bailiff began to pull out names at random. Those whose names were called proceeded to the jury box.

Twelve jurors would be chosen to sit through the trial. Two alternates were needed just in case an unforeseen event occurred, such as illness of a juror. Ten jurors must be unanimous for a verdict question.

The jurors were asked if they had a reason to be excused. One gentleman worked in a hotel and was obviously Filipino. He had many personal obligations pending with no time to spare for a trial that could last for days.

I was pleased he was allowed to go. He must have heard of me. He could have accompanied his relatives to my huge office. The Filipino hotel workers called me their personal injury attorney. It would have been too embarrassing if he stayed.

By procedure, O'Brien began the process. He used the podium. He asked the panel routine questions found in the law books. He was also allowed some time to talk to each juror individually.

It was Roy's turn. He also used the podium. He had similar questions for the panel. Most questions dealt with their prejudice and bias in life. He had the same style as O'Brien.

No attorney ever claimed to read the minds of jurors. And people had varied reasons to sit or not to sit in the panel. It was dreadful for some, an adventure for others, and for many, an opportunity to see that justice occurs.

It would be immoral for a juror to sit with strong undisclosed feelings for or against a party in a trial.

Harvey and I observed each person in the jury box. We exchanged short notes as to whether Roy should exercise a challenge.

* * *

It took the whole day for the jury selection. Both sides exhausted their challenges. Finally, there were enough numbers. The jury was impaneled.

Judge Marks thanked the people who were not chosen, and excused them from the courtroom.

We stood up and again turned to them until the last one stepped out and the door was closed.

"Are you comfortable with the panel?" Roy asked as he looked at the men and women seated in the jury box.

"They're okay," I said.

But there was a gentleman with lots of engineering background. The engineer's report of my opponents would be in the jury room. It was paper evidence that the judge admitted into evidence without giving me the opportunity to cross-examine the expert. The report was in the bulks of papers Harvey referred to and allowed by the judge for my opponents without live testimony. I had never seen this kind of trial in my law practice, and it had to personally happen to me.

"Where is my trial where I could at least confront the engineer who claims the machine was defective? He's not here. He just made an affidavit that he was paid for," I whispered.

Harvey just listened. He and Roy did not realize the impact of the judge's rulings against me. They seemed completely unaware that the paper exhibits could be read repeatedly by the jury during their deliberation.

More than ever, I knew that my suspicion could be right. My attorneys were not that skillful in jury trials. But it may be best I just shut up—in a lions' den.

I just looked at Harvey and said, "I know what you're thinking. The judge is entitled to her own opinion and it is her role to make the rulings, and there is always an appeal."

If my attorneys were not that good at trial, I hoped they would be better at appeal briefs since they always mentioned appeal.

The trial was anticipated to last approximately one week. Proceedings were to commence at 9:00 in the morning, with short breaks in between, lunch recess, then continue until 4:15 p.m.

The case was simple enough. But my opponents created an appearance of complexity by a multitude of counts against me and many defendants who were my former associate attorneys. Harvey named it false grandeur.

* * *

On the second day, my attorneys had become more at ease with the courtroom atmosphere.

The core of trial began.

O'Brien made his opening statement. He told the jury what he expected his evidence would prove.

I thought he was simply repeating what he argued to Mr. Davis when the case was arbitrated. I scribbled another note to Harvey. "Where's his evidence? He's saying the same thing he told the arbitrator and he lost."

Harvey nodded and scribbled back, "That's good for us."

Roy prepared for a strong opening statement. That had always been a lawyer's first opportunity to tell the jury good things about the client and the evidence.

The judge looked at Roy. "Opening statement?" Roy stood.

I knew what he was to say. He had it all written down. I did more than what other attorneys would have done when the only liable company was incorporated in Japan. I filed the federal case for product defect and gave the Barnedos hope while they benefited from the generosity of worker's compensation laws in the U.S. for many years.

The presentation of O'Brien's evidence began.

Mrs. Barnedo was led to the witness stand. Harvey and I whispered, "What for?"

We read each other's mind. Mrs. Barnedo's affidavit and her medical records—her papers—had already been allowed by the judge. We agreed that her testimony was for sympathy.

Harvey whispered, "Her husband will do the same—for emotions and court performance. Mark my word."

Mrs. Barnedo began to testify. She was endearing. No doubt, she was taught to project herself that way to the jury. But she had always been shy. She was not faking her behavior.

Mrs. Barnedo was asked by her attorney to step down from the witness stand. She graciously complied and walked to the center of the room and stood in front of the jury box.

She extended her right hand and showed it to the jury panel. Two and a half fingers were removed. Her deformity was in clear view. The jurors' eyes were focused.

"Why is she standing there so long?" I whispered to Harvey.

"Shh, pay attention."

Finally, Mrs. Barnedo walked back to the witness stand. She was asked about her injuries. She said her whole hand was still painful and that kids were afraid of her. "Really?" I scribbled on my notepad.

Next, Roy cross-examined Mrs. Barnedo. He was ready with the same questions I asked when I took her deposition, and her answers were the same.

Her injury from the noodle machine was in 1989. She had been paid about $200,000 in disability benefits. After settlement, she never went back to her doctor for pain. Her current job was taking care of kids in kindergarten. Now in 2003, fourteen years from her accident, we were holding her trial against me.

"Do you believe the trial we are going through?" I whispered.

Harvey whispered back, "I hope the jury sees through her claim, about the pain and the kids' fright. It's been fourteen years from her accident. When will she recover? That's so unfair to you, Erlinda."

On the witness stand, Mrs. Barnedo talked of the suit papers, in Japanese, that they received by mail from Japan. She told the jury that I laughed and told them to simply ignore the papers.

I felt the clear message of her testimony—that I ridiculed and despised the Japanese procedures.

"That's a lie." I scribbled my note to Harvey. "There are Japanese people in the jury. I respect them. She is inserting race. That would prejudice me."

Harvey simply whispered, "I agree, but you will have your opportunity to testify."

It was Mr. Barnedo's turn. His testimony was virtually a duplicate of what his wife had said.

He convinced the American Consulate that he was a religious man whose presence was necessary at a Pennsylvania convention.

The trip made him ill, he said. He ended up staying with his wife in Hawaii, without attending his mission. He never returned to the Philippines.

Deportation proceedings were brought against him. He had been an overstaying alien in the United States for about a decade and a half. He depended on his wife for visible support. He was still an alien while he was testifying.

He described his wife's injury and began to cry. This time, it was Harvey who turned to me and whispered, "He does not have to do that on the witness stand."

With my instinctive defense for a previous client, my response was immediate. "Harvey, those tears are not fake. He means it."

Mr. Barnedo's testimony was over.

There was a break. I knew I was next in line. O'Brien would be presenting me as a hostile witness.

"Erlinda, if you're asked, tell them you did not go to the Japanese Court to defend Mr. Barnedo when he was countersued because he was deportable and he could not travel with you," said Roy.

"That's not true, Roy. His alienage did not cross my mind. They had a different attorney for all those immigration intricacies. I was not aware of his problems when I was hired. The fact that I had no license in Japan and they never found out what happened in Japan should be more than enough."

"Don't be stubborn, Erlinda. I'm sure that was one of your reasons. You just don't recall it now. Don't worsen your case. You will recall that when you testify."

Before I knew it, I was on the witness stand. I said what Roy wanted me to. He convinced me he was right.

I saw Mr. and Mrs. Barnedo look at each other surprised. They knew what I said could not be true. But Roy was pleased, and it was important to me to make my attorneys happy.

Then, I was asked who else was involved in the case. I testified about my business relationship with Pohl.

Roy was shaking his head. He slightly knocked the table with his closed fist. The papers muffled the sound. He did not like what I said.

The jury was looking at me, but the judge was watching the lawyers' desks. She must have seen Roy. I thought to myself, A trial lawyer should never show his disagreement with a client!

My testimony was long. O'Brien was not only interrogating. He was arguing with me—a witness—with improper and repetitious questions. I looked at Roy to object. He did not.

My attorneys' participation was hardly there. It seemed that they had left me alone to defend myself on the witness stand. They were my audience and my cheering squad, that was all that it looked like.

"You did fine, Erlinda. We will not have to present you when our turn comes," said Harvey as soon as I returned to my seat beside him.

We were ending the day. As usual, the judge instructed the jurors not to talk about the case among themselves or to anyone.

Roy and Harvey organized their records and big charts and carried them on rolling carts to their car. That was expected to happen every single day until trial was over.

I followed my attorneys to their office. My former manager, Mila, was there waiting for me. She was instructed to be invisible so she wouldn't be subpoenaed by my opponents and presented as their witness. They did not know she was in town.

"Mila, it's like fighting a ghost. The opponents have only legal theories, no evidence. They have guesses and assumptions that the judge is allowing. Roy and Harvey are very indefinite in their explanations to me."

She did not understand. I did not expect her to.

She offered to treat me to dinner. I offered the fast food inn then drove around.

I drove to the Kahala Hilton Hotel where we watched the dolphins play in the pool. Then, to Mokapu. The hang gliders were high up in the sky with their colorful chutes. They looked so free and untouchable. They must be happy.

We went to the Waikiki Beach and mingled with the crowd. A few feet away from our bench on the sidewalk were women in their string bikinis. I felt funny in my formal suit attire.

"You can join them if you want," I said. "All you have to do is take off your pants." But she preferred to talk.

We started to reminisce about our office...during my hey-days...before it was taken over by the law firm of Pohl.

The employees and our friends who came in all forms—carpenters, nuns, radio announcers, leaders in the community, doctors, hotel workers, and so on—we remembered them all.

Multitudes of clients. They were precious in a professional and personal way. We talked with nostalgia—remembering how our toils helped them fulfill the American dream—buy their houses or send their children to school even with their severe disabilities. That was our break for happiness from my ordeal of the trial.

"Why is this happening to you, Erlinda?" asked Mila.

"I wish I knew."

"Why not Pohl instead of you? They took over your office and managed the cases."

Mila did not know about Pohl's tolling agreement that left me to be sued alone. She had no idea that Roy and Harvey refused to involve Pohl for me.

"My law office had been the front line, Mila. As you know, Pohl used my name, Law Offices of Erlinda Dominguez. I am sued alone. But you are right. They should be here instead of me. At the very least, they should help me."

"Remember the China Airlines disaster?" she asked.

I knew she was recalling her exhausting trip to Manila with Ken of the Pohl firm where they signed up retainers for the clients using my name.

"You should have dropped your name as their counsel to ensure that you stayed out of trouble. After our exhausting trip, Pohl did not return their calls at all," she said.

"They found out that I was right. There could be no jurisdiction in Hawaii. But they did not bother to explain to the clients. I dropped my involvement, and regretted that we bothered so many people in the Philippines."

The sun was setting. The most beautiful sunset in the world, so we were told. Awesome. Beautiful.

"This is one of the things I miss about Hawaii," said Mila. "If only things did not happen the way they did when you merged with Pohl, I would still be working for you and enjoying our clients. They were our family.

"Recall our escapades?" she asked. "We would go to the malls and shop until we dropped. We threw parties in the office. We worked, worked, worked so hard up to late evenings for the clients. They loved us!"

She was still speaking English like a Filipino. But she could be well understood.

"Then, Pohl came and things were no longer the same," I added. "We even disappointed the Filipinos who corresponded with us from other countries. I hope they have forgiven."

"That's right, how well do you recall," she said with a tint of sadness in her voice.

"Their cards and social letters got to me too late. And I never knew if my responses were mailed out. Pohl managed everything, as if they owned everyone including me. I never thought my life would turn out that way."

"You should have demanded that our office would resume its normal style and procedure of handling things," said Mila.

"I offended Sharon. She said there could only be one captain of the ship, and she was the one. East is east…have you heard of that expression?"

"But it was your office, Erlinda, and Sharon was hardly there to see what was going on."

"Let's not talk about that anymore. I was glued to the contract, my worst regret in my legal career. I did not predict that I would be somebody's glamorized slave and a puppet. I am not cut out that way, even when flaunted with the glitter of tons of money."

We stayed longer than planned. I knew that we should rest for what might happen tomorrow. The trial was far from over.

Chapter Eleven

The next morning, we returned to the courthouse. I avoided jurors taking the elevators. There were just too many people. Sometimes, we would be side by side and it could not be avoided. We should not be friendly to each other.

I wondered what they could be thinking about me. So far, they had heard the evidence of my opponents.

We had time to discuss the case while waiting for the calendar to be called.

"I don't mean to intrude in your trial style," I told Harvey. "The jurors cannot read all the charts when Roy points at them while he talks. They will be distracted."

Again, Roy and Harvey looked at me with no response.

Harvey's briefcase was open on the table. I saw a huge *American Jurisprudence* book inside. He noticed I was looking. "Oh, that's for their legal expert," he said.

"He will really give his own interpretation of the Hague Convention Treaty?" I asked knowing that the judge had already allowed him to. "And expect the jury to understand the book of *American Jurisprudence* when many lawyers can't? It's unfair to the jury, it will be too burdensome, and it's unconstitutional."

"Yes, a hundred times, I already answered yes," said Harvey and he raised his voice somewhat.

It was again time for me to be quiet.

The jury walked back into the courtroom. They were already familiar with their respective seats. They had become friendly with each other, as long as they did not yet discuss the case.

The jurors avoided looking straight at the attorneys and the parties. And we did the same. There really had to be no silent communications among us.

I never knew if that was part of the indoctrination provided to the jurors before their selection. I never was a juror, and would have been disqualified because I was a lawyer.

The jurors were in for a big surprise. They would construe and define the meaning of the masterpiece of worldwide delegates who labored decades ago to create the international law of the Hague Convention Treaty. Something that no jury anywhere in the entire United States was ever allowed to do.

O'Brien called his legal expert to the witness stand. It was Allen Williams. I never saw him before. He had no special qualifications. He was simply an attorney, just like my attorneys, Roy and Harvey. Just like my former associate attorneys, and me.

Roy decided there was no need to cross-examine Williams on his flunking the California Bar Examinations. "A matter of courtesy," whispered Harvey.

Then, I thought, if all is just courtesy in courts, nobody may win a case on the merits.

There were films and slides propped up against the board. On the witness stand, Williams explained how wrong I was to follow the orders of the federal court to publish the summons and to send it by certified mail to the Japanese Company.

He claimed that the orders did not conform to his own interpretation of the Hague Treaty, and what my office did was contrary to his interpretation.

"What an embarrassment to the federal court. And the Japanese people don't even know this is happening to me. Don't you agree?" I whispered quickly to Harvey.

"Shh, let's just listen," said Harvey. He looked almost happy, as if the whole trial was an added experience to his legal career. And that my interest was farthest from his mind.

"A jury could not extend justice if they do not understand the witness," I still managed to scribble.

I looked at the faces of the jurors. Almost equally divided between men and women, and a good mix of color. They were doing their best to listen and understand.

Their heads turned from left to right as they watched the two attorneys battle over the correct interpretation of the Hague Treaty on how to serve a complaint upon a foreign defendant.

One attorney was on the witness stand and the other was at the podium. I was sure the jurors were thinking, Is this really our job? How confusing, complicated, strange and scary! We thought attorneys and judges do that!

Finally, Roy pulled out the *American Jurisprudence* book, raised it high above his head, then opened it for Williams.

At the risk of contempt of court, I was tempted to yell, "Stop! Stop! This is not how a jury trial is, courts interpret laws, not the laymen jury. What is happening to me is obviously unconstitutional, can't you see?"

The cross examination continued, verbatim:

MR. CHANG: And United States is a contracting state; is that right?

MR. WILLIAMS: Yes.

Q. So is Japan?

A. Yes.

Q. Now, Mr. Williams, if the Hague Convention did not require a return receipt of a signed letter and Hawaii law on the other hand does require that, which law takes precedence?

A. The issue of whether the Hague--whether you can serve by--mail, I--I'm losing you in that because I--there is a question--

Q. Let me refer --

A. --as to the service of a complaint.

Q. Let me--

A. Let me finish.

As to the service of a complaint whether that is proper under the provisions of Article 10.

Q. But my question relates to Article 15, all right? And my question was: If the Hague Convention does not require a returned receipt or a signed returned receipt and Hawai'i law does require a returned receipt that is signed, which of the two laws takes precedence?

A. For the purpose of exercising jurisdiction and the enforceability of an action, you would have to look to the Hague.

Q. Because the Hague supersedes any state procedural law; isn't that right?

A. Not in total.

Q. Well, let me read you this. And again, I'm taking this from the AmJur, the same treatise we have here. It states that because the Hague Convention is a treaty--

MR. O'BRIEN: Objection, Your Honor. If we're going to read something, could we have a citation and section so there's a record of it.

MR. CHANG: I'm sorry.

THE COURT: Please.

MR. CHANG: AmJur Second, Section 379 under the Process section of the AmJur.

THE WITNESS: Uh-huh.

I whispered, "The judge must now be seeing the obvious. It is purely a legal question for the court's legal construction, not the jury."

Harvey scribbled, "Shh!"

My mind started to play tricks. I imagined me standing up and yelling, "Objection! Objection! Objection! You cannot do this in a court. You cannot practice your law profession on me. Choose another case for that! Wake up! Wake up! Wake up!"

I looked at Harvey and pleaded in a whisper, "I need help. I'm seeing marsupials in the room, kicking me on the face. And they are all in technicolor. I must be hallucinating."

"Mine are giraffes and they are polka-dotted." Harvey appeared to be sneering and enjoying the show as he said that, almost without thinking.

Obviously, Harvey did not believe me. He forgot I had the same human frailties. I could have been delirious—he would not know.

Williams' testimony was finally over. The room was chilly with the strong air conditioning of a Hawaiian court, but Harvey appeared to be perspiring.

"Harvey, I really saw marsupials. I don't want to go crazy and neither do you. It's no time to be joking."

"Erlinda, behave yourself."

"I'm behaved, the situation was unbearable. I think there were students in the room. I hope that they did not get the wrong impression of the role of a court and that of a jury."

"How true. But the judge must have realized that the Hague law interpretation was out for grabs. This trial was not a total waste. I'll ask Roy what could be done now. Are you okay, Erlinda? We could ask for a long court recess, you know."

"Thanks for your concern. Please tell Roy I ask for at least a mistrial. The judge saw what happened: two attorneys doing all they can to convince the jury of their interpretation of the Hague Treaty. Was that two hours of testimony?"

Harvey moved closer to me. "Don't mention this to Roy, but a female juror was almost in tears watching that display of interrogation. She was clearly traumatized trying to understand those technical words and to do her job—to impart justice."

If she cried, there might be a mistrial. On second thought, my opponents could fabricate evidence and attempt to cure all their mistakes the second time around. They might even sue Pohl. Then, Pohl would sue me, and my legal enemies would multiply.

* * *

Recess time. We were outside the courtroom.

"Roy, all those highly legal words like enforceability, supersedes, preempt, Article 10, Convention, and so on—you find those in the law dictionary. They are immediate eye-openers. You were asking the jury to interpret the law with a book! How can anyone not see that with the long testmony of Williams? Law students are in and out of the courtroom. This will adversely affect their future profession."

"That's true, Erlinda, but what is done is done."

"Everyone has constitutional due process rights to a competent trial. That's why we are lawyers, to debate the meaning of the law in courts. You never interpret the law to the jury! You even asked Williams what law prevails—the Hague Treaty or the Hawaii law. What a crying shame!"

Roy raised his voice. "We're doing what we can as the judge has ordered, okay?"

"I don't mean any disrespect. If I was not the defendant, it was so laughable watching you lecture to Williams with the *AmJur* book before the jury. But nobody was laughing. You are the first, Roy. You have to be last for that kind of spectacle."

"I said, I'm just following court orders. Let's move on! You're talking too much. Perhaps, you could do better, huh?"

I became subdued and simply asked, "Now that the judge saw what happened, don't you think she should dismiss the case or declare a mistrial?"

"That does not happen. Judges don't reverse their own rulings to accommodate you, Erlinda!"

Yeah—Who is Erlinda Dominguez anyway? She's nothing.

Roy was red in the face. He was again getting very irritated. I understood the tension of the trial. But it seemed Roy and Harvey were more concerned about their physical performance with an audience, instead of me. Or, was I so paranoid?

"So sorry, Roy. Are they about done with their witnesses?"

"They will present the daughter of Mrs. Barnedo's previous employer who owned the noodle machine. The father passed away."

"What for? We know what she will say. Her affidavit is clear that the Hawaii Royal Trading Company did not sell the machine. That's good for us."

"To confuse the jury," said Harvey.

I asked Roy to go through an offer of proof. We would admit the truth of the affidavit and dispense with the witness. This could avoid more confusion and guesswork.

Roy was about to snap, I could tell. I was intruding into his style and business of defending me.

It appeared I was making complete nonsense to him. Then I remembered that shortly before trial, I insisted that Roy and Harvey must have the witness sign an affidavit. It was a scary thought. If she did not, she could say anything on the witness stand.

I began to think of ways to take over my defense. But that would be disruptive of the proceedings.

Mistake or no mistake, let the show continue—I hired them to defend me and as they said, Roy is doing what he can.

There was a short recess. Everyone got out of the courtroom to stretch their legs and use the restrooms. Roy whispered something to Harvey. They did not tell me what it was.

O'Brien was in the company of his clients, the Barnedos. I was by myself.

Roy and Harvey walked to the farthest end of the hallway without me. I could not hear a word they were saying.

I wished they wouldn't show our distance to the jurors. We were in their plain view. I could only imagine what the jurors were thinking. The attorneys do not get along with their own client. There must really be something wrong with the defendant.

I was non-existent. I worried that my relationship with my attorneys had begun to adversely affect my case. The jurors were human—a word that Roy had repeatedly used.

The recess took more time than usual. O'Brien approached Roy standing in the hallway. His back was turned against me. I could not read his lips. They talked softly. Roy nodded and both proceeded to the courtroom passing by me on the bench. I stood up and followed them.

The jury was not allowed to listen to discussions among attorneys and the judge. They remained outside.

O'Brien told the judge that the parties had reached a stipulation, an agreement. He was holding a copy of the Hawaii Royal

Trading Company's insurance policy, showing the company's liability insurance coverage for millions of dollars.

Roy was already standing, then, he addressed the judge. He agreed with what O'Brien said. The policy was authentic. It could get to the jury as evidence for my opponents.

"Why is Roy doing this?" I asked Harvey in a low tone. "The jury will think this is a battle between huge insurance companies. I'm not even insured. They would give their verdict to Mrs. Barnedo who has a deformed hand."

Harvey listened, then scribbled, "Shh, quiet, quiet!"

I quickly scribbled a note back to him. "We excluded insurance topic through motions—and now this? Why?"

Harvey did not look at my notepad, which I intentionally pushed under his nose.

I felt trapped in the hands of my attorneys. I started to question if Roy was doing things on purpose. He was damaging my case in the most basic and fundamental points. But he seemed to fight for me in other aspects.

What exactly were my attorneys doing?

God, don't allow them to completely betray me.

As we left the courtroom for lunch, my attorneys talked in whispers facing each other. In a few minutes, they disappeared. I assumed they went back to their office—a short walking distance.

I immediately contacted my researcher, Jennifer Smith. I asked her to locate legal authorities disallowing the insurance policy from evidence.

The law library was steps away. In minutes, Jennifer met me in the courthouse. Her research was complete.

"What's going on, Erlinda?" she asked. "Presence of insurance will really hurt your defense. This is not a suit with the insurance company."

"I know, Jennifer. My case is being tried on sympathy and prejudice. I'm so disadvantaged, a defendant-lawyer. I'm facing the emotional ammunitions of my opponents—a deformed hand of a laborer, huge insurance policy, my laughing at the Japanese court procedures, and my lawyers showing their rudeness to me."

"Why do your attorneys make it so easy for your opponents to get what they want? It looks like you are pleading no contest to a murder case. It's so unfair and tragic."

"Jennifer, they have avoided me. They must feel I am disruptive of their style."

"Arrogance has no place to protect a client. You should have defended yourself alone. You were the best lawyer for you. It baffles my thinking that you did not."

"Jennifer, you know what they say. If you are a doctor, don't do surgery to yourself. I am taking care of clients who are depending on me. I have hardly enough time for my case. Don't discourage me over something that's beyond my control. There are many things in my life that I can't change, and what you just said is one of them."

"I have to go. They might see me here. Good luck!"

I looked at Jennifer hurriedly walking away. Another small fry in the community.

* * *

The lunch break was over. Roy and Harvey stepped out of the elevator and approached the courtroom. I was seated on a bench and stood up to greet them.

I handed Jennifer's research to Harvey and a copy to Roy. I asked Roy to please do something. That was a fatal mistake.

"Please don't take offense, we are in this together, I'm just trying to help my case," I said almost in fear.

Roy yanked the papers from my hand and shoved them into his briefcase. I suspected he knew the repercussions of what he did, but it was much too late.

My attorneys did not say a word. They just proceeded to their desks in the courtroom.

I remained seated on the bench in the lobby. The two people who were defending me had been alienated.

The bailiff called for me, "Ms. Dominguez? We're ready, please come in." I walked in politely and formally. As a lawyer defendant.

The advertisement of Allstate Insurance Company on TV was frequently aired. The host did it so well…"The courtroom is a lonely place to be if you are sued…Allstate will defend and protect you…you are not alone, you are in good hands."

The ad could be a tearjerker. My first job in the United States was with Allstate.

Of course, I was sued. Of course, the courtroom is a very lonely place to be. But to answer the question, "Am I in good hands?" I did not need an answer, or, I really did not know.

I maintained a cordial relationship with Roy and Harvey. We were in the middle of trial. I found it hard to believe that I was getting afraid of my own lawyers whom I hired and paid. Their efforts for me were not on account of friendship. I was their client. Not the Barnedos, not Pohl, not anyone else.

* * *

We were again in a trial recess. Mila dropped by to see me in my attorneys' office. She wanted to know if she would be presented as a witness. Washington State was her home. The week would be over and I had not started my defense.

We were seated quietly in the waiting room. The elevator door opened and Kenneth Okamoto stepped out.

He seemed surprised.

"Ken, how are you?" I asked excitedly. He must have come to give me moral support and was not aware that Mila was around. Their Pohl law firm knew that my trial was ongoing. They monitored the progress of the trial.

"Oh, hello there, and nice to see you both. How have you been?" he asked.

"We are fine."

The secretary immediately escorted Ken into Roy's room at the far end of the office. She closed the door.

Mila's surprised reaction was immediate. "Why are you not with them in Roy's room?"

"I don't know," I said. "I really don't know."

"You are a lawyer, and you never did that to any of our clients."

"I'm not invited. Don't worry about it, Mila."

It was a strange feeling. I remembered when Sharon Himeno of the Pohl firm telephoned Roy when we were filing my answer to the malpractice complaint.

That same feeling when the case started now overwhelmed me and grew more unbearable with each minute that Ken was in Roy's room. And we were nearing the end of trial.

After some time in Roy's room, Ken came out and proceeded to the elevator. He smiled but did not stop to talk. He raised his right thumb as he passed by us, looked at me and said, "Your attorneys are okay. They are really good. Don't worry."

Then, the elevator door closed and he was gone.

We prepared to get back to the courthouse.

"Let's go," said Harvey.

"Will I testify?" Mila asked quickly.

"No need. They have not proven anything. They presented no evidence, just theories through their legal expert. We should not glamorize what they have," said Roy.

"Ken was here. What was that all about?" I asked.

"Oh, that? It was just a small talk about the case. He was subpoenaed by the opponent. He will testify in your favor."

The assurance of Roy stopped me from asking one more time for the judge to step aside because her husband works in Ken's office. And his words were comforting and hopeful—She could be in your corner, she may have something up her sleeve!

I had come to completely understand the meaning of that metaphor, but not how it precisely related to a court case.

Each passing day, I worried that my confusion was doubling—about everything, including my attorneys. And for reasons I could not define, I felt more and more hypocritical of myself.

* * *

The Court was again in session. The jurors were waiting outside the courtroom.

O'Brien stood up and told the judge that his next witness was Kenneth Okamoto.

Then, Judge Marks looked around the courtroom making sure no jurors were in the room and the door was closed. She looked at the attorneys and began to speak. Very quickly, she said that her husband, Robert Marks, was working in the office of Price Okamoto Himeno & Lum.

She did not say that she was married to a high partner of the Pohl office who was the Attorney General after Warren Price, something I found out not from my attorneys, and shortly before the trial.

The judge paused a bit, then added that she had disclosed her spousal relationship in the very beginning of the case, and that nobody objected. With a tone of confidence, she claimed that it would be the same now—nobody would object to her presiding. Of course, I would object!

But I thought I was dreaming. I was flabbergasted! It seemed that the judge was putting ideas in Roy's brain. Or Roy and Harvey were continuously lying to me. They repeatedly said that the judge never disclosed anything, never offered to step aside, and that I would antagonize her if I attempted a disqualification.

My complete ignorance was so shameful. Shame! Shame! Shame!

O'Brien immediately stood up and said he had no objections.

Roy quickly looked at me. I was reading his mind and hoping against hope: Now is the time, Erlinda. I will keep my promise to you that I will ask the judge to get out of the case.

I nodded and without hesitation, uttered softly the words, "Please object, please object," with a silent message—Let her go. Another judge will pick up the pieces. Help me, Roy, let her go. Don't be afraid. Nothing bad will happen in your legal practice.

Roy addressed the judge. I was melting as I heard his words—as he agreed with all that the judge said. And that it was true, we had no objections! Roy sounded like he was actually pleading for the judge to stay in my case.

If only I could say it to Roy, but I did not—"What a ... you are! How can you be so ...!"

I looked at Harvey seated beside me. "This is beyond belief! This is beyond belief!"

Harvey was silent except one word he mumbled, almost inaudibly, "Well?" And he glanced at me as I kept stabbing my pad of paper with the sharp end of my pen.

The courtroom door was closed. I wanted to just walk away. I did not. I could be held in contempt of court for disrupting the proceedings.

The trial was quickly back on track. The jurors walked in. They did not hear and see what happened. I had to regain my composure quickly for their entry—with the usual standing up until each juror was comfortably seated in the jury box. The judge closed the session and wished the jurors a good weekend. Before any more confrontation, Roy and Harvey were quickly gone.

I spent the long break taking care of my clients and convincing myself Ken will not betray me. Maybe then, the judge will perform a miracle as Roy predicted.

Back to court!

Ken Okamoto was waiting outside the room for his turn to testify. The judge asked the bailiff to bring him in.

Ken passed by our desk and proceeded directly to the witness stand. He was sworn in.

Please, please say good things of me, Ken. Tell the truth, even if it's for old time's sake.

O'Brien's questions were short. Ken testified that he tried to help me and my office to see the prospects of collection for the Barnedos' case in 1993. Beyond that, he and Pohl were not involved.

Some parts of what Ken said were good for me. But he made me look like a liar to the jury. My testimony was different: that I co-counseled with Pohl before the federal judgment, and they continued with the case until my opponents took over.

Ken omitted the events of our partnership. He limited Pohl's involvement to that short circumstance of attempting to collect.

He looked at me when he was done with his testimony. I did not show any reaction.

Ken stepped down from the witness stand. As he passed by our table on his way out of the courtroom, he smiled at Roy and raised his right thumb. Roy smiled back. And so did Harvey. I just looked at him while he disappeared from view.

There was no further need to confront my attorneys. I knew what they would say: that they have no control over what a witness says. Questioning Roy would only make our relationship more tumultuous and perhaps, hopeless.

My fate was now completely in the hands of God. There must be justice beyond whatever was being played out in an American Hall of Justice.

Chapter Twelve

My opponents were running out of live witnesses. Nobody arrived from Japan to explain the Japanese court procedure. And they were comfortable with the volumes of paper evidence admitted by the judge as their evidence.

They did not need to present a single doctor, nurse, custodian, or therapist. They did not need an engineer. They had more than enough uncross-examined papers that the judge allowed and more where my own attorney, Roy Chang, quickly agreed to, without involving me. The entire transcript of hearing in the federal court got in with no effort by O'Brien.

My opponents were completely excused from the trial requirement of proving reasonable medical probability for all the medical expenses and condition of Mrs. Barnedo. Virtually excused from the need of live witnesses. Excused from burdens of proof, from the rigid requirements of trial we learned in law school on how to prove a case.

Linda Matsuo, the daughter of Mrs. Barnedo's previous employer, was O'Brien's last witness. She testified almost verbatim as what her affidavit said: Royal Trading supplied food for her father's business. It did not sell the noodle machine.

As she explained things on the witness stand, I remembered what Arbitrator Davis said. It was so obvious. It did not have to be argued. Royal Trading was not the seller. No need for a jury trial. No need for days of debating and lawyers' performances. I thought, that should only happen on stages in Broadway.

But Matsuu bolstered the dwindling number of O'Brien's live witnesses—that was what it did—for appearances.

The judge gave O'Brien some time to assess his performance and see if anything more was needed to be done. O'Brien claimed he had presented all his witnesses.

I looked at Harvey and said, "Before the trial, O'Brien listed about a hundred witnesses, even more. He presented only six. Where did the rest go? What a bluff!"

"No need, Erlinda, his bulks of papers were admitted by the judge without live witnesses, remember?"

Finally, O'Brien rested his case.

* * *

We were having a break. The jury was not in.

I reminded Harvey to renew the request for dismissal as a matter of law by directed verdict. My opponents had no factual evidence to prove their case. The decision on my case should be directed away from the jury. The jury does not make or guess facts. That would be unconstitutional.

Harvey was reviewing his arguments hours before. Again, he looked at Roy for an okay. Roy told him to go ahead.

They were suddenly involving me again in their discussion of what they would do. I was encouraged and pleased.

"Erlinda, I'll tell the judge that whatever your office did or did not do, there's no evidence of damage to the clients. Your fate can't be decided on guesses on what occurred in the Japan court. Even their expert did not know what happened there. All they claim is that the Barnedos were sued in Japan."

"Okay, I wish us the best. Be very respectful, Harvey. You certainly know how. You already know that the judge does a lot of guessing which she admitted. She told you that she does not know when and how to decide the law- she was honest to you, to Roy and to O'Brien. But this is scary because who would decide the law except the judge? Please do what you can and let's hope for the best!"

I glanced at Harvey's notes. He focused on the absolute inaction of O'Brien to collect the federal default judgment and find out what occurred in the Japanese countersuit. Who won in Japan—the clients or the Japanese company? Or was the countersuit dismissed for whatever reason? Nobody knew.

Worse still, was that even an issue? Everything seemed to be guesses and story-telling even at such a late stage.

O'Brien skipped each and all of those steps and sued me instead. He basically did nothing except call on his friend, Williams, to be a legal expert who testified on guesses and assumptions on what could have happened in Japan—as if that was even an issue in a court in America. Everything was a confusing mess.

"The opponents cut all corners. Be simple in your arguments," Roy told Harvey. "Our case is resting on that attorney who has less qualifications than any attorney in this room. None of us flunked the Bar Exams."

"Roy, I wish you cross-examined him on that, so the jury would know what you just said—but never mind, that's okay."

Harvey again turned to me. "I also have to be clear that the judge is wrong to believe that attorneys are presumed guilty of malpractice the moment they earn default judgments for their clients. That is unheard of. It's not how legal practice works."

"Yes, Harvey, that never happens anywhere in the world, otherwise, legal practice will condemn all successful attorneys."

"And she's wrong to think that the jury should interpret the Hague law and the Japanese laws. That's for the courts," said Roy in a last minute effort for my salvation.

This time, my attorneys were almost too friendly to me. I could not help but recall what Roy said, The judge might be in your corner…has something up her sleeve.

I managed to add, "Be careful, Harvey. Don't corner her in your arguments. Remember the word of Roy, human."

Harvey began to argue. He asked the judge to dismiss the case. The jury should not be involved any further. All issues are legal.

A portion of what Harvey described as basic arguments appear on the trial transcript of March 12, 2003, verbatim.

THE COURT: No, I'm saying there's a prima facie case made out that the defendant was negligent in her dealings with the clients.

MR. DEMETRAKOPOULOS: I fully understand that, Judge. Could you go one step further and tell me is the Court saying there's evidence before it now that the negligence caused harm to the Barnedos based upon the results or non results in Japan? Because that's the part we don't have anything on.

THE COURT: Well, you may want to dissect it in that fashion. I'm saying prima facie case is judgment hasn't been collected.

MR. DEMETRAKOPOULOS: But don't—okay. May I offer one analogy, Judge, though?

THE COURT: Be my guest.

MR. DEMETRAKOPOULOS: That's similar to saying the proof is that Ms. Dominguez was driving on the wrong side of the road at 80 miles an hour in a 50 zone. She was weaving all over the place, skidding her car but there's no proof she hit anyone. There's no proof she injured anyone. There's no proof she crashed on anyone. We don't have that—

THE COURT: I don't think that's a valid analogy.

MR. DEMETRAKOPOULOS: No damage is caused is what I'm saying.

THE COURT: Well, we can agree to disagree.

MR. DEMETRAKOPOULOS: Thank you, Judge. Thank you for indulging me.

I thought to myself, Is that all that the judge can say—we can agree to disagree—while my entire career is in jeopardy? What if this is a murder case? Would the accused lose his life with a no debate? With no law and no facts? And why is Harvey so subservient—he does not sound that way in the office?

Roy, Harvey and I looked at each other in helplessness. We read each other's minds. I predicted what they would say.

"The judge concludes without dissecting the issue as other judges do. I'm groping in the dark. I'm terribly sorry, I tried." Harvey sounded extremely apologetic. "I gave it my best shot. I can't read her mind."

"That's her style, she does not have to conform with other judges," said Roy softly.

"That's alright, Harvey, I'm not faulting you. She has her style as Roy said. Let's leave it at that. I only wish there was a way to get out of this guessing situation! I don't feel like I am in a court in the United States of America. Forgive my feeling, but I am almost believing that people in other countries have more due process."

I recalled what I told Mila, "It's like fighting a ghost, no evidence, no facts, just theories and guesses, and undefined issues."

My tiny consolation was that my attorneys agreed with me.

* * *

There was a break from the trial. I was again with my attorneys in their conference room for discussion. They decided that they would not present any live witness except our engineering expert.

"He will contradict the uncross-examined engineer's affidavit you filed in the federal court a decade ago, which our opponents now utilize as their evidence and ammunition against you," said Roy.

"Imagine the severe inconsistency that you are in, Erlinda? And you now have the burden of proof, instead of your opponents who sued you," said Harvey. "And we are still unclear on the issues against you."

"It would have been better that I did not fight for my clients in the federal court and presented nothing. Then, they cannot use anything. There would be no *prima facie* malpractice case, using the words of the judge," I said in desperation. "We don't know what law or rule she goes by. As you said, she hardly explains anything."

"You still have to pay for our experts. They reserved their time just for your case," reminded Roy.

I could afford the expenses. They were not a problem. But I dared not inquire too much on why we were suddenly cutting down on my witnesses when they had been paid. I felt so deprived.

At intervals, Roy's patience seemed to be stretched to the limit and I did not want my entire trial to collapse.

Mila decided to stay for moral support and to help me with small things, such as organizing my papers. She sensed what was going on.

"Mila, I'm not in good hands! I have no friends in the courtroom. Not even my attorneys! It's a lonely feeling—as the Allstate spokesperson says on TV."

"Couldn't you do anything?" she asked.

"Trial is ongoing. I can't."

"Erlinda, whenever you went to trial, your clients were your best friends. You showed them you were completely on their side. Remember? Your staff would sneak out of the office to watch you perform, and everyone was giving moral support to the clients."

"Lawyers are made of a different cloth."

"Is it cultural?"

"No, I don't think so! I hope not!"

Trial continued day by day. Toward my attorneys, I acted as if nothing had changed. I knew the jurors were observing.

Roy and Harvey continued to keep their distance from me.

Sometimes, O'Brien would join them and they talked more loudly than usual but not about the case. They socialized in plain view of the jurors who were taking their breaks outside the courtroom.

They laughed at their jokes. It was clear that Roy and Harvey wanted me to see them that way. Like I should not bother them with my concerns, that I was not relevant. They seemed to have forgotten the reason they were there—for me!

But at those moments in hell, I could not allow myself to sink in helpless confusion.

* * *

We were back in the courtroom.

Our engineering expert, Dr. Richard Gill, had arrived from California. He was well qualified. He published articles and was hired by both plaintiff and defense attorneys.

Through his testimony, I had to overcome the affidavit of my opponent's engineer—the engineer I hired in the federal court to prosecute the Barnedos' case against the Japan company. He had long since passed away.

Dr. Gill brought a big fan and let it stand in front of the jury panel. He performed a demonstration for the jury.

He attached the fan to the electric outlet. He pushed the button and the blades rolled. He began to insert his fingers and immediately retrieved them uninjured. It was very subtle, quick, and professionally done.

Some jurors smiled. There was nothing wrong with the fan, no product defect. It would have been his fault if he injured his fingers. That was the same with the noodle machine that caused Mrs. Barnedo her injuries.

I predicted that in his closing argument, O'Brien would tell the jury that I lied. The affidavit of the engineer I hired in the Barnedos' case against the Japanese company in the federal court said there was product defect. My second engineer, now that I was being sued by the Barnedos, said there was no product defect.

"I told you, the rulings of the judge placed you in an impossible position, Erlinda," again whispered Harvey. "And you are fighting tons of papers and no witnesses."

"I know, Harvey. I never thought this judicial nightmare would happen to me."

Testimonies of live witnesses were over.

Roy asked, "What do you think, Erlinda?"

"I don't know what to think. The instructions of the judge to the jury will kill my defenses. I just read them. Thanks for asking me. I wish something could still be done."

The judge asked Roy if he had any more live witnesses. Roy responded that he did not, and he rested his case.

The judge gave the final instructions to the jury. She read from the standard forms, such as, "You are the judges of the credibility of the witnesses."

I scribbled to myself, "Credibility for what? That I had two inconsistent engineers and I am a liar?"

The judge continued to read and said, "Special damages are those damages which can be calculated with reasonable certainty from the evidence."

I whispered to Harvey, "They have no evidence. Where will they get the figures? No doctor, no medical witness, not even the keeper of the records, nothing!"

I was pleasantly surprised that Harvey whispered back, "Right, just bulks of papers that your office filed in the federal court ten years ago, and the computation of the federal judge in deciding against the Japanese company! Tragic! Really tragic!"

"This isn't a legal trial. Law students have better trials in their moot courts!" I wrote down in desperation.

Harvey glanced at my notes and nodded mildly.

The jury instructions on burden of proof were mixed up. My opponents had the burden, and on some issues, I had the burden.

A listening juror could have easily understood that I had to prove my innocence. It would jibe with the thinking of the judge that I committed a *prima facie* malpractice the moment I earned the federal default judgment against the Japanese company.

"It would have been better if she did not read any instructions, don't you think? The instructions are confusing and so unclear. It's so unfair."

Harvey did not respond. My attorneys formed the jury instructions with the judge and my opponents. They could have done a much better job for me—I did not know. I wasn't with them in those pre-trial conferences.

It was the final performance of O'Brien and Roy before the jury. They would discuss the evidence that had been presented in their closing arguments.

They would try to convince the jury to take their sides. O'Brien represented the plaintiffs, and the law allowed him two opportunities to speak, the first and the third. He was supposed to have the burden to prove his case.

I pleaded with Roy to give it his best.

O'Brien stood up and walked to the podium. He asked the jury to decide that I violated the Hague Treaty—just as his legal expert, Williams, explained.

He said that I was negligent for not defending the clients in the Japanese court when they were countersued.

I again whispered to Harvey, "He's asking the jury to guess. What kind of trial is this? So what if I did not send anyone to Japan?"

O'Brien told the jury that the machine was defective, just as my first engineer said in an affidavit that was adapted by the federal judge in the uncontested suit my office filed against the Japanese company over a decade ago.

"You're right, Harvey," I said softly and quickly. "He's making me look like a liar because I hired an engineer to support the product defect case I filed for the Barnedos in the federal court. The court put me in a no way out."

Then, O'Brien talked of the source of the noodle machine and exclaimed in a much louder tone that I have admitted knowing that Royal Trading sold the machine!

"That's a lie. Nothing but a lie! How desperate could he get. Roy, please object!" I was talking from my seat, almost standing up, but Harvey stopped me.

Roy did not object. A matter of courtesy, whispered Harvey. He simply allowed O'Brien to say everything he wanted to say, even if it was not in evidence—even if it was not true—even if they were guesses and assumptions. And how to construe the Hague Treaty, and the judge was just listening!

"You might be heard by the jury," cautioned Harvey. Then, he quickly scribbled, "contempt of court!"

O'Brien then reminded the jury of the millions of dollars in insurance that the Hawaii company, Royal Trading, had. He said the money should belong to his clients, the Barnedos, if not for my mistakes.

I remembered how easily Roy agreed to the insurance policy, and that he yanked the research of Jennifer from my hand. He agreed to the whole nine yards of papers he said the judge admitted—as if it was all the judge's fault. O'Brien's closing argument was hurtful to watch!

Then, I wondered if that was the same inaction that Roy and Harvey showed the judge during the pre-trial hearings. The reason they did not want me to be with them. Is it possible that they said Amen to all the judge wanted?

I began to feel I was just a captive audience. Melting away while I watched a horror movie of me and my legal career played out in an American Hall of Justice.

It was our turn for closing arguments. Roy stood up and walked to the podium. Harvey had already placed their charts before the jury, including many on how to interpret the Hague Treaty.

Roy argued how the Hague should be interpreted by the jury, which was exactly as my office and the federal court had interpreted it.

He told the jury that my opponents did nothing to attempt to collect in Japan, did not even set foot in the Japanese court. Their evidence was guesses and assumptions.

He had good and logical arguments, but my mind was screaming, How can my fate be in the hands of lay people for all these legal issues and guesses? I have no due process. Am I really in court?

I sympathized with the jurors. Although competent and chosen, I imagined what they were thinking with their solemn faces: What did he say? What does it mean? Where do we begin? Where do we end? Is this our role to analyze for the courts what laws mean? I never thought.

And as for the Hawaiian company, Royal Trading, Roy reminded the jury that it sold foods and not noodle machines.

At that point, I imagined what Mr. Davis said during the arbitration—The owner of the Royal Trading was not a seller. He was simply a travel companion in Japan. How clear could it be!

I could not help but think—Did my attorneys fail to insist on the dismissal of my case for the glamour of performance before a jury, and for their learning experience?

An insane and tragic thought! Both were lawyers for many years.

Immediately after the closing arguments, the judge addressed the jury panel with a routine comment utilized by many judges:

"Okay. I want to thank counsel and the parties. This case was tried very professionally, and I appreciate the good work that everyone has done," she said.

Good work for whom? Where do I fit in all of these? I felt sorry for myself, and somehow, for Roy and Harvey as well, whatever their reasons were for being in court that moment.

Finally, the jurors were sent to their room to deliberate and reach a verdict.

The attorneys were requested to remain in the courthouse for a while. They needed to be available to respond to any urgent message from the jury. I was an attorney and I decided to stay.

The jurors selected a female foreperson and soon after deliberations began, the jury's communication number 1 was out. They wanted to see the Treaty of the 1970 Hague Convention.

The judge directed the jury to the confusing law in the Hague Treaty text that had never been interpreted by the Hawaii Supreme Court and was already in the jury room.

"Why didn't my opponents just drag the entire Supreme Court library to the jury room?" I said.

Roy and Harvey somewhat resumed their style of talking to me again in jest. The trial was over.

"Better yet, the entire Library of Congress for the jury to review," retorted Harvey.

"The jury is inside the room figuring out what is the correct legal method of summoning a foreign corporation. Aren't you scared?"

"Erlinda, it might work to our advantage if they do not know how to interpret the law, or if they are so confused," answered Roy.

"I don't want my justice to come that way. The law gets interpreted by the courts. The jury determines facts from the evidence. They do not determine laws. They must be wondering what the questions on the verdict form mean. The verdict questions do not relate to a cause of action against me, the defendant."

"We know, but trial is over. Let's just wait and see. Who knows, there could be conflicting interpretations of the Hague Treaty among the jurors. Some could believe Roy and some may believe Williams, and we'll have a hung jury," added Harvey.

"You mean, among other issues—including the Japan judgment that nobody knows if it exists," I said. "The issues are not defined. You are veteran attorneys, you know that."

Roy and Harvey were silent. It was a signal for me to be quiet. I just said, "Thanks, if anything comes up, I'll be in my office," and we dispersed.

I had time to get back to my office and return accumulated calls. Roy and Harvey would probably do the same. We expected more questions to come from the jury.

The other jury questions were for clarifications. I knew they were extremely confused. Communication No. 2 was, "We need clarification of question 8-A."

Question 8-A of the jury verdict form was for the interpretation of the International Law of the Treaty of Hague.

The verdict form asked, "Was the Defendant, Erlinda Dominguez, negligent in representing the Plaintiffs, Junie Barnedo and Juan Barnedo by choosing service by mail and/or service by publication regarding Marukiku Menki Company, Ltd?"

The answer of the judge to the jury was, "Rely on your collective memory of the evidence."

"Roy, that textbook response of the judge does not give an answer to the jury's question. The jury is asking for clarification. Their communication has nothing to do with collective memory. Question 8-A of the verdict form asks for the interpretation of the Hague Treaty. The jury is in agony. Can't you see? It's time to push the court to dismiss." Nothing could be clearer than the severe confusion of the jury at this time.

I may have said more than I intended because Roy's response was, "Erlinda, you could represent yourself, you know!"

That was a slap on my face although I knew Roy did not mean it. He was still tense from the trial and was just unwinding.

By procedure, the judge always gave the attorneys an opportunity to voice their opinion on the verdict form and how to answer the jurors' questions.

Roy must have felt I was blaming him. He was given that opportunity and he agreed with the judge.

I continued to be an annoyance to him even after the trial.

* * *

The wait for the verdict was long.

There was no verdict on the first day of deliberations. We expected that. Each day, the jurors would be discharged if they could not decide by 4:15 in the afternoon.

It was the second day and they had not decided.

"We have reached the third day. If they don't decide today, I'm sure they are still reading the fine letters of the Hague Treaty," said Harvey. "Something that the courts should do, not lay people. That was an entire class in law school and I still did not understand it when I graduated."

"Could you imagine the jurors reading the entire text of the Hague Treaty in the jury room for days?" I said with growing alarm.

By late afternoon of the third day, the court's clerk called my attorneys. The jury was excused for the day. No verdict.

The following morning, I was in my lawyers' office as they requested. It was possible that we would hear from the court on something. It was the fourth day.

"Did you ever have a jury deliberation that took this long?" Harvey asked me. "We've had the jury decide in hours or a day, but never this long."

"None," I said. "The only case that would compare was when I was court-appointed to defend Rolando Navarette, the world lightweight boxing champion. An entire week was gone and the jury could not decide. A mistrial was about to be declared."

"What happened in that case anyway?" asked Harvey.

"He was acquitted but not of a lesser offense. I believe it was trespassing. Our jury may now be looking for a reason to award money to the Barnedos. The jurors are human. They must think I would not be hurt because I have insurance. But I don't have. Insurance talk impacted the trial and has poisoned my case. I think sympathy and prejudice got in."

Roy was upset. He walked away, leaving me alone with Harvey. He must have remembered how easily he had agreed to let the jury see Royal Trading's insurance policy without telling me.

"I will not leave the building. You know where to reach me," I said. I took the elevator and went down to my office.

Mila dropped by to see how things were going. "We should go up to your attorneys' office and wait for news," she suggested. "How do you feel?" she asked.

"I don't know, Mila, it's sad. This day might be over without a verdict. If there is no verdict, I don't want to go through another trial. As we speak, the jury is deadlocked. You heard of jurors handing out a verdict in just a few hours even in a capital offense of murder with death penalty. It's not happening in my case. I'm really worried. They must now have reached the point of exhaustion and feel compelled to decide. The sympathy factor goes to my accusers, our previous clients."

We sat in my attorneys' waiting room and chatted. Finally, the phone rang. "The jury reached a verdict. You are to proceed to the court immediately," said Roy's secretary.

"Good luck," said Mila.

I was very unhopeful.

It's so unfair that lay people agonized over the Hague Treaty for several days, when the United States Supreme Court hasn't even chosen a correct interpretation. So unconstitutional!

Mr. and Mrs. Barnedo were in the courtroom with their attorney when we arrived. Everyone was ready. There were a few people in the audience.

There was a woman seated behind the Barnedos. I did not know her but she was certainly Filipino. Obviously local, what people call the Hawaii born.

Judge Marks asked the jury if they had reached a verdict. The foreperson stood up and said, "Yes."

The bailiff reached for the verdict form from the foreperson then handed it to the judge. The judge smiled almost unnoticed, then the verdict was read aloud.

Chapter Thirteen

The jury was polled. There was a split, but my opponents got the required votes.

The jury decided that I was negligent. I violated the Hague Treaty. They believed Williams, not Roy, or they did not understand the issue. At least, I had that thought even before the verdict.

The jury also decided that I was negligent in my conduct regarding the Japanese lawsuit that was brought against the Barnedos. I thought they meant my failure to represent the Barnedos in a Japanese Court. The verdict form was too vague. Worse still, they could have meant my laughing at the Japanese procedure—as the Barnedos said on the witness stand.

I did not know how defective the verdict form was until the case was handed over to the jury for their decision. I suspected the attorneys I hired were fearful to insist upon the judge. The judge even used disjuncture words of "and/or" making the questions almost impossible or non-sensible to answer. I was distraught.

Finally, the jury decided that the Hawaii Royal Trading Company was not a seller and was not in the chain of distribution of the noodle machine that injured Mrs. Barnedo. But they said I was still negligent in not suing it.

I knew the jury was so wrong and I could not blame them. I realized how critical it is to have a competent and reasonably unblemished judicial system. It could destroy innocent lives and reward the undeserving.

Harvey whispered, "They're so confused. Really so very confused. What a big mess this is!"

I whispered back, "They must believe it's just a battle of insurance companies!"

My mind was racing. They decided against me. How much? The clerk continued to read the verdict.

The amount was for $483,875.09, exactly the same amount as the federal default judgment my office earned against the Japanese Company a decade ago, shown to the jury by the court over the objections of my attorneys.

The reading of the verdict was over.

"What happened to the nationwide authority of Loube versus Loube, where a default uncontested judgment can never be used to measure damages in a subsequent malpractice case? The jury just followed the federal default judgment I earned for the clients against the Japan company," I whispered to Harvey who looked as desperate as I was.

"I had told you that before, Erlinda, the judge said she did not read it, she did not have the time to read it, even if I provided a copy to her. If you doubt me, you can confirm what she said from the transcripts."

My God, this is the kind of trial you gave me in the United States of America!

"Don't worry," immediately whispered Harvey. "By law, the judge will have to deduct what the worker's compensation paid. After deduction, her judgment will be around $285,000 only. And we still have the right to appeal. This trial is unbelievable!"

The reading of the verdict was over.

Mr. and Mrs. Barnedo were excited. They screamed, then hugged each other. They bowed and thanked the judge.

The jury had completed its job.

One by one, the jurors smiled at the Barnedos as they left the courtroom. We did a good job—that must have been their collective thought. At least, they tried.

The court was adjourned. The room was cleared.

Mr. Barnedo was more emotional than his wife. In an instant, he reached out and we both hugged mildly. As if he had a message: We are not enemies and we don't understand all that is going on. We are sorry for you, Attorney, but we won.

Mrs. Barnedo did the same, she hugged me very hurriedly. She just said "Attorney" softly, then let out a sigh of relief. She had always been respectful.

I managed to whisper, *"Sigi lang,"* Filipino words meaning, "It's alright."

There was nothing more to say. O'Brien and my attorneys looked at each other. Everyone walked out of the courtroom, then the door was locked.

"Don't despair. The appeal court will overturn the verdict. That's what happens when the jury is compelled to decide legal issues and guess from lack of evidence. The errors are obvious," said Harvey, also consoling himself and Roy.

"Remind me again of what you mean by plain and obvious errors that the appellate court will see—in our desperate situation."

"Meaning, anyone could see it, even if your appeal brief is turned upside down!" said Harvey.

The Filipino woman from the audience was speaking to O'Brien. She turned out to be a newspaper reporter and the daughter of a former client whose personal injury claim I handled so well.

The day after, the verdict appeared in a major newspaper in Hawaii, the *Honolulu Star Bulletin*. It was broadcasted on the local radio stations. A Honolulu attorney is guilty of legal malpractice and the clients burst into tears.

It was bigger news than a doctor who was found guilty of medical malpractice with a bigger verdict in a different courtroom.

In my apartment complex, people looked at me in a sad way. My next door neighbor, Mr. Ponsen, said, "Erlinda, the news of your trial is wildfire in the building. We are extremely sorry."

Mr. Dearing, another neighbor, was an executive for the insurance company. I knew he meant to ease my emotions with his comment, "Take it this way, there is no shame in going bankrupt. It's what you are, not what you have."

My neighbors and friends did not know what happened in my case, nor did they know the truth. But they meant well when they looked away from me.

Roy and Harvey showed some hesitation accepting another check for their fees. They felt guilty for losing. But if I had paid less, who knows if my case would have gone from worse to worst.

Mila decided to stay for a few additional days. I could use her services for things to be typed, delivered, or filed.

"It's sinful that you lost," she said. "You are punished for nothing you did wrong. You are also defending your former associates who betrayed you. You are even defending Pohl."

"That's life. In a blink of an eye, everything you worked for could be gone—your name, your career, your money—even in a Hall of American justice. Your whole life and your world could just collapse. You don't even know what hit you."

"Does the identity of a party have anything to do with the case? I thought cases are decided on the truth," said Mila.

"The truth could be very subjective, Mila. To others, there's not just one, but many truths about the same thing, depending on mental and moral factors. Our system is not perfect. Don't forget human factors in your concept of justice. I have heard this often and still don't know its actual extent in courts."

"Please work on your appeal right away," she said.

"That's what Roy and Harvey promised. They're sure I will find justice in the highest State court, the ultimate guardian of justice, protector of the Constitution, the laws, everyone's rights—and it oversees the actions of the lower courts."

"Sorry, Erlinda. I wish I understood all this legal stuff. I'm not much help."

I was making Mila my sounding board. That was all.

* * *

Jennifer Smith was still doing research for me. I was about ready to go to the office one morning shortly after trial when my phone rang. "Are you sitting down?" she asked.

"Why, what's wrong?"

"The judge in your case is the first Hawaii jurist of the year. I saw that on the internet!"

"What does that have to do with my case?"

"Well, she must be the jurist of the entire Hawaiian State, and I thought you should know, that's all."

My attorneys had to be told. The tension of the trial had somewhat left them. They began to socialize with me again. As if the trial never happened.

I called up Harvey and told him the news. "The malpractice judge is the Hawaii jurist of the year."

"Wow!" he said with a sound of mild fright in his voice.

"What do you mean, wow?"

"Nothing...she may be more believable."

"Than me, you mean? She is not a party to the case."

"She made the rulings and chose the evidence. That's what we are going to appeal."

"But the Supreme Court will go by the merits of my case, and not base their decision on the fact that she happens to be the jurist of the year."

"That's true, that's true. You're so right."

I sensed that Harvey was again on the loudspeaker. Roy was with him.

"I'm sure the justices, judges and their personnel will be there during her coronation. Some nearby offices might close early and send their employees over," said Harvey excitedly.

"She will be crowned?" I asked without really thinking.

"Don't be silly. You're too literal, Erlinda. You must be joking. She will certainly get something. Maybe a plaque or a trophy. I don't know."

"What does it take for someone to be the jurist of the year?" I asked.

"Lots of community service, long hours in the courtroom, the rulings made, letters of recommendations...that kind of thing." said Harvey.

"What recommendations?"

"From any lawyer who wants to recommend her like perhaps O'Brien," said Harvey, obviously kidding around. "I will certainly be there. It will be held at the judiciary building."

"Who appoints one to that position?" I asked.

"The Hawaii Supreme Court," said Roy without hesitation.

"Isn't that where my appeal is going?"

"Yes, and now you know what I mean."

"Roy, I really don't know what you mean. You have always spoken in riddles. And don't remind me of my case this time."

"I'm just trying to keep the mood light, that's all. No serious topic. Do you want to go the ceremony, Erlinda? You can be with Harvey."

"No, thank you."

Our conversation ended and I imagined my attorneys relaxing in the comfort of their office. Roy with his shoes on his desk and reclining on his chair, and Harvey as comfortable, seated in front of him with no papers to read, with just a cup of coffee. The two of them—just talking of any story.

I thought, that must be what judges do when they have no case to hear—just like what Roy explained when Judge Marks seemed to know too much about me—that I was hated by the jury—and that I was afraid someone will steal my coffer—in my successful and extensive legal practice in Hawaii!

I decided that Pohl should now be involved. We had been in partnership. They managed my office and my cases. They signed the tolling agreement not to be sued with me, let me go through hell, while they stayed in the background and monitored the trial.

The letter I wrote to Pohl was a mild threat: I would go to court to vindicate my rights if I had to.

Mila delivered a copy of the letter to Roy. I was still required to tell them all that I was doing to avoid any confusion.

Mila walked into their office building while I waited in my car in the parking lot. She came back and Roy and Harvey were with her. They looked worried, annoyed, and even frightened.

"Don't deliver that to Pohl," said Harvey, "or I will topple Mila down." He spoke sternly but was smiling.

"Why…you think it will complicate matters? It's too late for that. The trial is over and you never sued them…I'm just asking for their help. They have insurance and I don't. I have become a derelict without harming anybody."

"They are many and they are powerful. You are by yourself. They will turn you into mince-meat," said Roy.

"That's not what you said when I hired you, Roy. You promised to protect my rights. You said you would not hesitate to include Pohl in the suit if you had to. You never did. You confuse me with your conflicting signals of your concern for me, your clout with the judges, and your expertise in the law."

"We'll do what we can to settle," Harvey quickly interrupted. "There's really no reason for you to lose on our appeal. The errors are plain even with the haphazard briefs we prepared for you. The appeal courts are experts on the issues. They could see them with their eyes closed."

"Set that letter aside meantime," said Roy. "You're only frustrating our efforts on the post-trial motions and appeal."

"How?"

"You should completely know what we mean at this time."

"No, I don't know. But okay. Perhaps I'll just do that—set it aside for now and continue to allow myself to be destroyed?"

Roy and Harvey watched me drive away from the parking lot.

"Erlinda, you are crazy if you listen to every word that Roy tells you. He used to work on your cases. I think that all is not well in your defense even if I'm not a lawyer," said Mila.

"Don't say that. Please don't erase my hope in them. Otherwise, everything for me seems too late. Nobody will help me this late!"

She shook her head. "You have been a very aggressive lawyer for our office clients. But you are intimidated by Roy and Harvey. It seems they are your Gods. What's wrong with you? I will deliver your letter to Pohl. I'll do it right now!"

* * *

Hardly a week passed since the verdict. I had my phone lines open for any call from my attorneys or legal researchers, perhaps, even from Pohl.

I was on my way to the office. The phone rang. It was a long distance call from my sister, Helen, in the Philippines. "Our mother is sinking. She was rushed to the hospital."

"Oh, my God. What happened?"

"She heard about the verdict. It did not come from us. We tried to keep it from her. She collapsed." My sister was sobbing.

"May I speak to her, please? I am appealing. Tell her not to worry, not to be ashamed. Tell her to be happy."

"She must not be disturbed. She is resting."

I went to the Waikiki church nearby. I asked to talk to a priest. Nobody was around. I contacted my friends and relatives to pray for my mother.

The next day, my sister called. "Mamang has passed away."

How I wished I was never a lawyer in Hawaii, the United States of America. How I wished I never listened to my father when he said that it had the greatest and fairest legal system in the whole world, and that is where I could really use my mental and moral skills.

I told Roy and Harvey that I had to leave for the interment of my mother. I was worried that in my absence, the judgment would be filed.

"There should be no judgment over my head. It will crash my remaining credit, my name, my profession, everything I worked for. This case has already destroyed me."

My attorneys agreed to seek a status conference with the judge. The filing of the judgment should be held off until all parties had the opportunity to explore settlement upon my return from the Philippines.

* * *

The trip was difficult. Passengers had to wear masks because of the SARS virus. I arrived in Manila and proceeded to Baguio City where the wake services were occurring.

I entered the funeral home in the late evening, tired and haggard. The room was crowded with relatives, friends, and well wishers. Many were in their Igorot tribal costumes and chanting native songs. Their eyes were focused on me. I proceeded to the coffin where my mother lay.

My mother's face was peaceful now. I whispered, "Please forgive me, Mamang, for causing your death! I must tell you—I am not guilty of any wrongdoing. I am just the victim of ugly circumstances. You are again wearing your *terno* as the crowned Philippine Mother of the Year. I promise, you will not be disappointed and your many friends will know what some Hawaii people did to me!"

Back in Hawaii, I did not tell my attorneys that the verdict was my mother's death sentence. She was a strong woman. Besides, the news would reach my many enemies that early, including my opponents. That could be one of their trophies over me.

Our post-trial motions for judgment notwithstanding the verdict and for the judge to grant me a new trial would soon be heard. The motions were based on several grounds and asked the judge to decide the dismissal of the case as a matter of law.

Both of my attorneys promised to help each other in the arguments.

I continued to drain more litigation expenses. I desperately wanted the problem to end. At the very least, the problem should now be in the appellate court where Roy and Harvey always said the errors would be so plain.

"You better not attend the hearing on the motions, Erlinda," said Roy. "You may just be aggravated."

"Are both of you going for the arguments?"

"Yes. You should place all your trust in us," said Harvey. "There is just no point in adding to your concerns."

"I can't fathom why you would say that, unless you feel that I should have a reason. Do I?"

"I'm just assuring you since you've been through a lot."

"Just tell me what you want. More research? Duplicate transcripts? I am here to help. I am the defendant."

* * *

Days and weeks passed by. I contacted my attorneys sparingly and had to keep my thoughts of the case at a minimum. I still had many clients. Perhaps, they misunderstood the news in the newspapers and radio stations or hopefully, they continued to believe in my competence and integrity.

One day, Harvey called. "You have to come see us."

I hurriedly left for their office.

He was in the conference room with Roy and they looked very serious and grim.

"We lost in all the motions. The judge still believes the Hague Treaty Law interpretation is not her role. She also thinks you should have appeared in the Japanese court or sent somebody, even if nobody knows what happened in that court and your opponents did not have a Japanese judgment," said Harvey.

"That's not a legal case," I exclaimed.

"I know."

"How about the Royal Trading issue? The jury decided it was not within the chain of distribution. It was not the seller!"

"The judge said the jury had already decided that you were negligent in not suing the company even if it was not the seller, even if it had no connection to the noodle machine that injured Barnedo. So, the court won't dismiss that count," Harvey said.

"But the jury is plainly inconsistent and the verdict is legally illogical. Otherwise, I had no target, wildly suing the whole unconnected world. Remember how the judge described herself in her previous ruling—shooting from the hips? I did not want to be that way for my clients. If she won't dismiss because the jury decided, there's no purpose for post-trial motions that the laws and rules provide."

"How true. But we can take it up on appeal. That's why there are appellate courts," Roy again assured me.

"What laws is the judge basing her rulings on? I don't understand. Am I missing something?"

"We don't completely understand either, but that is her role as the judge. We're very confused with nothing we could do."

"My motion for new trial was denied just like that?"

"Erlinda, our written briefs and oral arguments were long and extensive. We did what we could do for you," said Harvey.

Later, I read the transcript of that hearing, held on August 1, 2003, which reads verbatim:

THE COURT: I've reviewed everything that's been submitted. Basically you're asking me to find that my rulings on evidence resulted in an unfair trial for the defendant. And in my discretion, I don't quite see it that way. So my inclination is to deny the motion. If you want to make any further arguments, I'm happy to hear it.

MR. DEMETRAKOPOULOS: Actually, Your honor, I think we pretty much covered our arguments in the written submission. So I'll leave it at that.

There was nowhere in the less than two pages of transcript for my new trial where both my attorneys, Roy and Harvey, made an oral argument for me as they said they did. And as they described to be long and extensive—doing what they could for me. And I suddenly remembered how truly critical are the rules on recusal and disqualification of judges.. Though it may not happen, the public would always suspect the judge's discretion was used for a sibling, a friend, a spouse and so on.

My attorneys were tongue-tied in court. They were too fearful. It could have been intentional. I would never know.

What a fool I was—the word of Roy.

One early morning, Nikki called. "Roy and Harvey want you to come today if possible."

Again, it was time to talk. I suspected why.

"Your opponents have filed motions for pre-judgment interest, for fees, and for their expenses. We just want you to know. Perhaps you could add to your settlement offer," said Roy.

"I assume that the judge would not give them any interest," said Harvey. "You did not cause any delay in litigation."

"They were the ones who delayed when their attorneys lost the records they got from Pohl's office," I said.

"But we are sure the judge would allow their expenses. That's routine," added Roy.

We had calculators and notepads and did some computing. The opponents did not have many expenses. They had one legal expert, but he may not have been paid his fees. He was a friend of the attorneys for the Barnedos.

I looked at Roy and Harvey as they watched me with their apparent sympathy and apprehension.

"I will ask my bank's assistance. My opponents might accept half of the verdict amount. By law, the worker's compensation lien is deductible which will bring down the payable verdict to less than $300,000. Half is $150,000 which I may be able to offer."

"That's the only valid computation and extremely generous to your opponents," said Harvey.

"It might make things worse if I come with you. I still shiver at the words of the judge before the trial: Split the baby," I said.

There was not much to talk about. My attorneys just wanted assurance that I was still willing to discuss settlement.

We waited for the hearing on the motions. I thought to myself, it should not be more than what we computed. The judge won't give them interest and fees, only their expenses, which was not too much. With the worker's compensation deduction, I could bond myself for just over two hundred thousand dollars.

I organized my bank records, made some computations for my bond while I appealed.

* * *

Days passed by. Roy called me. "I just want to go straight to the point, Erlinda. We're busy preparing your appeal briefs and pursuing your bond with the Supreme Court. You don't need to come see us at this time." They were on the loudspeaker.

"What is it?"

"Judge Marks granted all their motions to the penny."

"Please wait for me. I won't talk about this over the phone. I have to see you in person."

Roy and Harvey were silent as I reached their conference room. They looked hesitant to speak. They stood up to meet me. "Have a seat, Erlinda." And they closed the door.

"Something severely serious?"

"Yes. Judge Marks gave the opponents everything they asked for in fees and expenses, without a breakdown and without invoices. She also did not deduct the worker's compensation payments," said Roy.

"And the judge awarded them ten years of pre-judgment interest over the verdict," added Harvey, and he looked at my reaction with his deep concern.

"The ten years of pre-judgment interest is equivalent to another half a million. Oh, my God! My God! Why? Why?"

"With everything the judge awarded, and running interest on a daily basis, the judgment of Judge Marks against you will be way over a million, possibly close to 1.5 million dollars," said Harvey. "That's almost four times the total jury verdict."

My whole world collapsed!

"What does the judge have against me? I didn't kill anyone. I did nothing wrong to her or to Pohl where her husband works! You had said this is a nonsense malpractice case. I'm sure that was the thinking of Arbitrator Davis who decided for me. Now, I'm facing some 1.5 million judgment for a nonsense? Help me!"

"We're as devastated as you are. We don't know what to say. Perhaps, because you refused to settle, who knows," Harvey said.

"Erlinda, we are not prophets. If you settled a long time ago, none of this would have happened," added Roy.

I stared at Roy and said, "File a motion for Judge Marks' recusal right away. She never disclosed her conflict that she's married to an attorney in the Pohl firm, another former Attorney General. They are my ultimate legal opponents. The Barnedo case ended with them, even if they tolled their being sued. I'm so confused right now and I feel that the events in my case are so immoral and unethical."

Both of my attorneys looked seriously grim and worried. They were slightly nodding their heads like they agreed with all I said.

"I know that Pohl is very angry at me. But I have not made up the facts of their involvement in the malpractice, or of our partnership. They should help instead of going against me."

Roy's face turned pale! He did not know what to do.

"It's much too late, Erlinda. Judge Marks already made the rulings. You may be facing two million or more for such a late motion," said Roy.

Roy's two million was arbitrary and he did not mean it. I felt it was more like a threat, that I may be held in contempt of court, which had been at the judge's discretion.

"I don't care anymore," I said. "I did not have a true trial. The judge told you that I was hated by the jury long before trial began. But you know what? I think the hate is not from the jury at all! The hate may be so thick against me in the Pohl firm where the husband of the judge works and has his office."

"Don't make us look bad," said Roy indignantly. "That's not exactly how I said it—that you were hated by the jury."

"Harvey, you are my witness when you and Roy said that. I am willing to go through a lie detector test. Would you?"

"That's kid stuff, let's move on."

"If you have a conscience, you would admit that the judge never disclosed her spousal relationship with someone in Pohl's office and never offered to disqualify herself before the trial."

"That's our recollection. Her recollection is different. She thinks she disclosed, but she never did. That's the honest truth," said Roy defensively.

"Why did you not say that when she made the announcement at trial when Okamoto testified, Roy? You agreed with her. You were extremely afraid to offend her because of your legal practice. But did you think of me, your client? So, don't talk of honesty."

"We were in the middle of trial, Erlinda. I did not want to argue with the judge. That would create a scene and make things worse for you and your case. I was actually protecting you."

"Protecting me? You are amazing, Roy. How dare you!"

"We understand what you feel. All we can say now is that we are doing our best for your appeal. It's never too late. Your justice will come, we assure you. We ask for your patience."

"I'm sorry," I said. "I may be so confused and distraught right now. I feel I am overwhelmed by intense immorality. But I should not allow myself to believe this or be paranoid because I am in America, a country I so respect."

Chapter Fourteen

I spent days preparing for my bond. I felt I was surrounded by enemies and pulled from all sides. Another day, another conference.

"Your bond will be in cash for the amount of the entire judgment, perhaps more, all within the discretion of Judge Marks. We know that she will not accept real properties and will eventually pin you down into pure cash," said Harvey.

"They might as well guillotine me for something I never did. If I murdered somebody, the bond would be much less than 1.5 million. I was never charged with any crime in my entire life. Never! It seems every step I took to fight for my rights had an adverse reaction with the judge. She should have stepped aside because she is the wife of my legal opponent's partner, and it is obvious she could not stand me. That's just my opinion and you are entitled to your own opinion. As the judge said during the trial, "We can agree to disagree.""

Amazingly, Roy and Harvey just looked at each other and did not respond. They knew I was distraught and desperate.

"If the bonding company helps you, the premium will be something like seventy thousand dollars a year," said Harvey.

"What happens if my appeal takes five years, or forever?"

"We have no control over that. You can still settle now."

"You know what a settlement means, Roy. My opponents will release everyone, including Pohl, all of Pohl's partners, attorneys, and their employees. That is really what this boils down to, isn't it?"

"That is the end result, Erlinda. We cannot deny that. We will tell the judge that even her husband who works in Pohl's office will be completely released when you settle."

"You just spelled it out, Roy! I'm pressured to settle to appease the opponents and to release Pohl, including Judge Marks' husband, isn't it? You said it so well, it could not be clearer than that, can it? The husband may have worked in the Barnedo case. Remember Sharon Himeno's memo I found? Please share with me your honest thoughts."

Again, Roy and Harvey were silent. They had nothing to say. They looked guilty for not having been candid with me, their client.

"As for the cash bond, I have divulged my assets. Whatever you will say and do in court, I will not be with you. The judge seems to prefer it that way, and I think I know why," I said.

"Erlinda, the judge has control over the bond issue. We know you are extremely distraught, but be careful of your conduct. You may be facing a court contempt instead of just money!"

My own attorneys were threatening me, their client, who was hanging by a thread in my desparate and helpless state.

"Roy, it's time that Pohl helps me on this. You know that we were in the Barnedo case together."

"We cannot speak for you, Erlinda. You should do it yourself. Perhaps they will help if you talk to them nicely."

"You mean beg? You had always talked to them about the case. Why won't you speak on my behalf now that I lost? They monitored the progress of the malpractice case through you!"

"It would be an embarrassing situation, Erlinda. The husband of Judge Marks is in Pohl's office. It will appear that we are personally going after the judge and we are your lawyers."

"Roy, you should have told me that when I hired you. You, promised to be my protector all the way! But I am in a desperate situation. I have no choice but to work with you."

They were surprisingly calm in spite of my anger. They must have thought I would report their conduct to the Office of the Disciplinary Board, but I had no such intentions—to add to the long list of my enemies.

"We want to work with you, too, Erlinda. Just keep personal things away from us, that's all we ask."

* * *

Harvey called. My opponents warned us that they would file the judgment immediately if we could not settle before the judge.

"Please feel what they could accept. Maybe a figure less than the verdict amount? Something I could afford. I will plead with my bank to help me. My cellular is open. Call me."

"We will tell the judge that you were punished enough. You had to sell your empty lot to finance your case. We will be clear to her that you will also release her husband who works with Pohl. She will do her best to settle the case, but so much will depend on your opponents," said Roy.

The day after the conference with the judge, Harvey called. They again wanted to see me in their office.

"The opponents are talking $750,000. They feel they earned every penny of the million plus that Judge Marks awarded them and are asking half to help you out. If settled, they will release everyone involved."

"Helping me out? Forget settling, Roy. Let them file the judgment. Please appeal immediately. I'm already giving up on everybody. But as you said, I will find my justice on appeal!"

"You see, Erlinda, if you settle for less than what they want, they will claim the difference from the others, such as your former associate attorneys."

"But they were dismissed from the suit."

"That was without prejudice to re-filing. Or the opponents could maneuver where you will still be bothered as a witness or a third party defendant in a separate case."

"I know what you mean, Roy. They might now sue Pohl and prepare for a good case. They learned from my trial. If I don't settle, I will be sued by Pohl as a third party defendant? Is that what you're saying?"

"That's not exactly what I said."

"Well, Pohl is not yet free. What else could you mean?"

"We all know the phrase…that's water under the bridge. As we said, nobody is a prophet who can predict, and that includes us."

The topic of settlement was aggravating to the three of us. We would just do what we had to do: prepare post-trial motions.

As I walked out of their office, I despised my luck in meeting some people in my life. I despised my past desires to better my practice for the hundreds of clients who were underdogs.

Most especially, I despised my guiding light in my career—that America has the greatest and fairest judicial system in the whole wide world—the belief of my father when he was alive.

Then, I consoled myself. There is always an appeal. Hawaii belongs to everyone, and is not the entire America.

* * *

Pohl did not respond to my letters. I called and I called. I insisted on an appointment with their office. They set up some time with Ken and Sharon. I was early.

They noticed my black attire. "We heard of your mother's demise. Please accept our condolences," said Sharon.

"Thank you."

The conference room was closed. Nobody could see us. We discussed the verdict.

"That was in the news, we're sorry," said Sharon as if to tell me her source was only the newspaper.

I reminded them of how we thought the case was senseless, and the letter from Warren Price to O'Brien before I was sued where he said, guesswork and theories do not make a malpractice.

They remembered their tolling agreement so that they would not be sued while I went through the trial alone.

They had no comment about the unannounced transfer of the case from Judge Del Rosario to Judge Marks, whose husband works in their office.

I looked at both Ken and Sharon seated side-by-side, and politely said, "In your minds and in your hearts, you know you were involved. We are knowledgeable of the insurance law. The duty of the insurer to defend is greater than its duty to indemnify. Your insurer should help. I don't know what to do."

Ken and Sharon were solemn. They wanted me to do the talking. It was almost scary, but it never crossed my mind that they could have tape recorders on.

"Judge Marks will soon execute on her judgment and the opponents will collect against all my assets. You know that I have no insurance," I said. "Please hurry up. Please hurry up!"

I felt awkward mentioning the name of Judge Marks. That very moment, Robert Marks, her husband, could be with Warren

Price, steps away from the conference room—knowing I was there discussing the almost 1.5 million malpractice judgment of his wife against me.

How fitting that they are now together in practice. They were both the Attorney General, one after the other. How lucky they were. They have everything this planet could offer!

"We'll see what we can do," said Ken.

Sharon asked to be excused. She had to see members of her family. I continued to talk a little with Ken.

"I was never told of any disclosure done by Judge Marks that her husband is with you in this office until your testimony in court, Ken. I did not know. I'm in turmoil. I need help. I'm so confused about what is ethical and what is not. In fairness to the judge, she said she disclosed, but her disclosure was not in the records or in anybody's notes."

Ken was silent and was just observing me.

"I never encountered this situation in my career. Is Mr. Marks in your office right now? Are you going to tell him what we discussed?" I worriedly asked.

Ken said, "We don't talk of outside things, and we know that Robert Marks does not talk to his wife about your case or any cases for that matter. Very respectable couple."

It was obvious that he wanted me to leave, but was polite.

"Good day, Erlinda. We have to call up our insurer and get back to you," Ken said as he walked me to the elevator.

Mr. Marks does not talk to his wife about cases and both of them are lawyers—one a past Attorney General and the other, a relatively new trial judge?

As I walked back to my office, I knew that I just did not fit into that kind of a highly civilized society. As I heard said before, not in their circle.

In a few days, another conference was held in my attorneys' office. We knew the very critical situation I was facing.

Roy said, "It was wishful thinking that you be released on your own recognizance even if you are a practicing attorney and will not leave this State. In fact, Judge Marks denied the bond."

"She wants cash now," continued Harvey. "You will have to reveal every cent of your assets, locate all your checks in the past years—that kind of thing. Prove to your opponents that you have not hidden any money anywhere in this world."

"Pohl must really want me dead, dead, they're merciless!"

"You are again bringing up Pohl, you are unfocused," said Roy.

"Roy and Harvey, my feelings may be wrong and confused. Just like you, I am also a human being—I hope," I said, almost without any further strength to discuss the matter with them.

"We will pursue an emergency stay and affordable *supersedeas* bond with the State Supreme Court even if your opponents are glued to the over a million dollar judgment of Judge Marks. We may have sympathy from the Supreme Court. You were never disbarred or suspended from the Bar," said Roy.

"First, I have to testify on examination of debtor, isn't that the procedure before they garnish, so they know exactly where to send the summons and subpoenas?" I asked.

"Yes. They will only garnish where your assets are."

"My assets were listed in my affidavit you filed in court."

"Your two banks, the First Hawaiian and the American Savings, will be served the garnishee summons and subpoenas. But your debtor examination is yet to be scheduled, so that the court will not guess and could pin down the location of your assets."

"They will not wait for the decision of the State Supreme Court on our motion for the bond and the stay of the judgment?"

"They don't have to. The bond issue is still under the control of the lower court through Judge Marks," said Harvey.

"Erlinda, after we go through your examination of debtor, you should warn your banks of the garnishee summons and subpoenas. You have a good name with your banks," said Roy.

All three of us were out of words. Then, I said softly, "I feel like a fly caught in a spider's web, I wish I predicted this much earlier...I was too naive, very naive!"

After a while, Roy said, "You should consult with a bankruptcy attorney. We hear the automatic stay in bankruptcy is effective upon filing. Nobody can collect from you."

"Bankruptcy? Never! It will ruin my credit and livelihood. I have helped thousands of people. I have not done anything wrong, and now, bankruptcy? That's unfair to my legitimate creditors!"

We agreed to wait for the schedule of my formal examination of debtor. I was not worried about committing perjury. My filed affidavits were accurate. I did not hide anything.

I was now a debtor for about a million and a half dollars in cold cash, payable immediately at the whim of my previous clients! That was the procedure, even if I was pursuing an appeal.

In the words of Harvey, my opponents were dangling me on a string. I retorted with a "No, it's not them, it's the system!"

* * *

Days and weeks were passing by quickly. I was still frequently in court for my clients' cases.

Attorneys shunned me. I knew they were embarrassed for me—too embarrassed to even say hello. It was obvious they knew the humiliation I had been through.

I saw lawyers with whom I shared mutual respect. I had to avoid them when we were in the courthouse.

Others preferred to have nothing to do with me. Their legal practice didn't need the added burden of being blacklisted as mine had been.

I was clearing up my office one morning and saw the telephone number of Lillian Uy. She was a family court judge and a friend. We had lunch at the Kahala Waialae Club.

I sensed there were things she wanted to say about our legal profession, but she did not. We talked of better times.

There were other family court judges in the club. They stopped by our table to greet Lillian. She did not introduce me to them. I preferred it that way.

Lawrence Cohen and I had a quick snack. He was hired by Pohl years ago to work on my cases. He was now a *per diem* State district court judge. I knew he wanted to help. But he did not know of any lawyer who would file suit for me against Pohl.

One afternoon, I was in the court parking garage. Richard Griffith was getting into his car and saw me. He used to be the in-house counsel of First Insurance Company, where I worked as an adjuster before I became a Hawaii lawyer.

Now, he was a solo practitioner, had a small downtown office, and used to do contract work for me.

"I have not seen you for some time. How's everything?" I asked.

"Fine, fine…still in the same office."

"Bad things have happened to me," I said.

"When I saw the papers, I thought you were dead meat."

"Could you co-counsel with me in my claim against the Price Okamoto Himeno & Lum law firm? It is public knowledge that they absorbed my entire office."

"You and Pohl are both my friends, Erlinda. Unfortunately, I can't go against Warren Price. You understand."

"Yes, Richard. I do now. Can you refer another lawyer? I'm so busy with my small practice. I can hardly attend to my personal case. I have people to help in the research and briefs."

"I honestly doubt you will find anyone to sue Price."

"That's the bitter truth, isn't it?"

"Your case is very odd. I'm sorry. It's a nightmare, but hang in there, Erlinda."

Even court reporters hesitated to greet me. Surely, to spare my feelings. And they probably wondered how I could still function in my legal practice.

The tone of insurance adjusters changed. I was discussing a claim with Dina McGarrity of the American Insurance Guaranty.

She casually asked, "How are you doing? You're the talk of the insurance companies all the way from AIG through Allstate, State Farm, Geico, Traveler's, Hartford, you name it."

"They don't know the extent of what I went through, Dina."

Then she said, "Erlinda, I'm not a lawyer, but I have some idea of court trials. Why did the jury interpret the meaning of the Hague Treaty? And the judge refused to discard a patently inconsistent verdict? How did your attorneys allow that to happen?"

"I give you credit for the courage of your question. In this place, everyone has some unseen fear of something."

Ann Fallon was an attorney working for GEICO. She seemed cautious at first.

Then, she said, "Everyone here read the Personal Injury Judgments compiled by Neal Simon. When I saw the verdict and found out that the jurors were made to construe the Hague Treaty and decide other legal issues, I just could not believe it!"

"Yes, Ann, truth is stranger than fiction, isn't it? But as my attorneys said, it's not the end, the system allows us to appeal, and they are doing what they can."

* * *

The year would soon be over. There was no news of the schedule for my debtor examination.

My opponents must be waiting for the ruling of the Supreme Court on the bond issue. A matter of courtesy to the courts.

"The sword of Damocles will soon decapitate you," joked Jennifer as she handed me more of her research work. "The bond issue is within the discretion of the trial judge. It will never be granted, I predict."

"Don't worry, Jennifer. You will be paid in cash for your work. I just have to go to the bank. I have had no time to do personal stuff."

I walked over to the First Hawaiian Bank. Years before, I called their attention to a mistaken million dollar deposit into my account. They never forgot my immediate reaction.

Tricia, the teller, recognized me. There was no need for ID. She looked at the check, her computer, then stared at the screen. "Just a moment, Ms. Dominguez."

She stood up and talked to her supervisor, Iris. I could see them checking the computer and reading some records.

Then, Tricia walked to me and said, "We're so sorry, all your accounts have been garnished in a case against you and your office. We're sorry, the bank has to comply with court orders."

I could not immediately speak.

"Does that include my clients' trust account?"

"Yes, Ms. Dominguez. All of your accounts, including your clients' trust account."

"But that belongs to my clients...my God!"

While in the bank, I contacted Roy. "All of my accounts have been garnished, didn't you know? Even my clients' trust account is frozen. That means, I cannot practice law."

Roy was in a panic. "That's impossible. That can not be done. How? When? That's illegal. That's really unethical. The bank should ignore that."

"I'm coming to your office right away."

Roy and Harvey were waiting for me.

"How can I survive? I don't have a penny in my pocket!"

"We'll talk to your opponents and see if they will agree to ask Judge Marks to lift her Orders," said Roy.

"My gosh!" exclaimed Harvey as he browsed through the website. "There must be a hundred garnishee summons and subpoenas against you circulated in the State of Hawaii! We were not even notified by our opponents or by the court."

"Let me see," said Roy. He joined Harvey in reading the long list. They were both literally in horror.

My opponents served their garnishee summons and subpoenas to the schools, the police department, travel agencies, hotels, banks, credit unions—and many companies all over Hawaii.

"That's pure harassment," I said. "I have no money in those entities. They don't even know me. I'm being humiliated throughout this State. They want my practice to be crippled. My opponents know where my accounts are. They are in the records."

"Judge Marks approved all the summons and subpoenas, Erlinda. If a judge signs the orders, there's no harassment."

"They're in control. I have nothing."

"Our opponents must have delivered their *ex-parte*, one-sided motions in chambers. The judge had to act on them," continued Roy. "She cannot procrastinate."

"Roy, she had other things to do. Why did she rush on my execution without even notice?" I asked. He did not respond.

"They had no basis whatsoever. How tragic," said Harvey. As he looked at me, he again showed sympathy.

"The court calendar and my case will be yelled aloud in the courthouse as many times as there are people summoned. That's still the normal procedure as I know it. They really want to humiliate and step all over me when I'm already down," I said. My attorneys were speechless.

Roy and Harvey were really of no help. I felt I was alone.

We did not want to talk anymore. They asked me to see them when they figured out what was happening. They were bothered that the examination of debtor was skipped against their prediction.

The day after, I was back in my attorneys' office.

"How can I pay my creditors? My office space? My litigation expenses? Even basic necessities? I have only two bucks in my wallet, and my car is running out of gas. I want you to know that I will refuse any hand-out from you and your staff," I said.

"Erlinda, it's a friendly reminder to file for bankruptcy immediately, but we don't handle that kind of case," said Roy with a tone of sadness.

Their secretaries watched me as I walked toward the elevator to get to my office. I was imagining what they were thinking.

There goes a beggar! She is making the competition in this small Hawaii legal community happy! Her clients' trust account has been garnished! She cannot continue with her practice!

"Bankruptcy is the answer." I recalled Roy's seriousness about appointments with a few attorneys for consultation. It was difficult to mention my name.

Khaled Mustaba waived his fee. He used to do contract work for me years ago before he established a lucrative law firm focusing in bankruptcy.

In fact, nobody else wanted to be paid. They all knew me or had heard of my tragedy.

They asked lots of questions. Their inquiries were relevant to losses and receivables in the context of my problem.

All of them said bankruptcy was not for me. And many remarked, "If it is a reasonable option for you this late, you should immediately drop your malpractice attorneys!"

I concluded that I was too trusting and naive, possibly even idiotic, and it was transparent to the bankruptcy attorneys and to others—but not to me.

But I should not punish myself with guilt. I was lulled into confidence with the hot then cold, cold then hot attitude of my attorneys, and reinforced by my clear success in the arbitration.

"Drop them at a time like this? They started my appeal. And things could be made worse for me. Who knows!"

I told Roy and Harvey what the bankruptcy attorneys suggested—that the Pohl firm would be listed as my potential receivable if I decided to go bankrupt. I watched Roy's face turn pale again. He had suggested bankruptcy but did not like what he was hearing, the involvement of Pohl. I was tempted to say that I should fire them as my attorneys. I did not. Who knows what they could do for or against me.

* * *

Pohl was not responding to my letters and calls anymore. I decided to sue them. I knew I would have a hard time looking for someone to sign the complaint or co-counsel with me.

Back at my office, I prepared the complaint against Pohl.

Soon, it would be filed. I hand-delivered a copy to my attorneys.

Roy read my complaint. "Don't do it, Erlinda. Those people have very close friends all over."

"I don't know what you are implying. Their multitude of lawyers? Their witnesses? You always use the word friends. I don't think their friends will murder me even if I'm just a small fry in this community."

"You are going against our advice as your attorneys."

"This is not a nation where people take the law into their own hands! Hawaii is part of America, Roy, or did you forget?"

"Well, please set the matter aside for the meantime. You are treading on thin ice. Some better things are bound to happen in your case. It could not go any worse."

"Like what, and please don't be metaphorical?"

"We already said there's no reason you should lose in your appeal, although it is unethical to use the word, guarantee. You are a lawyer, so you know that."

"You speak of ethics in relation to one word, guarantee, after all that I've been through? What kind of ethical system do we have anyway?"

Roy did not respond.

"Isn't it strange? I have to sue Pohl to pay me back the unbearable judgment amount rendered by the judge against me, and her husband is part of Pohl. And Pohl must have thought I will succumb to settlement and all problems will go away!"

"We understand that, but please—it will be scandalous, and you will be in a lot of trouble if you sued them."

"Roy and Harvey, if you were in my shoes, I don't know what you would have done!"

Our conversation ended without accomplishing anything.

And as I stepped back into the elevator, I imagined both of my attorneys hanging from the ceiling of their office with ropes around their necks and piles of law books kicked underneath.

But they were not in my shoes!

Chapter Fifteen

I called up a friend, Ben Martin. He had a small, but thriving general law practice. He might handle bankruptcy and could have a different perspective of the situation I was in.

"I will refer you to Dana Smith. Bankruptcy is his specialty along with divorce. He is a friend and we often consult with each other. I will accompany you to his office a few floors above," Ben said.

"I think I know him. I referred divorce cases to him when I was in the same Century Square building during the early years of my practice," I said.

That day, I was with Ben in Mr. Smith's office. The office was small with only one secretary. He seemed to do almost everything, including paperwork.

Smith immediately invited us to his room. There were many bankruptcy and divorce manuals on his credenza behind his chair.

He had heard of my tragedy. He did not disclose his source.

Smith asked detailed questions, such as what assets I had, if I was divorced, and so on.

It was somewhat embarrassing, but Ben was a friend and I did not mind if he heard everything.

On our way out, I asked Ben, "Am I right that Smith was out of line to tell me, 'I find you exotic,' in a serious discussion? His face was so close! Yuck! Or is he just a dirty you know what, with a sudden urge of you know what in the middle of the day?"

"Don't worry," said Ben laughing. "He was just putting you at ease. You are an attorney. Don't take things personally."

"You mean, I could ethically tell him that he is handsome and irresistible even if I did not mean any part of it?"

Ben just laughed.

"Hawaii is now my home, and I'm still not quite used to that."

"Neither am I even if I grew up here," said Ben.

"Attorneys here use slang in and out of the courtroom. I can't find that in the law books. But to them, it's both professional and civil. Confusing."

"Erlinda, do as the Romans do when you are in Rome!"

"Is Smith a successful, skilled attorney?" I asked.

"He must be, or he would not be surviving all these years."

"He does not even validate parking tickets. I used to do that for everyone with no exception who came to my office."

"I never validated parking," said Ben.

"You're right. Parking validations may not be relevant to skills and success. I just wondered, that's all."

Days after, Smith called. He wanted me to sign a retainer. He offered to be my counsel in my civil suit against Pohl. He would use his litigation skills to help me, he said.

I quickly met with him in his office and paid the required deposit. His fee would be by the hour. Smith asked to see my small real estate holdings so he could prepare my bankruptcy papers.

I agreed to drive him around Waikiki while he relaxed as nothing more than a passenger.

He then suggested I withdraw all my investment money from the banks and create a trust fund in his name to protect my litigation fees. The account could be protected from garnishment.

Smith sounded very serious. But I thought he could not really mean what he said. There was a religious icon in his office. And what he suggested was a fraud upon the courts.

One day, Smith called me again and sounded excited. He had scheduled a meeting with William McCorriston, the attorney hired by the insurance company to defend Pohl in my suit for indemnification of the malpractice judgment.

He thought that perhaps Pohl's insurer would pay his fees.

"I'm so angry at Price Mikimoto for what they're doing to you. I'm also very angry at your malpractice attorneys. What were their names again? Ching? Chung? Chang and Demetrious? I'll show them," he said.

I could hear him breathing heavily.

"Thank you very much, Mr. Smith. But their names are Price and Okamoto, not Mikimoto. And my attorneys are Roy Chang and Harvey Demetrakopoulus, not Ching and not Demetrious. Their names are all over the records on top of your desk."

"Erlinda, please call me Dana, okay? I will be your protector. Call me any time, morning, afternoon, even nighttime. Here is my cell number."

I would have nothing to tell him at nighttime, but I noted down his cellular number anyway.

Days later, Smith's secretary called. I was to go to Smith's office immediately. Smith and McCorriston had spoken, and there was extremely significant information waiting for me.

As soon as I arrived, Smith invited me into his room.

"Erlinda, you should dismiss your case against Pohl right away, or you will be sanctioned."

"What?"

"Just like I said. You should withdraw your case against Pohl immediately."

"What happened in your conference with McCorriston, Dana?"

"Bill convinced me that you will be fighting an uphill battle and you will not sustain your case. Last Friday evening, he discussed it with his clients in the office of Warren Price."

"The opponent convinced you and now you're giving up? You are now calling Mr. McCorriston by his first name. You know him?"

"He's my friend. He defended me a few years ago."

"Defended you? What kind of case?"

"Legal malpractice."

"You were sued for legal malpractice? You were defended by McCorriston who is my opponent, and you never told me!"

"I'm sorry, I forgot. Erlinda, forgive me?"

"Mr. Smith, I will not ask you how many times you were sued for legal malpractice, but I don't think our business relationship should continue. Goodbye!"

I left his room in a hurry and as I closed the door, I said loud and clear, "No, I will not dismiss my case against Pohl. And I will not pay you for your socializing with McCorriston. You can sue me if you want. Understand what I mean?"

His room was silent except for the sound of crumpled papers one after another thrown into the trash can like a ball.

Then, Smith stepped out to invite his next client, who looked very much at peace as he was escorted by him, into his room. I recalled Ben saying, "Do as the Romans do."

But in my vocabulary, I could not ever be one of them. Smith and the rest were no Romans.

* * *

My worry over my clients' checks was overwhelming. I dropped by my attorneys' office without an appointment.

The Office of Disciplinary Counsel Board had to be told. My clients' trust account had been garnished. I would be in trouble if a check bounced.

"You will make another big mistake. We think O'Brien's assistant is an ODC counsel," said Harvey.

"So what? You mean, I have no place to run to?"

"You have to cooperate with us, Erlinda. We're already talking to your opponents to lift the hold on your accounts," said Roy. "Don't do anything to frustrate our efforts.

"You will sign an affidavit that you will deliver to them any income you receive from your office from hereon," he added. "They may be generous to you."

"I will actually be their slave? I have not done anything wrong to anyone, including you and Pohl," I said in total desperation. "I feel I'm being cooked alive."

Roy was visibly annoyed and said, "Perhaps, you should handle this issue yourself. Garnishment is not our expertise and that was not what you hired us for." He looked at Harvey to get confirmation of what he just said.

"What you mean, Roy, is that I should have handled my defense from the very beginning. I could have saved myself lots of money and anguish and probably even won, who knows."

"Well, we don't know what else to say and do. It seems we disagree on just about everything," said Harvey.

"There's something you could do—file the motion to recuse the judge today. We have all the reasons for her to step aside—imagine being the wife of an attorney in Pohl's office?"

"We don't believe that her intentions were corrupt, so we can't do that," said Roy, sounding more irritated.

"I never said anything about corrupt intentions. There are things that should not have happened, but I never labeled anyone corrupt. Never! I am for the appearance of propriety and I know I have the right to think this way."

"The judge is really a nice person. Our children are close friends, I know her family," said Roy as if in a complete daze.

"What did you say, Roy? You know her family, after all?"

"Good day, Erlinda, I have things to do." He stood up and walked out of the conference room. He was so pale.

Roy had made a slip of the tongue. He was obviously overwhelmed by the problem, but he was not talking in his sleep.

I looked at Harvey and suddenly remembered what he once told me in jest, "In the future, Erlinda, you might be calling Roy `Your Honor.'"

* * *

Many clients were still interested in hiring me, and I needed the revenue. I reviewed my office calendar. The case of my client, Ganoy, was coming up for jury trial. He was a child who had suffered severe brain injuries in a traffic accident.

The case was assigned to Judge Marks. I had to get out.

My motion to withdraw as the attorney for Ganoy was heard as another week was ending. It was a mere formality as Federizo, my researcher, agreed to continue with the case. He was simply locating another attorney to handle the trial.

My withdrawal had to be supported with good reason. The judge prodded me to explain. There was no audience. I had concerns regarding her spousal relationship in the malpractice case against me. I would not be comfortable in her courtroom.

Judge Marks took my explanation in good order. I was respectful. I was not there to offend her or myself, just to protect my client's best interests.

Early morning in the following week, Roy and Harvey called me at home. They were on loudspeaker in their office. Something important must be happening.

"We want you to come with us to court immediately. Judge Marks scheduled a conference about your malpractice case."

"What about?"

"We don't know. It has something to do with what you said in her court last week in another case."

"Okay, I'm coming."

I reached Roy and Harvey's office and was led to the conference room. They were obviously talking about me and my case and looked more concerned than usual.

"Erlinda, the judge's clerk called. You don't need to come with us, after all. You are not really needed. Just the attorneys. We will be there and also O'Brien," said Harvey.

"I am not just the defendant. I happen to be an attorney. I'm coming."

Roy and Harvey looked at each other. "You can only come if you do not say anything provoking," said Roy.

"I beg your pardon? I have the right to hear everything said of me in my own case. This time, I can say whatever I want and still be professional."

We proceeded to the courtroom. We took our seats in the same order as when the case was tried.

The clerk came out and checked to see who was in the room. She saw me. She went back to the chambers of the judge. I was sure she told her, "I informed the attorneys, but Ms. Dominguez came anyway. She is out there!"

The clerk invited all of us into the judge's chambers. The judge explained that I was extremely respectful and professional in her courtroom the week before. But I had said something that needed clarification.

We proceeded to the courtroom and the calendar was called. There was no audience. We all stood up as a matter of procedure and announced our identities.

Judge Marks had, minutes ago, handed out copies of the portion of the trial transcript when Kenneth Okamoto was about to testify. She claimed that it proved her previous disclosure of her spousal relationship and that nobody objected.

I thought to myself, the judge must have had the court reporter prepare that over the weekend.

She wanted to know if I was now asking her to step aside.

Roy requested some time to confer with me in private. We talked outside the courtroom.

"Roy, the transcript that she handed to you was her disclosure during the trial when Ken Okamoto testified, not before. There is no record of disclosure before that."

"You can ask her to step aside now. But she can still deny your request. Simply put, Erlinda, you can continue to antagonize her, or we can just move on."

"I never did anything wrong to her, to Pohl, to you and Harvey, or to anyone. My world is turning upside down. Pohl is the core of my case even if they were not named in the suit, and the judge is married to a partner in Pohl's law office."

"Judge Marks can still change her rulings on the bond issue in your favor. A new judge could make the situation worse. There's no reason that we should lose in your appeal. Please help us mitigate your losses," said Roy. He was really pleading.

Roy's persuasiveness added to my confusion. But I wondered how I could be patient with the garnishment, the over a million cash judgment and bond, all from the rulings of the judge. Now, I was told that it could be even worse if she stepped aside?

"I feel so helpless...I leave it up to you, Roy. What's happening is not in the agenda. I was not informed and had to push my way to come here this morning, even if I was not invited and you discouraged my coming. I have no ready answers."

We went back into the courtroom. Roy did not wish to do the talking. Harvey told the judge that we were asking her to stay.

"She has exhausted all her power and discretion. She cannot make your situation any worse. We made the right decision to have her stay," assured Roy, doing all he could to give me hope.

I went home hating myself. What a wimp and a hypocrite I had become! How ugly had I made myself!

There was a possibility that the judge would have stepped aside. I should have taken a stand insisting that she did.

* * *

My resources were draining. Not only was I paying my attorneys, but the court reporters and my varied researchers, many on a rush basis—to research on conflicts, recusals or disqualifications of judges.

"Erlinda, your case is stranger than fiction…the one and only. We can't locate a case in the whole United States similar to yours on judges' disqualifications," said Jennifer, who was still doing research for me.

"Because there never was?"

The records of the court from the time the malpractice case was filed against me were reviewed. There was no disclosure of the spousal relationship by the judge before the trial.

Then, I thought although it seemed unreal to me because there were no filed Orders or Minute Texts, the judge may have truly recalled differently, as Roy said. Her due process would come through my motion to recuse her, during the hearing.

My written motion was completed. I approached Roy and asked him to sign it.

"You are making a big mistake," he said. "She has friends all over. I will not sign that and put myself in trouble."

"I still don't understand what you're saying. I wish you were more clear."

"Those people are human."

"That does not make it clearer."

"Recusal and disqualification matters are personal. You're attacking the judge is what we mean," said Harvey.

"I beg to disagree with you completely. You know what I am going through. My life has been wrecked. The system will not improve if litigants are stopped from doing the right thing."

"Word travels fast among judges, even through other circuits—in the other islands. You will destroy yourself. That's what you seem to want to do. A death wish! Your malpractice case must be known to all Hawaii judges."

I paused a bit and knew Roy was correct.

In one of my recent jury trials in another island, I was severely sanctioned because the judge saw something nobody else saw: that I was making flying motions in the middle of a jury trial while I was listening to a witness from my desk. Something too impossible for me to do. But that was the judge's true perception of my conduct. And he was the judge and I was just an attorney in his court.

And in an in-chambers Minute Text, the same judge described me as, "in all her shining glory," to which I had no opportunity to defend myself because I saw the text long after the case was appealed. I blamed inconsistent perceptions on the stress of the profession.

Everything was in the eye of the beholder. What happened to the rules and the laws on due process, and why would Roy always mention humans, am I not one of them?

The malpractice case had now been titled, The Whole World versus Erlinda Dominguez, alone.

"Roy, I am talking law, which is what our profession is all about. That's what the courts are for. I can't help it if the facts are personal," I said.

Harvey again extended a bit of sympathy. "Erlinda, I think you have become the release valve of anger from different sources, including the courts. With the hectic pace of the law profession, they need release valves, they are human. We are truly sorry if it had to be you."

I left thinking, I could not believe that. How could I be hated by those who hardly know me? And me…a release valve?

And I remembered what was once told me by my grandmother when I was little: "You are either loved or hated. There is no in between. No person is without emotions, and emotions must have a resting place. Be careful among people whoever they are."

I was not careful enough.

* * *

Neither Roy or Harvey wanted to have anything to do with my motion for the judge to step aside. I signed and filed it myself, served my opponents, waited for their response and the hearing.

Then, Harvey called. They wanted to see me right away.

"A letter arrived from O'Brien," said Roy, holding the letter and looking very confused and apprehensive.

"You are my attorneys." I said. "He is putting ideas in your brains, describing when the disclosure of the judge happened. You can't be afraid of the truth. I don't mean to preach, but that was the vow we took as lawyers."

"We're asking you one more time, Erlinda, withdraw your motion. You're losing all your chances in court."

"I really don't see the connection, Roy. Honestly!"

"The judge has friends. We told you that many times before. You are not listening to your attorneys. You are stubborn."

"I am the defendant. I have rights just like anyone else. You always speak in parables. I am your client and your services have never been free! I treat animals better than you treat me."

I made sure to leave before Roy and Harvey could respond.

Days after, the anger of my attorneys showed on the phone. They had been subpoenaed by O'Brien to testify during the hearing on my motion to recuse the judge. The other attorneys were not, they were all my legal enemies anyway. And I was sure they did not hear the judge disclose anything.

"My opponents subpoenaed you. Don't vent your anger on me. I'm not asking you to lie on my account. You will still have an excellent private practice. For me, it all seems very late."

The hearing arrived. I was on time.

Roy and Harvey were seated outside the courtroom. They came as witnesses but were attired as attorneys.

They saw me approach. We looked at each other.

"Hi," I said.

"Hi," they greeted me back as I continued to walk into the courtroom. I showed no resentment. I did not know what they would say, perhaps some truth, which would be in my favor.

O'Brien was already seated. I did not greet him, nor did he greet me. It was just the two of us in the courtroom with the clerk and the court reporter.

My case was alone on the calendar. It avoided embarrassment.

As we waited for the judge, it felt strange that my two attorneys, Roy and Harvey, were not seated beside me. Instead, they were outside the courtroom as witnesses for my opponents and for the judge.

My mind reflected back to better times, when they both said I was their client and they would do everything to protect me. In return, I worked so hard to pay their attorneys' fees.

The clerk announced that the witnesses had arrived and everyone was ready.

Judge Marks entered her courtroom. The calendar was called. I greeted her as the defendant and as my own attorney.

It was my motion and a very delicate one. I vowed to myself that whatever happened, I would not show any emotion.

I would be respectful. With my accent, I could stumble on a few words, but would strive to be clearly understood.

The records were my ally. I just needed to be factual.

Professionally, I requested that my motion be decided by another judge.

Judge Marks noted my request and denied it.

I objected to the testimony of my attorneys. I invoked my attorney-client privilege. I was overruled. The judge wanted to hear testimonies first, then make her rulings.

As the movant, and pursuant to procedure, I was ready to present my evidence ahead of O'Brien. He was my hostile and only witness. I asked the court that I proceed. My request was denied.

This is what appears in the recusal hearing transcript of February 25, 2004, verbatim:

THE COURT: We're going to take up Mr. Chang and Mr. Demetrakopoulos.

MS. DOMINGUEZ: Your Honor, please, I want Mr. O'Brien to testify first.

COURT: Well, --

MR. O'BRIEN: I'm not under subpoena, Your Honor.

MS. DOMINGUEZ: Yeah, he is in court.

THE COURT: Just wait. I want people to take things one at a time. I'm trying not to interrupt you. I'm trying to allow you to make your record. Don't interrupt me.

MS. DOMINGUEZ: I'm sorry.

THE COURT: Mr. Chang, Mr. Demetrakopoulus.

MR. O'BRIEN: Thank you, your Honor.

MS. DOMINGUEZ: Excuse me, your Honor. Since they will be--apparently they--they may be witnesses, I want the one witness to be excluded meantime the other is testifying, if you allow them to testify.

THE COURT: Yes.

THE BAILIFF: Your Honor, Mr. Demetrakopoulos is requesting that he go first.

The words of the judge and the way she looked at me were terrifying. We were just beginning, and already, I realized that I was fighting an uphill, impossible fight. Roy could have been right in all his warnings, but I had to do what I had to do. *After all, I was in an American Hall of Justice. I had the freedom of speech that other countries did not have.*

The bailiff opened the door and asked Harvey to enter while Roy waited outside the courtroom. A witness was not supposed to hear the testimony of another.

The judge allowed my request for witness exclusion. That was part of my constitutional right to due process.

Harvey walked to the witness stand. He did not look at me or at O'Brien. He remained standing. The clerk administered the oath for him to tell the truth.

Then, he took his seat and faced the judge.

O'Brien presented Harvey as a hostile witness. That way, he could ask leading questions, a style of questioning normally re-served for cross-examination.

Chapter Sixteen

Harvey began his testimony, almost in a shy way. He was continually smiling, injecting mild jokes. Possibly to relieve his tension. He made it look like everything was casual.

He claimed that the judge disclosed her spousal relationship not just once before the trial, but twice.

I concluded that Harvey was accommodating the version of the judge and O'Brien. He could not identify dates and places, but claimed that when the judge disclosed, he said, "No Problem," and he was speaking for me, his client.

It was my turn to cross-examine.

My greatest temptation was to tell Harvey to stop his silly grins on the witness stand. We were in court.

I asked if he made notes of the disclosure and his comment to the judge that there would be "No Problem."

As shown in the hearing transcript that day, his verbatim response was:

"The only notations I can recall coming from that would have been noting the trial date, and, with a smile, I recall also the issue of the expert disclosure deadline that was originally set and which was subsequently reset by agreement of the parties."

Harvey sounded so silly. He even literally described himself on the witness stand with his words, "with a smile."

He was referring to the first conference with the judge, where trial scheduling was discussed. I was present.

I could attest that the judge did not make a disclosure. But the Court Minutes Text meticulously prepared by the clerk was more than enough to prove this.

My mind raced. Look at me straight in the face, Harvey! I am your client and that's not what you and Roy had been telling me, as God is my witness!

Then, I processed the events. I was drowning in lies among people who took the vow of allegiance to the flag of the United States of America and all that it stands for.

My cross-examination of Harvey continued.

"Okay. Now, you are an attorney, as I know you, Harvey, otherwise, I didn't retain you; right? And I believe that you are a- - you have capabilities getting into the computer- - I think you call it website- - because I'm sort of computer illiterate?" I asked.

"I've gotten- - I know how to access the State of Hawaii judiciary website, yes," was his answer.

"From there you would get the court minutes text?"

"Just to clarify, this is all public record, I'm not a hacker," Harvey jokingly said with a big grin.

"Yes. I didn't mean that. But if I may approach the witness, Your Honor?" I asked. Judge Marks approved my request.

When the Court Minutes Texts were shown to him, Harvey continued with his smiles.

I wondered if I would have been treated differently, with a sanction, if I was in his place.

He did not deny that the trial transcript I was holding was authentic. I read the transcript for the judge to hear what she said during the malpractice trial.

"THE COURT:...I don't think I've put this on the record. I think when I first met with counsel in chambers to schedule a trial date, I had indicated that my spouse now works with Price, Okamoto, Himeno and Lum. I don't think I ever put that on the record but I disclosed it at the very beginning and I believe that the--certainly counsel and I'm assuming the parties know that and have no objection to that?"

I had with me the earliest transcripts that the judge meant where she disclosed her spousal relationship.

The earliest Court Minutes Text of the status conference on July 19, 2001, where I and many attorneys were present was shown to Harvey. There was nothing said about disclosure by the judge.

I showed him the next Court Minutes Text of the pre-trial conference on September 5, 2001, again showing the presence of attorneys. Nothing was said about the disclosure by the judge.

Both texts were detailed on speakers and what they said, and timed to the minute, even seconds.

A reconstruction expert would agree that there was no slot where the discussion of disclosure could fit in the Court Minutes Texts, especially with the multitude of attorneys present.

But that could not be my argument. I did not hire a reconstruction expert. It might not even be admissible in a disqualification hearing where ethics was so involved.

I was still a stickler for the rules of evidence—for constitutional due process—even when I hit rock bottom.

On the witness stand, Harvey was becoming increasingly uneasy. He did not smile as often and his jokes disappeared.

It was at the height of my cross-examination when he asked Judge Marks to allow him to talk to Roy, his partner, who he claimed was now acting as his attorney and was outside the courtroom. His attorney? I thought Roy was my attorney!

Both were witnesses. They should not be talking to each other while testimony was ongoing. Harvey was manufacturing his testimony on the witness stand—and under oath. I was in shock, and my objection showed it!

The hearing transcript of Harvey's testimony reads verbatim:

THE WITNESS: Any possibility that I can have a short moment? Because this is an issue I need to discuss with my partner acting as my attorney.

THE COURT: Sure. We'll take a break.

MS. DOMINGUEZ: Excuse me. Just a moment, your Honor. These two people are witnesses.

THE COURT: Excuse me. We're taking a break.

MS. DOMINGUEZ: I'm just objecting, Your Honor, that he will contact the other witness in this case.

THE COURT: I will allow him to do that. There are sensitive issues obviously about attorney-client. I'll allow him to do it. We'll take a break. I think we've been going, at least, for the court reporter and the court, certainly more than an hour.

THE BAILIFF: All rise. Court stands in recess.

I literally pictured the books of professional conduct and ethics governing attorneys thrown in front of me, mocked and ridiculed, kicked then burned—in a hall of justice—where lawyers practice their profession. And the lawyers, like Harvey, were all smiling and laughing at their own client!

What a mockery of the rules! Roy and Harvey seemed to have their thrills from conflict after conflict. And with all his jokes and smiles, it seemed Harvey did not respect the proceedings.

Then, I thought, what law of procedure were my attorneys and the judge going by? They did not say. I wish I knew. It was like fighting something unseen, something that was not there.

I berated myself. Why am I afraid to insist on an answer? Why am I afraid to ask for an explanation? What happened to me?

What was clear was, my words and conduct extremely irritated the judge. I tried to assess my tone of voice and my accent. I remembered what Harvey and Roy threatened: contempt of court.

If I would be dragged to jail, at least, I still had that one phone call that I hear inmates were entitled to. But who was I going to call? What Hawaii attorney would help me? Small fries.

And I thought, The law protects me, regardless of my color and my creed. After all, even if my language is not American, I have always been civil and respectful and it is not my words, conduct and accent that are being tried. I have American Justice.

Harvey walked out of the room. I proceeded to the court lobby and saw Roy whispering to Harvey. They were seated side-by-side on the bench and obviously in serious discussion. I knew they were deciding on how to answer my questions.

As I looked at them, memories of the trial flashed back to the isolated breaks, where they walked to the opposite end of the hallway, excluded me from their conversations, and shared jokes with my opponent, O'Brien, all in view of the jurors.

Roy and Harvey were still talking when I returned. They did not look at me as I passed by their bench on my way to the courtroom. They continued to whisper.

Then, the clerk announced that the judge was ready to resume. We took our respective seats. Roy remained outside.

Again, Judge Marks entered her courtroom and Harvey resumed his testimony under the same oath to tell the truth.

As soon as he took his seat on the witness stand, Harvey told the judge that they were withdrawing as my attorneys. They were dropping me in the middle of a horrible mess, and in the middle of my cross-examination.

I objected and I was overruled. Again, the judge agreed with Harvey. She asked him to file any motion they wanted. I worriedly thought, Will Roy and Harvey now ask the judge to sanction me for fees? Worse still, could they ask the judge to hold me in contempt of court, the words they loved to use? And I wouldn't know what rules or law they would go by.

Any further testimony would have been rehearsed with Roy. I quickly finished my questioning.

Harvey was again looking straight at the door as he hurriedly walked out of the room.

O'Brien told the judge that he had no other witness and did not need to present Roy Chang.

Why should he? There would be a risk of inconsistencies. I decided against presenting Roy. For some reason, I feared his testimony would demolish me and my defenses.

It was an eerie feeling that I could not explain. After all, they were still my attorneys on record in the appellate court and, as Harvey once said, I might be addressing Roy as "Your Honor" in the future.

Was it possible that Roy could get involved in deciding my appeal? Of course, it was an insane thought.

It was my turn to present my evidence. I asked O'Brien to take the witness stand. He immediately objected.

The judge appeared to hesitate, then allowed his testimony. There was no need for a subpoena, he was in the courtroom.

O'Brien heard all that Harvey said when he testified. I knew O'Brien would testify the same way, perhaps, use the same words.

He walked to the witness stand, raised his right hand, and swore to tell the truth.

His testimony was basically a mirror image of what Harvey said: two disclosures before trial, No Problem, and so on! He also could not recall dates and people in attendance.

Those two words decided my fate and my life: No Problem! Words that did not seem to fit in a formal Hall of Justice.

And if that really happened, nobody cared to ask me, the defendant, what I thought. Did I want the wife of a partner of Pohl, my ultimate legal opponent in the case, to be my judge?

The transcript of that hearing on February 25, 2004, shows the following questions and answers, verbatim.

Q. (BY MS. DOMINGUEZ) Mr. O'Brien, you have represented the plaintiffs in this case, the Barnedos; true?

A. Yes.

Q. Okay. And, of course, you are still their attorney?

A. Yes.

Q. And you were here all the while listening to the testimony of the previous witness, Harvey Demetrakopoulos, and you heard all that he said; true?

A. Yes.

There were no difficulties understanding O'Brien. He talked like a purebred American born in the United States, and his testimony was loud and clear. Many of his answers were one word.

Then, O'Brien became emphatic. He showed anger, appeared to lose his composure, and agreed that remittals, disclosures and disqualifications of judges are exceedingly important.

The manner of his emotional answers, not just one-word responses, encouraged me to pursue my cross-examination.

Q. (BY MS. DOMINGUEZ) You know that that's important, don't you?

A. I consider it exceedingly important.

Q. Okay. Since you consider that disclosure and recusal, all of those exceedingly important, as an attorney, did you remind the Honorable Judge Marks, Judge, let's put this in writing, it's very important, it might decide the outcome of the case? Did you say anything like that?

A. There was no reason to.

Q. You did not in other words.

A. No, I did not.

Q. Even if you thought it was very important.

A. I did not think it was necessary.

Q. That's your best answer?

A. That's my only answer.

Q. Good.

I proceeded with my cross—examination.

Q. Okay. I'm not going to breach your privilege with your clients 'cause I know better than do that, Mr. O'Brien, but did you ever, ever ever put down in your notes, as an attorney, that Judge Marks disclosed her spousal relationship?

A. No, ma'am, I knew it anyway. I knew it —I've known Bob Marks for a long time. I knew where he worked.

Q. Thank you.

No words could describe what I felt at the ease with which O'Brien testified on his acquaintanceship with Mr. Marks in the Pohl office. We were before Mr. Marks' wife who was judging my case, making rulings, and I was fighting for my rights to have her step aside from my case.

There must be a reason why he was testifying with laxity and saying things on the record that the appellate courts would see.

I concluded that O'Brien's intent was a clear message designed only for me: that his relationship in the community was extensive and he had friends while I was obnoxious with enemies.

But it did seem clear that he somehow forgot we were in a Court of Law, not in a Court of Friendship and not in a Court of Who You Know. Then, I thought, he should call himself the uncivilized, not me.

My arguments were simple. I presented all the Court Minutes of every session with the judge. None showed any disclosure or semblance of the topic of disclosure.

O'Brien had no notes of any disclosure before trial.

Roy and Harvey had no notes of any disclosure before trial. The judge and her clerk had no notes of any disclosure before trial.

There was another piece of evidence I offered to Judge Marks. I told her that on a Friday, the Pohl partners met with their attorney, McCorriston, to discuss the malpractice case before her and the case I filed against Pohl for indemnification.

O'Brien had made sure to file and submit to the judge a copy of my complaint against Pohl where her husband worked.

Judge Marks was curiously listening without a hint of what I was going to say. I said that on the next business day, she signed the dozens of Garnishee Summons and Subpoenas against me. She did not wait for the recusal hearing to happen before she froze all of my accounts.

The judge showed extreme surprise, even shock—that I knew about the internal meeting between McCorriston and Pohl in the office where her husband worked.

O'Brien's anger mounted. He read my mind—I was angry that the judge made severe rulings against me before there was the possibility that another judge would take over.

On the witness stand, O'Brien's message was clear—that I was too uncivil, too rude and too disrespectful to the judge. He looked at the judge as if he wanted her to do something.

I knew that I was professional and respectful. But I had no control over anything. Automatically, I looked at the clerk and prepared myself to be handcuffed by a guard.

O'Brien continued to interrupt with objections before Judge Marks could respond. I was exercising my due process and having no regrets. I could not have argued the point in a more professional and respectful way.

Presentation of evidence and arguments was completed. The circumstances were to be assessed by the judge. That had always been the procedure.

It did not come as a surprise. My motion for her recusal was quickly denied. She was the judge of her fairness or unfairness as Roy and Harvey warned me about.

O'Brien expressed his full gratitude. "Thank you, Your Honor." The last thing I heard him say was for my payment of his fees and costs, and the judge wanted him to submit papers.

The proceedings were over. The judge left her seat. I gathered my papers, then slowly walked out of the courtroom.

I pulled over to a side street and stopped my car. I immediately called up Roy and Harvey on my cellular. They were in their office waiting for my call.

"Thanks for your testimony," I said sarcastically. "You are lucky I did not present you, Roy, to testify. And I was respectful to you, Harvey, was I not?"

"Thank you, Erlinda. We really appreciate it."

"Will you be asking for your fees and costs for testifying?"

"Of course not, but we have to really withdraw from the case. There is a tremendous conflict between us. We are extremely sorry, Erlinda. Very, very sorry."

Both seemed truly regretful that things developed that way. People have different recollections at different times, they said again, and I let it go that way. Tragedy was staring at me in the face and I had to be resigned.

I imagined unfortunate individuals all over the world with no more strength to fight the systems. I should not allow that thought to demolish me, or anyone I could help. This is America!

As I drove back home, I was thinking the worst that could happen if I was unkind to my attorneys. They had prepared my appeal documents. And my list of enemies was already a mile long.

Their withdrawal was immediately approved by the judge without my say. I was now left completely alone to defend myself, with volumes of papers delivered by Harvey to my messenger for me to read.

"We decided to stay as your attorneys only for the appeal," said Harvey in a phone call. "We should not dump all of those records on you at such a critical time in your life. You can review the briefs we will do and improve them if you wish."

"Thanks, Harvey, for your humanity."

A document was by my fax machine three days later. My case was transferred by order of Karen Blondin who was the Administrative Judge, from Judge Marks to Judge Gary Chang. No relation to my attorney, Roy Chang.

A full load of hard concrete was lifted off of my shoulders. I wondered what may have happened.

I immediately ordered the transcript of the hearing of my motion to recuse Judge Marks. At the very end of the transcript, it was noted that she was stepping aside, voluntarily.

I did not hear the judge say that during the recusal hearing. I was sure neither did O'Brien. If he did, he would have fought so hard to have her stay. After all, he subpoenaed my two attorneys to testify for that purpose.

The words of the judge's departure were at the very tail end of the transcript. The judge must have said the words softly in a very tense situation, and we did not hear. But it made no difference. My case was now in another court.

It was hardly a time to rejoice. Judge Marks issued a multitude of orders against me before her departure. No successor judge would overturn them. They had become the law of the case. Like midnight appointments of a President whose term was expiring.

Prior to his appointment to the bench, Judge Chang was my heavy opponent in my litigation practice of personal injury. He was always on the defense side and I was always for the plaintiffs. Many of our cases were bitterly fought.

The transfer of my case reminded me of a federal bench trial for insurance benefits I handled against two main partners of Judge Chang's firm years before. The injuries of my client from a car accident caused him to take his own life. The presiding Judge from the mainland ended the trial with a complimentary remark: "This must be the most interesting case I handled on the bench." He awarded me with substantial fees paid by the insurance company I sued. I was thinking of all these, apprehensive but so grateful that my malpractice case was finally removed into another court.

My trust in the system should be intact. The happenings in my malpractice case were coincidental. It's nobody's fault that the Hawaii legal community could be small in that respect.

* * *

Harvey called early in the morning. "Your appeal to the Supreme Court was dismissed."

"Why?"

"Don't worry, we can re-file. The suits against your former associate attorneys had not been properly identified in the judgment form. It is defective and our appeal is premature.

"The Supreme Court would probably deny your emergency motion to stay the judgment with a *supersedeas* bond," he added.

I thought to myself, If there is no valid judgment, there can be no garnishment, which can only come after judgment. That would be good for my clients' trust account that remained frozen.

My motion to lift all of the garnishee summons and subpoenas issued by Judge Marks was heard.

That was the first time I saw Judge Chang in years. I was before him as a defendant and not as his legal opponent.

The law was clear. There was no final judgment, there could be no execution. My motion was granted. The freeze on all my accounts, including my clients' trust account, was lifted.

Roy should be happy for me. I gave him a courtesy call. "Oh…it was Judge Chang…oh, well," was all that he said.

I filed a motion to bond myself. Judge Chang allowed cash and real properties for close to 1.5 million dollars to fully cover the judgment of Judge Marks against me.

Although my properties formed my bond, at least, I could now continue with my profession—lawyering. My clients' checks would not bounce.

Harvey called again. "Erlinda, you don't need us anymore. You have your researchers who can help with the briefs. We have given you our drafts. We will withdraw as your appeal counsel."

"You're asking for my permission? You did not need this when you told Judge Marks you were dropping me in her court right on the witness stand when you were testifying against me!"

"You are again dwelling. You can represent yourself in the Supreme Court. We have decided that we are out of your case completely, whether you like it or not!"

"Why?"

"Like we said, we don't see each other eye-to-eye!"

"Let's just file a stipulation or agreement, Harvey. It would not look to the Supreme Court justices that you dropped me because I am truly obnoxious. As Roy said, people are human, and he claimed he had close ties with some of the justices. I can't afford to antagonize anyone. In Roy's metaphor, I'm treading on thin ice."

"Okay, fair enough. We'll give you everything that we prepared. You can just review, add your research, finalize, sign and file the briefs!"

"It would not be as simple as that, but thanks."

* * *

My appellate briefs were done. My main argument was constitutional and jurisdictional. The argument that could have salvaged me immediately, but my attorneys refused to touch.

The defense that could have demolished the malpractice suit from its inception, but could not be found in all the appellate drafts written by Roy and Harvey.

United States District Courts, also known as Federal Courts, have limited jurisdiction given by the U.S. Constitution.

The federal court never had subject matter jurisdiction in the case brought by Mr. and Mrs. Barnedo against Marukiku where they said the malpractice happened, because the parties were all aliens. The Barnedos were Filipino citizens and Marukiku was a Japanese corporation.

In federal diversity cases as was that case of the Barnedos against the Japanese company, federal courts do not get involved in resolving problems among aliens. That is in the United States Constitution, the ultimate backbone law of the nation.

The Barnedos' case where they claim I failed to collect, was legally void or non-existent from the beginning. It was in violation of the Constitution of America!

There was an old Martindale Hubbell book in my office. It said that Justice James Duffy of the Hawaii Supreme Court had authored a book on constitutional subject matter jurisdiction. He agreed that without that jurisdiction, the case should be dismissed. There could be no malpractice committed in the void federal case.

The Constitution cannot be manipulated or defrauded. The issue could be raised at any time, even on appeal. Americans gave up their lives to protect the United States Constitution. I was then convinced that the State Supreme Court would vindicate me.

If Roy and Harvey had brought this up in court, the malpractice case should have been dismissed a long time ago, as early as when Judge Del Rosario was presiding. No amount of judicial discretion could validate the contrary.

But the Barnedos could still sue Pohl who signed the tolling agreement, at any time, and change their strategy to overcome the jurisdictional issue even if the malpractice case against me was dismissed.

I felt severely betrayed including by my own attorneys.

Chapter Seventeen

Weeks passed by. I was busy in my private practice. My researchers spent time assisting me with the briefs. Duplicate transcripts from the court reporters added to my already burdensome expenses.

One day, a document arrived from the appeal court. Justice Simeon Acoba of the Supreme Court was recusing himself and was voluntarily stepping aside from my case. He was the only Justice with Filipino roots. The document did not say why.

My respect for Justice Acoba only doubled. He was avoiding any appearance of impropriety with his keen sense of morality.

But I worried who the replacement would be. In weeks, I received another document. Judge Randall Lee was to take over Justice Acoba's chair.

Judge Lee was newly appointed to the circuit bench. He used to be a public defender. What if he bends under pressure? He is a new circuit judge. He must have a room beside the other judges' rooms as Roy described.

How stupid could I be to even consider that thought!

What did Roy and Harvey do to me? Why am I afraid to even think my thoughts?

I waited for the appellate decision in the malpractice case while events were rapidly moving in the suit that I filed for indemnification against Pohl. It seemed that the whole Hawaii legal community was intensely waiting for- what would happen to Erlinda Dominguez? Why doesn't she stop and be realistic?

My case was Dominguez versus Price Okamoto Himeno & Lum, a law corporation. Pohl managed the Barnedo case where Judge Marks' jury found me negligent—that was my case against Pohl.

William McCorriston who was Pohl's attorney called it the Pohl case to distinguish it from the Barnedo malpractice case.

The Pohl case was assigned to Judge Sabrina McKenna. She immediately stepped aside because of her friendship with Sharon Himeno, a main Pohl partner.

The judge's integrity was clear. Nobody was misled.

Then, the Pohl case was re-assigned to Judge Elizabeth Hifo. I checked the records. The case was transferred to her twice. The documents did not say why.

Again, I wondered how judges were chosen and why there had to be an assurance that Judge Hifo would take over the Pohl case by two assignments.

I did not know her, and did not recall appearing before her. I speculated that she was not a circuit court judge during my liaison with Pohl and when I began my sabbatical leave.

"Judge Hifo used to be a part-time TV announcer and her name then was Bambie Weil, that's all I know," said John Yuen.

"Why the change from that name to Elizabeth Eden Hifo, a long and very unique name?"

John did not know and I did not expect him to. The judge must be quite familiar with the Pohl firm. The Pohl partners were always in the news, especially Warren Price and Robert Marks, when they were Attorney Generals for the State of Hawaii. And she was a newscaster.

But I could not allow myself to imply anything. It would be unfair to pre-judge anyone. How well did I know!

* * *

It was now 2005. In the Pohl case, status conference statements had been filed by both sides in preparation for our first session with Judge Hifo. All parties involved were clearly identified with their names and addresses.

The judge held the conference in her chambers.

That was the first time I met the judge. Days before, I handed her a legal document, thinking she was the head clerk. She was wearing a long Hawaiian muumuu dress and was socializing with her staff outside of her chambers during a court break.

I hoped she had forgotten my unintended behavior.

The status conference signaled our time to seriously prepare for trial. The judge was polite and pondered each word she said.

Kenneth Mansfield represented Pohl. I was by myself, my own attorney, commonly called *pro se*. It boiled down to scheduling, nothing complicated.

The meeting was over. I left the courtroom feeling that I was in good hands. The judge certainly knew the facts of the case.

She had with her the documents submitted by both sides.

Roy Chang and Harvey Demetrakopoulos were listed as witnesses by Mansfield. They were expected to testify on my liability and the damages that I caused Pohl.

Roy and Harvey whom I paid to defend me in the legal malpractice suit would have another opportunity to demolish me. It was difficult to swallow.

Also in Pohl's witness list was O'Brien along with my former associate attorneys who were sued with me in the malpractice, many of whom had cross claimed against me.

All had become my legal enemies. They appeared too eager to throw mud in my face.

I remembered things I used to hear before: Pohl is very powerful, with a multitude of attorneys, and many friends all over.
They will mince-meat you. And I could imagine the face of Roy
while he said those words—worried and alarmed, but sincere.

And here I was, just me, fighting to survive the system!

There was nothing to hide. I decided that I would make a
blanket waiver of my attorney-client privileges.

Roy and Harvey could say anything short of libel and defama-
tion. I would allow them to produce all my records, our letters,
memorandums, everything—to Pohl and their attorneys.

Go ahead, make your records public. Show the courts that I
am hated even by you, my paid attorneys, as long as the truth comes out and the laws will be applied with equality.

* * *

Months passed by quickly. Trial time was approaching in the
Pohl case. As a matter of procedure, a settlement conference was
scheduled. We filed the required documents.

The documents again told Judge Hifo the nature of the case,
claims and defenses, all the potential witnesses, what they were
expected to say, and the possibility of settlement.

The conference arrived. It would happen in the chambers of
the judge, just like the status conference months ago. But this
time, the judge was to explore any possibility of settlement.

Sharon Himeno of the Pohl firm came with two of her attorneys, William McCorriston and Kenneth Mansfield.

We quickly greeted each other as if nothing serious was happening. "Erlinda, how have you been?" and "Sharon, have you
been traveling?" A matter of courtesy.

Sharon formally introduced me to her attorneys. McCorriston
was a main partner of the big law firm of McCorriston Miho &
Miller. Mansfield was his lead associate attorney.

They had represented the insurance companies in a multitude of my past cases, and were always on the opposite side. They heard of me. I heard of them. We never knew each other.

We waited for the clerk to give us the signal. I was to go into the judge's chambers first. Judge Hifo would talk to me then to my opponents, then to all of us. That was the procedure.

As we waited, I was imagining the judge browsing through the records in preparation for speaking to everyone.

In a few minutes, Judge Hifo came out of her chambers. She was steps away from us. She looked at me and beckoned that I enter her room. She did not have her clerk do that. She was very humble and looked pleasant. "Please come in, Ms. Dominguez."

I followed the judge. I remained standing at the end of her long table. Nobody else was there. She closed the door.

Then, she walked toward me and began to touch my clothing. She gently stroked the collar of my blouse as if she was fixing it. I wondered what was going on.

Her hand was still on my collar when she moved close to my ears and whispered, "I believe you…I understand…if you only know what I also went through in life."

I was just listening and observing, and looked into her eyes. She was so sincere. Nothing about her was fake.

The judge offered me a chair next to her. She took a box of tissues beside her chair, pulled out two, one for her and one for me. I did not know why.

She was not crying and neither was I. My face could not be smeared, I did not wear eye shadow or lipstick.

It was confusing for me, a legal practitioner. No judge, male or female, had ever shown me such endearment during a proceeding.

Judge Hifo looked extremely sad as she scanned through the records in front of her.

I remembered the words of Roy Chang: People are human!

Finally, there was someone who believes in me and my case, when not even my attorneys did, who could read between the lines, who knows what I had been through…and it was my judge.

Judge Hifo and I were both seated. We proceeded to discuss the Pohl indemnification case.

She appeared versed in the facts and was well informed that the case was for Pohl to pay and reimburse me for the almost 1.5 million malpractice judgment that Judge Marks rendered.

But we knew that any settlement discussion was premature. My appeal in the malpractice case was still pending.

Then, the judge was solemn. She wanted to know if she could inquire on something that was not connected to the conference. "Fine with me, Your Honor."

She asked if my malpractice attorneys brought up the issue of the diversity subject matter jurisdiction of the federal court. The alien versus alien defense that would have made the federal case disappear, along with my malpractice that my opponents claimed happened in that federal case.

I responded with a simple, "No."

She mumbled, "My, my," again almost inaudibly.

Then she asked, "Did you, at least, address it in your malpractice appellate briefs?"

"Yes, Judge. My briefs were very clear, with the testimonies of the Barnedos that they were Filipinos, and they sued a Japanese company. It's a basic one plus one equals two."

"Right, right."

"But Judge, there is nowhere in the trial court records to point to where Roy Chang and Harvey Dematrakopoulus brought up the issue because they never did."

Judge Hifo listened, seemingly perplexed and bewildered.

"But it is a constitutional fatal flaw in the federal court's subject matter jurisdiction issue. It can be brought up for the first time even on appeal. This is unanimous nationwide. Case authorities say that the strength and integrity of the U.S. Constitution must always be protected by strict adherence."

The judge was seriously looking at me while I spoke.

"In fact, it is the duty of attorneys who are aware of the violation of the Constitution, to call it to the attention of the courts. Otherwise, there will be that rotten data in the dockets. I read the research materials. Some call it an ultimate raw evil against the U.S. Constitution that should be discarded."

Judge Hifo was nodding her head, and again, very softly murmured, "Right, right. If there was no federal case, there is no malpractice in a void federal case. That's logical."

Then, she said she did not know how to help.

"Judge, my appeal in the malpractice has not yet been decided, and you are handling the indemnification part. I need assistance from Pohl's insurer for my bond so that I'd be somewhat unburdened."

"Is it alright, Ms. Dominguez, if we remove the confidentiality of this conference? I'll tell you what they said and I'll tell them what you said, and nothing will be hidden or confidential in this room. We can function better that way."

"Thank you, Judge. Whatever you think is best."

"Everything you have in mind, just say it. I will understand both sides better; anyway, we are not yet at trial," she said.

"Your Honor, I feel severely betrayed. My attorneys backed up Judge Marks. However, there were no notes, no records that before the malpractice trial, she disclosed her spousal relationship with a previous Attorney General, also in the law firm of my present opponents. My attorneys made me look stupid and a liar, and I felt trapped, and please, don't ask me to explain. It's traumatic."

"Yes, yes, I take judicial notice of the events in that case. They are all public records and I know them," she said.

And she began to pull another tissue paper, but I said, "It's alright, Judge, that's not for me."

I thought, How truly considerate and thorough, how can I be so blessed with a judge talking to me this way! She must have browsed through the computers while we waited for her outside.

I was still talking when Judge Hifo clapped her hands three times, then waved her fingers in the air. I stared at her wondering what was going on. I looked around. Nobody else was there except the two of us.

Then, she resumed the conversation.

"I'll have to discuss this with the other side, the Price firm. Since this is hardly a true settlement conference and nothing is confidential, I can tell them all you said?"

"Of course, Your Honor. They had an unlimited flow of communication with my malpractice attorneys anyway."

"I will also tell you what they have to say."

"Thank you, Judge."

She again clapped her hands and waved her fingers above her head as if there were insects there.

I was curious and again, I looked around.

Then, the judge noticed my bewilderment at her actions and she explained that the electricity in her room was fading in and out. She had found a way to temporarily solve the problem by clapping her hands.

Electricity was farthest from my mind. But I wished that my malpractice case would soon be dismissed so I could make donations for electrical improvements. Only if not unethical.

I was on my best behavior, intently listening to the judge. "Relax, Ms. Dominguez. Everything will be alright."

Finally, Judge Hifo graciously dismissed me from her room and invited Sharon Himeno and her attorneys in. It was their turn. Minutes passed. It felt longer. Then, the judge's door opened. One more time, the judge came out of her chambers. She motioned for me to join them.

McCorriston and Mansfield were seated side-by-side. Sharon was seated behind McCorriston. They were all smiling, as if we were there on a true social visit.

I suspected that finally, their insurer would assist me.

The judge announced that the parties could not agree. She mentioned nothing specific.

"But I have something to place on the record," she said. She asked her clerk to contact the court reporter's office.

I wondered why. A Court Minutes Text was usually sufficient.

While we waited and for a while, Judge Hifo was in deep thought and everyone was silent, in obvious contemplation.

She was probably thinking, How in the world did Judge Marks get to be the presiding judge, making rulings on evidence and deciding motions and jury instructions in the malpractice case against Ms. Dominguez, when her husband is a partner in the Pohl office now sued for indemnification of her own judgement? Ms. Dominguez must have gone through hell!

Judge Hifo looked at all of us. Then, she said that she had to make disclosures so that the records would be clear. That should avoid problems in the future as to conflicts.

My mind was racing. She does not want to repeat the same problem in the malpractice case. Don't tell me that she is also married to an attorney in Pohl's office, not again!

Luckily, it had nothing to do with her husband. Judge Hifo disclosed that she socialized with Sharon Himeno. They belonged to the same social organization that would meet every month.

She said that she was present when Sharon got married to Warren Price and considered it a privilege to be invited among hundreds of guests.

Sharon was looking at the judge talking very graciously. "And who wouldn't know Warren Price anyway? He was the Attorney General!" the judge said, and she smiled at Sharon.

"And I also know Ms. Dominguez because she is a practicing attorney. I believe I successfully settled two of her previous cases with me." She also smiled at me.

That was all she knew of me—a practicing attorney. But there have been multitudes of practicing lawyers in and out of her courtroom. Could Roy be right that judges talk among themselves? Their rooms are side by side.

Then, Judge Hifo said that she worked in a law firm where Roy Chang was a partner before she was appointed to the bench.

She added that she was now making the disclosures because she just found out the identity of the players.

I was analyzing. The Dominguez versus Pohl case with Judge Hifo was filed in 2003. We're now in 2005. Everyone's names were in the records. My opponent, Sharon, and my former attorney, Roy, had been repeatedly mentioned. How did she not know?

But the judge said she did not discuss the case with Sharon even at their club meetings, and her past relationship with Roy would not influence her.

There was no doubt in my mind that she would be fair. She just treated me so affectionately in her chambers. I looked into her eyes and she was true and sincere.

It was the first time in a very long time that someone extended compassion to me as a human being in the mesh of the legal malpractice case. I would be crazy to complain.

"I can really be fair and impartial," the judge said, "but you have the right to object and I can step aside." She repeated what she had disclosed and her opinion that she could be fair, over and over, even after the court reporter left.

Her words were still clear as she was fixing my collar affectionately and whispered, "I believe you…I understand…if you only knew what I also went through in life."

"I have no objections. I ask that you please stay. Please stay," I said again without the slightest hesitation.

McCorriston did the same: "No objection, too, Your Honor."

On my way out of the courthouse, I realized that the judges in the malpractice case and the indemnification case were intimate with Pohl and I was just a practicing attorney!

But how lucky I was to have Judge Hifo. She was so fair and objective despite her relationships, no doubt about it! And she always looked so pleasant in her colorful long Hawaiian dresses. An added bonus in stressful situations.

* * *

Shortly thereafter, a document had to be delivered to Judge Hifo's staff. I did it myself. The court was near my office.

The chambers room was open. It was in clear view of whoever was in the staff's room, which was adjacent and steps away.

Judge Sabrina McKenna was seated in Judge Hifo's chambers, facing the door. She looked at me as I walked in. She knew me from my other cases in her court.

Judge Victoria Marks was seated beside her and was looking at Judge Hifo to her left. She appeared to be explaining something serious and did not seem to notice my presence. Judge Hifo could not be seen, but I knew that she was at the other end of the long table, presiding.

The clerks saw me glance at the open door of the judge's chambers. Their surprised reaction was obvious.

All three judges were there: Hifo, who had just made her disclosures of conflict and was the presiding judge in my case against Pohl for indemnification; McKennna, who recused herself and stepped aside because of her friendship with the Pohl firm; and Marks, who presided in the malpractice case against me and whose husband was working in Pohl's office. And all were female judges. Coincidentally, of course!

A few minutes later after I filed my court documents, I was back in Judge Hifo's office. The chambers was completely closed. One clerk turned her head to the chambers door, making sure nothing could be seen. I greeted the staff and they returned my greeting. "Have a nice day, Ms. Dominguez."

Roy was right. Judges are human, they cannot be reclusive. They talk, they just walk to the other's room. And as Harvey said, their court calendars were sometimes empty, especially when hearings were postponed or cancelled, with more free time to socialize.

I wondered who and what they were talking about. And why it would be none of my business when a minor appearance of impropriety by attorneys could subject them to disciplinary action!

Were we held to a much higher standard than judges? It did not make sense. It was becoming my impossible profession.

Then, I remembered what Judge Hifo said, that our discussions in her chambers were not hidden—we can function better that way. I left thinking all that she could have meant.

All three were past middle age. But Judge Hifo was older and had more experience. She must be telling them my sob story in the privacy of her chambers, presiding and advising.

Finally, I had someone on the side of the law and on my side.

* * *

Dominguez vs. Pohl. We were allowed a reasonable period to go through discovery, which entailed formal exchanges of pertinent evidence between the parties.

Retired Judge Patrick Yim was assigned the discovery master. Judge Hifo had no time to rule on potential objections arising from the proceedings.

Judge Yim explained in a detailed letter that he had no conflicts, no matter how remote, in both the malpractice case of Barnedo vs. Dominguez and the indemnification case of Dominguez vs. Price Okamoto Himeno & Lum.

Nor did he or any of his relatives stand to gain or lose anything, regardless of how he would rule, and he had no strong feelings for or against anyone involved.

I knew of Judge Yim's moral values and legal skills since years ago, as a practicing attorney in his court, which the judge also disclosed.

O'Brien, Barnedos' counsel in the malpractice case, had become a main witness for Pohl. I decided to discover what he had to say. Judge Yim would preside in the oral deposition.

The day of O'Brien's deposition arrived. O'Brien came with his lawyer, Dennis Potts, a Honolulu attorney who had a small office of what appeared to be general practice.

His testimony provided me with information I thought could never happen. O'Brien described a conference he had with Warren Price and Sharon Himeno days before he sued me for malpractice. Something I was never told.

He testified that in that conference, I was called crazy, confrontational, and had a tendency to blame other people—and it happened in the Pohl office.

So hurtful!

If that was true, that means, when I had that conference with Sharon, O'Brien and Fritz in Pohl's office before my office was sued, Pohl and my opponents had been talking about me behind my back. And here I was—with Roy and Harvey reporting everything they had to say to Pohl. Tragic!

It is of no wonder that Sharon did not say a word in my defense and hardly took down notes during that conference. Everything was in her mind. How could someone do such a thing!

What chance did I ever have in the malpractice case where Judge Marks presided, while her husband worked with Warren and Sharon in Pohl's office, a place where I was ridiculed and called names moments before I was sued?

If O'Brien was truthful, I had been sold to the enemy. That was not the way I conducted my relationships ever, where the glitter of money seems to replace traditional values in life.

I decided to clear up the truth. Warren Price hardly set foot in my office. I wanted to know his basis for such remarks, especially since I was their partner in my cases years before.

Warren's attorney would find it hard to object when my questions were fully supported by O'Brien's testimony.

The deposition transcript of O'Brien on August 9, 2005, reads, verbatim:

Q. (MS. DOMINGUEZ) Did Mr. Price or Sharon Himeno tell you in that telephone conference where they were on the speaker that they did not want to go through discovery or they don't want to be involved in any discovery of some sort?

A. (MR. O'BRIEN) They did not use those words.

Q. What words did they use?

MR. POTTS: Objection, asked and answered.

MR. YIM: You may answer.

THE WITNESS: Well, one of the things that Mr. Price said was that he thought you crazy.

Q. (By Ms. Dominguez) I was crazy?

A. Yes. And they had said that you were extremely difficult to deal with and that you tended to run and try and lay things on other people.

Q. He said all of that in that conversation?

A. I believe so.

Q.. Obviously I was not there to defend me, right?

A. You were not a party to the conversation.

O'Brien's social meeting with Judge Marks was not really bothersome. It happened before the judge was appointed to the circuit bench.

The transcript of O'Brien's deposition further reads, verbatim:

Q. (Ms. Dominguez): Did you socialize with Judge Marks?

A. The only time I can ever remember what you would call socializing with Judge Marks was that I attended—when Tom Sterling, Sterling & Kleintop opened their new offices at 1100 Alakea, I was there and I ran into her there and we both had a brief conversation while we were standing with a drink in our hand. That is the only time I ever remember socializing with her.

Potts was obviously frustrated with the complete ease with which his client, O'Brien, answered my questions.

O'Brien volunteered information with unresponsive answers. Potts turned his head to his client seated beside him. I could read his mind.

You're really long winded. Stop! Stop! She is not asking for those answers or your story-telling! Tell a case, not a story of your drinking with the judge!

I wanted O'Brien to change his testimony about the drinking, as it would be unfair to the judge. His testimony might be misconstrued. The transcripts were public records.

I had to continue with my questioning, but gave him a chance to clarify. He modified his response. I was pleased. The same transcript reads, verbatim:

Q. What did you say? Did you say with a drink in your hand?

A. Yes.

Q. How about her hand?

A. I believe she had one, too, but I don't remember.

Q. And you were talking together?

A. Yes, for maybe two or three minutes.

I observed O'Brien moving closer to Potts and my questioning continued.

Q. Do you know where Judge Marks was before she became a judge?

MR. POTTS: Objection, relevance, not calculated to lead to the discovery of admissible evidence.

MS. DOMINGUEZ: Why not?

MR. YIM: You may answer.

THE WITNESS: I'm not sure. I believe at one point or another she might have worked for David Turk. That is the memory I have, but I could be wrong.

Q. (By Ms. Dominguez): Did you see her at David Turk's office before?

A. No.

O'Brien was not just a friend of Robert Marks, the spouse of the presiding judge in my malpractice suit, but a friend of the Pohl partners who may have given Judge Marks the idea that I was afraid somebody would steal my coffer!

Those were the words the judge used to describe me and my practice in open court—meaning, a Silas Marner hoarding his gold, although Harvey said she did not mean it that way.

* * *

Pohl's attorneys agreed that Warren Price and the employees would testify in oral depositions. I had to grab at the opportunity before they changed their minds.

Warren Price's testimony was held in the Carnazzo Court Reporters' office. The reporters were utilized by my office and Pohl's office. No problems. No conflicts. They were skilled and professional.

Warren came with his attorneys, McCorriston and Mansfield. I was by myself.

It was an embarrassing and a lonely moment. I was face-to-face with someone so esteemed, who had agreed to partner with me in my cases in the recent past.

Warren was sworn in to testify. I asked the court reporter that we be off the record for a while.

I thanked Warren for calling the clerk of the Supreme Court, Mr. Makekao, on my behalf, to find out the requirements for an immigrant to take the Hawaii State Bar Exams many years ago.

That was when he was the attorney for Allstate and I was an adjuster. It just took a minute of his time. I never forgot.

Next, I began the proceedings. I tried my best to camouflage my slight Filipino accent. It could be misinterpreted as emotion, even anger, when it was really meaningless.

Almost all of my questions were answered by "I don't know" or "I don't remember," obviously discussed between Warren and McCorriston, his attorney.

Warren could not even recall that his firm had a contract with me and they used my entire office and employees for two years. I was such a small fry.

Unbelievable as it seemed, that was alright. I wanted some vindication from O'Brien's testimony.

Portion of the transcript of the oral deposition of Warren Price on January 17, 2006, reads, verbatim:

Q. (Ms. Dominguez) …You did say allegedly that I am crazy. Erlinda is crazy.

A. I have no recollection of saying that.

Q. Okay. And according to O'Brien, that you said that I am very confrontational.

A. I have no recollection of saying that.

Q. And that according to Mr. O'Brien, that I, Erlinda Dominguez, tend to lay the blame on people, something like that.

A. I have no recollection of saying that.

Q. Are you capable of saying those things?

A. You ask me to speculate.

Q. Well, you know yourself, so—

A. Am I capable of saying what things about what people? I mean, you're asking me to speculate about could I say something about someone generally?

Q. Well, about me, Mr. Price. Would you be—knowing what I am, okay? Do you think you would be capable of saying that Erlinda Dominguez is crazy to somebody?

A. Be capable of saying that?

Q. Uh-huh.

A. I—I can't answer that question.

Q. I mean, not physically, not physically. But you think you—

A. You're asking me to guess. You're asking me for at some point in time what my state of mind might have articulated something in my state of mind. I'm not going to guess.

I've answered your questions. I have no recollection of telling Mr. O'Brien any of those things that you just asked me about.

Q. Do you think I'm crazy?

A. You want me to answer that question? That's an improper question.

I pursued my questioning on the point, and McCorriston instructed Warren not to answer. I realized how really angry I was at O'Brien's description of me and I was afraid it showed.

The testimony was not bad. I felt some relief with the I don't remembers of Warren.

Any admission that I was crazy would have been devastating to me and even to Pohl—for having had me for an insane partner. Or, is the entire legal profession sane and I am the only one crazy?

There were a few things that Warren recalled during the break through the mesh of his failure to recall: that in our first adversarial civil case, my client collapsed in his office when he questioned her. "We both thought she would die," he said.

And he heard that I re-married during my sabbatical.

Is this what legal life is all about? I asked myself as I watched Warren, McCorriston and Mansfield walk out the door after the deposition.

A profession that could be so glamorous and at the same time could show the ugliest facet in life, with the worst impression of many in the public. I still did not want to believe that.

Chapter Eighteen

I made repeated requests for oral depositions of Sharon Himeno and Kenneth Okamoto. As a matter of courtesy, I agreed that I would avoid the force of a subpoena.

They were either on a cruise, out of state, ill, or busy with some other schedule. They were the best witnesses as the two Pohl partners with whom I discussed my contract years before.

The testimonies of my former employees hired by Pohl could fill in some gaps as Ken and Sharon remained unavailable.

A legal assistant, Janet Souza, still worked with Pohl. So did Youme Glanry who used to supervise the clerk division and helped in the receptionist area.

Linda Huang, my paralegal, had married and was working in San Francisco. Mila Cubero, my manager, remained in Washington. Both were available for oral depositions if necessary.

Luisa Rigney, who helped organize the mail and answered telephone calls, was a Hawaii resident and always ready.

Chris Dique, another legal assistant, had passed away. Some time after she signed an affidavit for me, her work situation in Pohl's office became so miserable, she collapsed right in Pohl's office. She had spent the remainder of her life fighting for her employee benefits. I felt guilty.

The oral depositions were scheduled in the same office of the Carnazzo Court Reporters.

It was a nostalgic feeling seeing my former employees again. But I felt uncomfortable.

Janet Souza and Youme Glanry felt the same way. They were accompanied by Pohl's manager, Wendy Inouye. All were listed as witnesses by both sides.

Wendy was visibly annoyed. I imagined she thought, What do you need me for? I was never your employee, Pohl had always been my boss, not you!

She was not aware of the intricacies of the case. However, my questions were mostly procedural. I did not expect her to testify on our contract.

Wendy testified last. She did not recall basics, such as the security cabinets where she stored employees' records and her personal stuff. She was protected by her obvious lack of recollection.

There was a lot of sadness on the faces of Janet and Youme. I knew what they were thinking. Why did it have to come to this, E.D.? That was what they used to fondly call me.

They knew that it was not a game for me, that I was in agony interrogating them.

At this moment, I was not their boss or a friend, as when The Law Offices of Erlinda Dominguez worked hard to help people, especially the underdogs and victims of obvious discrimination—and they then felt very rewarded.

Now, I was investigating and confronting them, and adversarial.

A few days after her testimony, Youme gave up her job and left the Pohl firm. She called Luisa Rigney who was still working for me on a contract basis.

"There's just too much politicking," Youme said. Luisa knew what she meant.

Youme was hurt. She must have decided to leave before she would duplicate the experience of Chris and collapse at her place of work in Pohl's office then fight for her employee benefits until her death.

Another guilt for me. And I could not do anything.

* * *

I had filed my Motions for Summary Judgment. I asked Judge Hifo to decide the issues summarily, based on the evidence both sides uncovered. She could make a judgment without the need of a jury trial. The facts were clear. There was nothing for the jury to determine. The jury decides the facts, not the laws.

Pohl filed their own Motions. They wanted the judge to dismiss my case.

The hearing was on January 19, 2006. Christmas and New Year holidays had just ended.

I had the plaintiff lawyers' table to myself, closest to the jury box. I was alone. I simply used a rolling cart for my bundles of records.

There were three lawyers for Pohl: William McCorriston, Kenneth Mansfield, and Becky Chestnut. They had multiple rolling carts and huge briefcases.

They carried a large chart that was turned upside down so that I could not see its contents until their argument. The chart was a long summary of their points. They used the defense lawyers' table and laid out all their records.

The courtroom was crowded with spectators. All of them were partners, friends, and supporters of Pohl. Even O'Brien was there. They were all seated behind Pohl's lawyers to show their support. Nobody was behind me.

Warren and Sharon left their seats and moved to a bench on my side. It avoided an imbalance that showed I had no friends, that I had no supporters. But we were in court, we were not in a political convention. Who would care?

I heard muffled laughter from the audience as Warren and Sharon slowly moved from one side of the courtroom to the other. They were the only two people who were physically in my corner. But it was out of necessity. There was no space on their side.

More people were coming in. I avoided looking back. They squeezed into the benches occupied by the Pohl supporters.

Was it possible that Pohl was waging legal and psychological warfare against me?

They should know better. My first oral argument in the Ninth Circuit Appellate Court for the U.S. District Court was before three male Justices. I was alone, with one associate attorney who helped me carry the files. There was a multitude of attorneys for my opponent, as Pohl was doing now. My opponents there ran out of time with the flashing light before they could begin with the meat of their arguments. The Justices were clearly annoyed.

I won on the merits and hoped the same would happen in my indemnification case against Pohl. I was asking for no favors!

Everyone was simply waiting for Judge Hifo to appear, open the session, and begin arguments.

Finally, she entered the courtroom in her robe. Her eyes were covered with thick dark glasses, which did little to hide the fact that she was sick.

I was alarmed that she was forcing herself to preside and impart justice even though she was very ill. What happened to her? How could she read anything from the volumes of exhibits if it was pointed to and argued?

It must have been quite serious, as practicing attorneys and witnesses were not allowed to use beach glasses or sunglasses in court, for eye-to-eye contact. I sympathized with the judge, hoping that nothing was terribly wrong with her.

Judge Hifo took her seat and turned her head in the direction of Warren and Sharon seated behind me. She mildly nodded to them, acknowledging their presence.

The calendar was called. The attorneys entered their appearances. I was the only attorney for myself.

The judge began the proceedings. She immediately apologized for her dark glasses, stating that her pupils were just dilated.

I wondered why she had to do that when heavy arguments would happen that day.

An optimistic thought ran through my mind. She would rule against Pohl and could not look at them eye-to-eye when announcing her ruling. I was pleased.

McCorriston and Mansfield handled the long arguments for Pohl. Their co-counsel, Becky Chestnut, was taking notes.

It was my turn. The judge asked if I wanted to use McCorriston's extremely large chart. I did not. It was just blocking my view. It might even fall onto me. Dean, the clerk of the court, dragged it away.

I argued for myself. I had no charts, but my evidence was organized.

During my arguments, as she did when Pohl's attorneys were arguing, the judge asked a few questions. I knew she had extreme difficulty reading the exhibits.

But I was pleased that she did not say I was afraid someone would steal my coffer, the words Judge Marks used to describe my legal practice in the malpractice case.

It helped put me at ease and boosted my confidence.

When an exhibit showed that I had over a thousand claims and cases when Pohl and I were partners, the audience merely gasped. "Over a thousand cases? Oh, wow!"

I was confident. I could still hear Judge Hifo's whisper in her chambers when nobody else was around, "I believe you...I understand..."

I was sending her my thoughts, Your Honor, you could see how I argued—organized, well researched, with complete evidence, I did not disappoint you. Thanks for believing in me and my case.

The judge heard everything and was ready to decide.

She looked at everyone in the audience, but with her dark and thick glasses, it was difficult to see where her vision really was.

Then, she turned to McCorriston and immediately announced her ruling in the many technical words that judges use for the same meaning, Case Dismissed!

I shook my head in disbelief.

The judge asked McCorriston and Mansfield to prepare and file her Order.

Judge Hifo just dismissed my case against Pohl. Her affectionate words and conduct in her chambers while she fixed my collar, minutes before she disclosed her friendship with Pohl and her close ties with Roy, my previous attorney, just melted away. I was virtually speechless.

The judge stood up to leave the courtroom and addressed McCorriston and Mansfield while she was stepping away. She wanted the Order to reflect that I did not abuse court process when I filed my complaint.

What was that remark for, a piece of candy for someone who was just beaten to a pulp?

But who knows. Judge Hifo could have truly believed that her rulings were correct although I would never understand why. The higher courts must decide. I could not just drop everything with all that had happened. I had to prepare the appeal. I was thinking about all of these while the crowd started to disintegrate.

Sharon looked at me intently and half-smiled. I was reading her thoughts—Pohl always gets its heart's desire. Poor, poor Erlinda, you should know that by now. Our know-how and tons of lawyers will demolish you... Roy and Harvey had been warning you, but you did not listen! That's what you get!

McCorriston and Mansfield walked over to me as I gathered my papers. They took turns shaking my hand. "Ms. Dominguez, congratulations for your excellent arguments, but sorry!"

* * *

Days thereafter, in the middle of the day, I was driving in heavy traffic. Judge Hifo's court clerk, Dean, called. I gave him my cellular number for court emergencies.

"Ms. Dominguez, you have to proceed to your office quickly for a conference call with the judge and the attorneys of Price Okamoto Himeno & Lum."

"What's the subject, Dean?"

"To schedule the jury trial for the damages of Price Okamoto Himeno & Lum."

"What damages?"

"I don't know, Ms. Dominguez. Sorry."

I worried. I damaged Pohl because I sued them? Am I to be further punished for approaching the court? And the jury will not decide if they were damaged, but just how much?

The phone was ringing as I reached my office.

"I wish to schedule the jury trial for the damages of defendant Price Okamoto & Lum to begin this coming Monday," said Judge Hifo.

"Their damages that I caused? Like what, Judge?"

"I want a jury trial for their fees and expenses—all their damages," said the judge very softly, but very bluntly.

"But Judge, you have dismissed my case and cancelled the scheduled trial. You have not heard my motions for reconsideration," I said, worrying that she had pre-decided without looking at the documents I just filed.

"I could rule on motions summarily, but we have to proceed on Monday."

"Monday is less than a week from now. We have only the weekend to prepare and I have the flu. You know it from my voice."

Mansfield was on the other end of the line and was listening.

A male associate was whispering to him. I did not know him. I knew that Mansfield pretended to be ready for trial. Judge Hifo insisted, hesitated, then ended the conference.

The jury trial was continued to another date in the future.

"Jury trial for attorney's fees? What does the jury know about attorney's fees and legal issues?" I asked Mansfield. "Is there such a thing?"

"No, I never heard of it."

I imagined him almost laughing, knowing that I was about to repeat my experience in the malpractice case—where the jury construed legal issues including the meaning of the Hague Treaty.

"Nonetheless, Pohl can make it easier for you, Ms. Dominguez. We will agree to a motion instead of a jury trial," he said.

"Mr. Mansfield, why did the judge suddenly put back a jury trial on the calendar when she cancelled it because she had already dismissed my case?"

"We don't know."

"And with such a short notice? Why?"

We ended the conversation and I could hear soft laughter from Mansfield's line.

Now that I had lost, the escalating fees and expenses of Pohl, especially with a jury trial, would potentially drain all of my revenues and time to attend to my private practice.

It could immediately stop my legal practice unless I dropped my case against Pohl.

Pohl and the judge knew that my assets were frozen as bond in the malpractice case. I was extremely deficient in resources, almost unable to pay my researchers and the court reporters.

I filed my motion for Judge Hifo to step aside. Roy and Harvey were no longer in my life to threaten me not to do so.

In my motion, I claimed that minutes before she disclosed her social ties with Pohl and her working relationship with Roy, I was misled by her affectionate words and conduct when we were alone in her chambers.

It also bothered me that I had confided in her my description of the poor performance of Roy in defending me before her disclosure that she had actually worked for him.

I expected what would happen. Judge Hifo denied my motion for her recusal. She claimed she had made her disclosures and I agreed. She was right. I even begged her to stay.

A petition for a writ of prohibition was my remedy. I filed one with the Hawaii Supreme Court. I asked that my case be in a different court. My opponents called it forum-shopping.

My petition was denied. I expected that.

The malpractice case and the Pohl case, what a double whammy! I succeeded in making more enemies in the State of Hawaii, just as was predicted by Roy and Harvey.

I had no place to go to. A complete stranger in a strange land. Worse than when I arrived from the Philippines many years ago.

But that time, I had the American dream. This time, everything was quickly evolving into a nightmare in the American Halls of Justice.

* * *

McCorriston called me. He proposed that we personally discuss both cases: the malpractice and the indemnification.

I suggested a neutral place, outside the courtroom of Judge Hifo. We could use one of the benches.

We met. He asked that I drop my case against Pohl and not appeal. Pohl would also have no claims against me. We would both walk away from each other just like that—and still be friends.

Somewhat in jest I said, "Otherwise, our present conversation will be taxed against me. Every word you say, even your breathing is being timed, so let's just get to the point."

"Erlinda, you are just draining your monies," said McCorriston.

"I would really be crazy to drop my case. Pohl used my name: The Law Offices of Erlinda Dominguez. If I made errors as Judge Marks insisted, Pohl could have corrected them in the many years they worked in the Barnedo case. You don't agree, so it will be up to the higher courts. We can't discuss it now because we disagree on almost all points and the records show that."

McCorriston was listening. Every now and then, he would greet his attorney friends as they passed by the bench. I wondered if he was fully concentrating on our topic.

My optimism and confidence in my appeal were obvious to him.

But I said, "The malpractice case is now in the hands of the State Supreme Court. They will either affirm or reverse. If it is affirmed for whatever reason, it will be between me and Pohl."

He was nodding.

"And that is a very long way to go," I added. "That's how our system works. We can't take the law into our own hands," and I observed his facial expression.

McCorriston smiled a little and remarked, "That's true. How right you are," as if he was talking to himself.

Then, he spoke softly. "Erlinda, your memorandums in this case are better than your appellate briefs in the malpractice. And we don't know when your appeal gets decided."

Why was he describing my malpractice appeal briefs?

I wanted to talk of the multitude of fatal errors in the trial court, but focused it on one that was so obviously strange, even McCorriston would have to agree.

"Judge Marks' jury construed the Hague Treaty law, something only the courts should do. Anyone who reads the verdict form will immediately know the blunder. I don't even think the appellate court would have to review the transcripts! You must agree, the verdict questions do not lead to what we call cause of action against the defendant."

"Well, things are so unpredictable. Your malpractice appeal could stop with the clerks of the appellate court. You never know."

I was stunned. I knew he meant the staff attorneys of the courts. They were known to do the research for the justices and draft the decisions.

"Did I hear you right? You mean, the Supreme Court Justices will not read my appeal briefs? Roy and Harvey said the errors of the trial court were so obvious, even if my briefs are turned upside down. Someone must hear me out, that's my constitutional right!"

"Well, of course, the justices read and they decide, but they have a huge case load, you know. The clerks have a big say, they are the justices' right hand."

"That's what the newspapers say, a heavy load. But if the clerks draft decisions for the justices to sign, the clerks may target typo errors, any kind of mistake even as to form. And I don't even know their names. I have a lot of legal enemies now."

"Oh, no, that's not what I mean. The justices read."

"I don't know what you mean, Bill...may I call you Bill? I can't be fair to anyone if I'm not fair to myself. I will lose all my self-respect if I do nothing. I'm sorry."

"Well, if you change your mind, just call me."

We cordially parted. I glanced at him while he walked back to his office, still greeting other attorneys who were walking in and out of the courthouse. He had many friends.

His office was just across the street from the courthouse. Then, he disappeared from my view.

What McCorriston said bothered me. Why would he be mentioning the court clerks and my malpractice appeal in the same breath? He was always in the news, yet, he found time to personally meet and socialize with me.

Whenever I called the court staff attorneys' office, the recording warned the caller not to discuss cases. Then, a staff attorney would help on matters of form.

Could some powerful law firm know what happens ahead of time? And if they could, do they get into the clerks' minds? Do they socialize? Do they laugh at their own jokes?

I didn't even know what an office of a Supreme Court Justice looked like, except when Justice Menor administered my lawyer's oath many years ago. I passed the Hawaii Bar Exams before my credentials arrived from the Philippines.

I have read the rules on professional conduct and lawyers' ethics. What I thought McCorriston implied doesn't happen.

But Roy's descriptions were still in my mind: People... Friends... Humans.

Then, I remembered how my opponents described me: an uncivilized, sub-standard attorney attacking at least two sitting Judges, previous U.S. Attorney and Attorney Generals.

They made sure to put that in writing for the courts, their clerks, and their staff attorneys to see.

And I did not know any of them.

My meeting with McCorriston made me worry. I tried to make sense of our conversation. I knew he did not intend to mention the clerks of the court, but he did.

The State Supreme Court's decision in my malpractice case was ready and I would lose, that was my feeling. And McCorriston knew it and I did not.

If he did, and how it was leaked to him, I may never know. Strangely, still without the appellate decision, I began to contact my researchers.

I asked them to research the procedure for a Petition for *Writ of Certiorari* with the United States Supreme Court. That was the last legal step I could do.

From what was called a senseless malpractice case, I was now potentially going to the United States Supreme Court in Washington, DC, the highest and final court of the nation.

My researchers were unknowledgeable. They had no previous experience on the topic.

Nationwide, attorneys hardly ever filed in the U.S. Supreme Court. Especially a solo practitioner representing herself in a civil case of malpractice. It probably never happened.

In a matter of weeks, the Hawaii Supreme Court staff left a message on my voice mail.

"This is a courtesy call, Ms. Dominguez. The decision of the trial court against you in your malpractice case was totally affirmed by the State Supreme Court. Your copy of the Summary Disposition Order is in your court jacket."

I lost in my malpractice appeal! It was summarily disposed. It did not even deserve a full appellate review on the merits. Everything seemed to be as a matter of form. And litigants like me cannot do anything to disagree with how they are portrayed by the appeal courts in their "internet" decisions, or to disagree with the laws and facts stated in their decision, right or wrong.

My conference with McCorriston was my prediction. It prepared me, and the decision did not come as a total surprise. I thought the news preceded his comments and he knew it all along.

Days thereafter, I dropped by the documents section of the Supreme Court.

My face had become familiar to Evelyn, Kathleen, Norma, and Eugene of that office.

They could not believe that I was now guilty of malpractice. I, who had such a high volume of cases, not once disciplined by the Board, contributed so much monetarily to the local community and to my native country, the Philippines!

I re-read the decision. The Summary Disposition Order was unanimous, signed by all five Justices.

The numerous rulings of Judge Marks that Roy and Harvey called basic and plain errors for her almost 1.5 million dollar judgment did not merit the appellate court's time to review.

The description by Harvey that the trial was absurd became meaningless. As if I did not appeal at all, and even worse!

Somehow, Google seemed to have created a website for me. My opponents' description of my arguments as uncivil to them, and the incompetence of my office—they were all there.

I never figured out what the relevance was. The appellate court did not touch on what I claimed to be the decay or the evil existing in the dockets of the federal court—the alien versus alien void case, to which my opponents had no defense. But their decision quoted a miniscule portion of my short conclusion in my fifty-paged appeal brief, in bold print:

There is evil that lurks underneath Appellees' claims. Covered with false grandeur, Appellees' case has no roots—It revealed its true insides when it spouted more venom. Appellees' case is inherently vicious but without life. A dead weight. Appellees' case molded its role in legal history—fictitious and tyrannical, hollow but oppressive.

Substance gave way to form, I concluded. Very quickly, I made my previous clients millionaires by order of the appellate court!

I signed the appellate brief, nobody else did. Everything was my responsibility, just as I absorbed any sins of my former associate attorneys. And as I had seen worse briefs, truly uncivil, my briefs did not even come close.

The evil I mentioned, which was the ultimate betrayal of the U.S. Constitution, was once more in the eye of the beholder.

But through all the preparation and signing, I failed to see that the Hawaii State Supreme Court had absolute and total power, the full discretion to read or not to read, to review or not to review an appeal. And the final say rested with them in the State level.

Total supremacy and total judicial discretion! I missed it all, and more!

That was part of McCorriston's message. I was just too slow to grasp it. And I wondered how connected Roy's many cautionary words were to me in the past...human, feelings, and so on.

But I also remembered how lawyers used vicious words, judges and practicing attorneys used metaphors and sometimes, distasteful remarks—especially in their offices.

They were not called uncivil. They were not called unethical. That professionalism was part of our legal practice. Highly adversarial and highly intense. And Roy and Harvey were no exception—even if they struggled to be overwhelmingly respectful in the courtroom. If the judges only knew all they had said!

Surely, the Supreme Court meant what they said in their decision—the errors were not pointed to in the records. The alien versus alien, my ultimate defense, was nowhere in the trial records of Roy and Harvey.

But what happened to the Constitution? I had to know.

The highest State court did not decide the most jurisdictional issue. I had to file a motion for reconsideration.

I asked the State Supreme Court to reconsider its appeal decision against me. In my motion, I ended up apologizing for my unintended uncivility to my opponents although I felt my words were just strong and adversarial, with no personal offense intended. Any uncivility of my briefs was not part of the issues in my case.

And attorneys, like O'Brien, bound by the strict rules of ethics and professional conduct, and the oath of allegiance to the flag, should never earn their millions by covering the raw evil of the violation of the U.S. Constitution! An unethical and illegal ultimate betrayal of the United States!

My motion was extremely short and clear. In diversity, aliens cannot sue another alien. A mandatory requirement of the Constitution, the ultimate law of the United States.

The unrefuted trial testimonies that all the parties were aliens were clearly in the records. My motion referred to them. I asked that the court decide, and not look the other way—even if Roy and Harvey refused to bring up this ultimate defense.

My hope was for Justice James Duffy to pen the decision. He was well versed on the issue of federal court subject matter jurisdiction as was proven by the book he authored. The jurisdiction cannot be compromised, cannot be waived, cannot be agreed to, cannot be ignored.

Again, the State Supreme Court quickly and summarily denied my motion. The Order did not say why. The Order was signed by Justice Duffy.

The U.S. Constitution was sacrificed because my brief was invective—that was merely my conclusion. But I found it impossible to equate this sin with a fraud upon the supreme law of the land, a betrayal from the roots of the case.

Was I just too idealistic, or was I really paranoid as even Roy and Harvey used to say! I could not force myself to believe that.

If my appeal argument was reviewed, the potential malpractice of my trial attorneys for their refusal to bring up the decay in the subject matter jurisdiction of the federal court where my opponents say the malpractice errors happened may have become so glaring and more pronounced.

I imagined Roy and Harvey, my previous defense attorneys, celebrating my extreme loss, even throwing a party in their office. The two people I paid and trusted were still drunk with success in their legal practice.

Where would I get the money to pay for some million and a half cash judgment? I did not have a fraction of the resources of O.J. Simpson, Michael Jackson, Donald Trump, or a huge corporation.

I was just a solo practitioner in the legal profession, who was unfortunately somewhat successful in Hawaii and who was called crazy, confrontational and a slave driver because I wanted everyone to excel with their knowledge of the law, instead of fortuitous events of sheer luck or power, or politics.

There was only one higher court remaining outside of the State of Hawaii: The United States Supreme Court.

My issues were not like those of the Al Gore and George Bush case. But I had to try or would blame myself, another guilt I should not have.

Chapter Nineteen

"**D**o you know how much chance you have for the U.S. Supreme Court to even look at your petition and grant you a review?" asked Connie Chun while we had lunch.

"One percent?"

"Less than zero."

Connie was the lawyer in the medical clinic owned by her husband in Honolulu. She used to be a State Representative.

"Before all your respect for me disappears, let me tell you again how grateful I am for your lending me your law books when I reviewed for the Hawaii Bar Exams," I said.

"Well, you made it as soon as the Supreme Court allowed immigrants to take the Bar Exams! Dean Jeremy Harris of the University of Hawaii was so proud of you when we visited your large office at the Commerce Tower, remember?"

Connie was consoling.

"Erlinda, you tend to be idealistic and strictly legal. You are in the world of reality, of legal life. Stop being naive."

"And what is the world of reality?"

"Just like in other walks of life, it takes all kinds in the law profession. Not all successful lawyers are competent or moral, and not all poor lawyers are dumb or immoral."

"But all lawyers have the moral vow to keep."

"That's literal and true, I cannot disagree with that."

"I admire your courage talking that way. Everyone should have forgiven my origin and gender. I had no say about that. And I hope you are not implying arrogance of racial superiority."

"There must be a reason, a purpose why things happened to you the way they did," she said.

I heard that said before by Harvey when things did not make sense to him. But as far as I knew, Harvey was not political and Connie had always been.

"Connie, it's not so much that I will end up a derelict on the street. It is my name and reputation."

"They can say anything. The truth is what matters."

"Thanks, you are a friend."

Connie deviated from the topic. She asked how my mother was. She saw her at the Hawaii Filipino functions receiving my awards.

"Mamang collapsed when she heard of the verdict, then died in three days. She never knew that the judge multiplied the amount of the jury verdict and ordered dozens of garnishee summons and subpoenas circulated throughout the whole State."

"See, Erlinda, that's one of God's blessings—that your mom never got to know that part. She would have been devastated."

"Connie, the jurors never intended to make the Barnedos millionaires and me a derelict."

"How long did they deliberate?"

"Four days."

"Then, I'm sure they did not act on hate as your previous attorneys had said. They probably thought you had a huge insurance policy, and they had to decide through their turmoil interpreting the Hague Treaty. Under time constraints, they did not wish to waste a mistrial," she said.

"They wanted to do the right thing, but unfortunately, it did not turn out that way." I am convinced I did not have a competent and quality trial—what we were taught in law school. Strangely, my previous attorneys, Roy and Harvey, always agreed.

"You're right, Erlinda, the jurors did their best or they would not have struggled for a verdict in several days."

"I never blamed the jury. Jurors follow court instructions even if they are wrong. I also never blamed the Barnedos. They were a very nice couple. They did not know what was happening. They must now really believe that my office made mistakes—even if they had no case. I never betrayed them, never betrayed a single client."

"What a tragic mockery of justice. If the jurors only knew what happened to you!"

"No, they don't know. Their participation ended when they filed their verdict."

"I feel so bad about your trial and that your appeal was not given due consideration," she added.

"Thanks. You were in my life when I began my legal practice and you are in my life now that I may have to end my practice."

Then, Connie looked at me intently. "I am not optimistic because of statistics, but I suggest you contact Professor Van Dyke of the University of Hawaii. He teaches constitutional law. I'll set up the appointment for you."

In a few days, I contacted Professor Van Dyke. He thought the case sounded very familiar. But he said, "Ms. Dominguez, you may be throwing away your money. Even if your case is very meritorious on the point of Alien versus Alien subject matter jurisdiction, the U.S. Supreme Court reviews a miniscule percentage of thousands of cases filed with them."

I contacted Connie.

"Knowing you, Erlinda, you will feel guilty if you don't take the last step. Perhaps, you just have to file with the U.S. Supreme Court. Be resigned that they will reject a review."

* * *

My friends advised me to stop fighting. They all said, "There's no way out."

But if I did nothing more, all the truth I knew would be meaningless. I had to keep trying. Someone would listen.

"Erlinda, I can't get involved in your personal cases. I know Mr. Price, I know Pohl. I can't go against them," Hawaii attorneys would say. Others, even those who socialized with me, never returned my calls.

All that was needed for my appearance as an attorney in the U.S. Supreme Court was an endorsement by two attorneys licensed to practice in that court.

Mr. Ron Oldenburg had always hung his certificate in his office for prestige even if he did not appear in the courts. He was proud to tell people that for a short time in the past, he was my boss and I was his subordinate.

"That's great," he said. "I have not seen you for years. Let me treat you to lunch. We'll meet in a nice restaurant. I'll bring two other attorneys. I'm sure they know you."

Days passed. He did not call and did not return my calls. Another small fry in the community.

There was no further need to waste my time. I decided to handle everything myself *Pro Se*, with my researchers.

Cockle Printing of Omaha, Nebraska, rushed to print and file my petition for a *Writ of Certiorari* with the United States Supreme Court.

Its staff members were extremely knowledgeable and thorough in legal briefs. They worked long hours and there was a personal touch to their professional services for all their clients. They must have spent some of their Christmas Eve in their office for my brief.

Cockle Printing filed my petition on time, December 26, 2006. It was seventeen short book pages. The issues were limited to the most basic topics. The U.S. Supreme Court had better things to do than read bulky briefs.

My petition was titled "On Petition For A Writ Of Certiorari To The Supreme Court Of The State Of Hawaii." I was technically going against the State Supreme Court, the highest Court for Hawaii. But I had no option.

At the very least, I had a message: Anyone could be instant millionaires by violating the United States Constitution with no U.S. citizenship in diversity cases and with uncontested affidavits in court, so long as their malpractice case is not dismissed.

There were no surprises. In weeks, a review was denied. Not because my petition was meritless. It just did not fall in the miniscule percentage of five percent or less for the valuable time of the United States Supreme Court. Just as Connie said. Just as Professor Van Dyke said.

Simply statistical.

My case against Pohl for indemnification of the malpractice judgment was pending. But meantime, I had to pay the malpractice judgment. I refinanced and sold my properties.

My small real estate holdings were walking distance to the most popular beach in the world, Waikiki. My opponents could not wait.

The manager of the First Hawaiian Bank, Chris Yamada, and his staff spent hours assisting me. I was beyond grateful.

The bank must have remembered the million dollars accidentally deposited into my account that I promptly returned.

Then, one afternoon, Manager Yamada called me on my cell. He was very concerned. All their efforts reached a stumbling block.

"Your loan transactions could not go through, Erlinda. Price Okamoto Himeno & Lum recorded their fees against you and it affects your real estate. Your opponents are executing on your assets. They subpoenaed our bank. How can we legally help you?"

I sought urgent meetings with my opponents and Judge Chang who replaced Judge Marks in my malpractice case. He reluctantly agreed to a few days extension, but not without words to describe me- that I was almost disingenuous for seeking refuge with the U.S. Supreme Court.

Well, he was the judge and I was just a litigant losing all that I had including my career, my property, my dignity, for something wrong I never did.

My thoughts were immediate, although I could have been paranoid as my opponents and previous attorneys described me.

How cruel could Pohl be? Even with all that I had gone through with Judge Marks who was married to a powerful attorney in their firm and rendered the million plus judgement, that wasn't enough for them. I was pursuing the rights of any citizen or human being in the United States.

They seemed to have one clear message: Nobody should mess around with us. We will mince-meat you if you do. Erlinda, you never listened to your attorneys. That's what you get for stepping on our toes.

I reflected back to years ago. I did not approach Pohl. They approached me for business, for profits, for more money over and above their lots of monies on this planet. They intruded into my zoo-like office, where my employees worked hard and made my clients content, happy, and welcome, where I practiced my law profession with honesty and dignity.

The Law Offices of Erlinda Dominguez disappeared. Pohl got their hearts' desires, familiar words I heard from various sources before my tragedy.

* * *

Mansfield, one of Pohl's attorneys, met me in the courthouse. He was eager to get paid for Pohl's fees and costs that Judge Hifo approved without a trial, without invoices, without explanations. And he claimed he should be paid his time talking to my previous attorneys, Roy and Harvey. He got what he wanted to the penny!

I handed him what Pohl desired: a crisp cashier's check for one hundred fifteen thousand dollars that the First Hawaiian Bank quickly and graciously extended to me to keep me afloat.

Mansfield hesitated to put the check in his folder. "What's wrong?" I asked. "Pohl must remove the recordation over my properties at the bureau right away. That check is immediately negotiable. Tell Pohl I did not learn my lesson. That should make them very happy through their lifetime, no matter how long that may be."

Mansfield was in deep thought. He seemed almost unsure of what to do with the check in his hand.

"Ms. Dominguez, Pohl wants to make certain that the signatures on the check are genuine. It will take some time."

I looked at him in total panic and desperation. He could be extremely insulting.

"They're now working with all my opponents to make me perish? If so, they must be a very cruel group, with all due respect to any past Attorney Generals and U.S. Attorneys comprising their firm. I'll drive you over to the bank. Please!"

"Thank you, but there's no need for that. I'll meet with Mr. Price, Sharon, and Ken. I'll expedite this with their permission. It's their call, not mine. I'll go to them now."

Mansfield began to walk away. Then, he immediately turned back. He spoke so slowly and calmly.

"Ms. Dominguez, you and Pohl had the aloha relationship before. Zurick Insurance Company pays all our fees and expenses. I'll suggest to Pohl that you drop your claims against each other so that everyone can move on with their lives."

"Life? What kind of life will that leave me, Mr. Mansfield? Just what kind of life?"

My mind flashed back to my malpractice trial.

Judge Victoria Marks made the rulings, rendered the million plus judgment without evidence of my opponents, garnished against me throughout Honolulu without my notice immediately after the conference between McCorriston and Pohl. Judge Marks was married to a silent partner of Pohl who despised me as crazy—according to O'Brien. She would walk over to Pohl's office to visit her husband, as I discovered when the employees testified in depositions. More importantly, the verdict killed my mother.

And I just handed a check to Mansfield—because I sued Pohl. I felt I was melting with all those flashbacks.

I stared at him and said, "To be honest with you, Mr. Mansfield, I could grant Price Okamoto Himeno & Lum their wish to drop my case—if the verdict did not kill my mother!"

"Ms. Dominguez, let's just move on, don't dwell."

"I'm having difficulties finding all the morality in what had happened. Is everything such a coincidence and I am just crazy and paranoid, like my opponents said? Is my perception of facts so wrong when they are happening in front of me?"

Mansfield almost seemed to sympathize. I knew it was merely for appearances. "I'm sorry, Ms. Dominguez, that you feel that way."

I knew what he wanted to say, but he was professional enough. He did not say it: "You are really out of reality, go to a dozen psychiatrists!"

But if he said that, I would say: "Go to hell and I'll meet all of you there!"

As I watched him disappear, I was thinking, There is more to money, power, and the profession. I may not have friends all over, and you may never agree with my standard of what is moral, right and decent. Perhaps, the climate will change and someone will listen, or at least, know! Don't cry for me because I actually pity you, Mr. Mansfield.

* * *

I began liquidating my law practice. I would miss my clients who remained true and faithful. But I chose to register myself with the Hawaii State Bar as voluntarily inactive since the year 2008.

My desks, chairs, and hundreds of legal books were given to lawyer friends.

They decided to continue with their American dream in very beautiful Hawaii!

Attorney friends from Manila knew that I was leaving. A small group scheduled a weekend trip to see me in Honolulu in the early part of March, 2008. All male. Female attorneys were still a minority.

I met them at the airport.

They were excited and the famous Manila attorney Pete Quadra exclaimed, "This is such a beautiful place, the sun is out and the skies are clear—there is only one season through the year!"

"You're right. One stagnant season through the year in Hawaii. And for decades, the season has been the same. I hope for a change in season. There must be a season for everything," I exclaimed, happy to see them.

They must have thought I was a bit crazy with all that I was mumbling—after the many years that they had not seen me.

We compared notes on the Philippine and the United States judicial systems. We realized that people everywhere tend to believe that an American jury is always right.

"Let me clarify that," I said. "Jurors generally want to do the right thing. If the laws, the verdict form, or the court instructions provided to them are wrong, confusing, or cannot be understood, severe injustice could happen."

"But that's the role of attorneys to guide and discuss their legal research with the judge. And in your case, the questions in the verdict form were not leading to a cause of action—why you were sued to begin with," they added.

"That's true, but it's the judges who make rulings, and we can't read minds, and it's difficult to read feelings either. As Roy said, we are not prophets. We could all be spinning our wheels and ruining lives, even in American justice."

"We heard that your judges have absolute immunity, they can rule any which way they want, in their judicial discretion, and cannot be sued."

"That's also what I know, otherwise, they would be disrupted in their roles of deciding people's lives. Unless it is a criminal offense, and who would think of suing a judge criminally? Besides, what they do is not criminal."

"Wow, your court system is better than a Las Vegas casino! It certainly breeds ugly connivance in the legal profession. Your U.S. Constitution is dead."

"Our Constitution is alive. We have to adhere to court decisions and go through any legal steps remaining. You can't take matters into your own hands. That's the hope in America," I exclaimed defensively.

"We would have preferred a death penalty," they added. "At least, there is hope that the fatal injection is recalled at the last minute when the DNA proves our innocence."

"Let's not be graphic, it's depressing."

Then, they said in astonishing seriousness: "Perhaps, not in our lifetime, cases will be tried by computers and robots. This will start in America, the world leader. Feelings of hate, love, contempt, respect, and judicial or legal skills will not be present. Just the facts and the laws determined by machines. Nobody will have to fear or adore the words, friends and humans—the favorite words of your attorneys."

Trial by computers? By Robots? I looked at my friends and said, "You are scary, but you may be right, very right indeed! Let's all look forward to the realization of that hope. What a dream that we, moral humans, can cling to!"

My Manila friends described how the Philippine judicial system had evolved through the recent years. As usual, judicial proceedings are in English. But still no jury. Just bench trials.

Their jurisprudence had been patterned after the United States. It was a system that developed while the Philippines was under America's control.

They had not forgotten General Douglas McArthur fighting side-by-side with them in the second world war. He was still their hero.

Then, they continued to talk. "It took us one minute to read the jury verdict questions in your trial. They were obviously legal questions and for the courts to decide. Imagine lay people interpreting the Hague Treaty? And the issues or questions about your alleged malpractice were not even identified. Are we missing something here?"

"No. I don't think you are."

"But the jury construed the law in your case and they are not even lawyers," they said. "Your Constitution does not allow that!"

"What hurts the most is that the Hague Treaty should not have been involved even if the judge insisted. Japan recognizes foreign judgments according to their laws without the Hague-Hague-Hague!" I explained in total frustration—I felt cheated.

"Your attorneys were not good to you, Erlinda. They did not even present your legal expert from Japan even though you already paid him."

" In the blink of an eye, your life could be at the mercy of others dangling a rope for your salvation, that's true."

"So, Erlinda, what do you think is the better and greater judicial system, the Philippines or the United States?"

It was an unfair question. My experiences were not ordinary. And my conclusions and feelings were just that. Besides, Hawaii is such a small portion of America. And no particular group is the owner of Hawaii.

I gave their question some thought, and then sadly responded, "I honestly don't know. You saw the transcripts; still, I don't want to be misquoted. I must introduce you to Roy and Harvey. They handled my defense. I'm sure there were things they knew that I was never told. You may be luckier finding this out from them."

"No, thank you. We don't want to meet them. They should be malpracticed, not you. Other people in your situation would take matters in their hands and that is so un-American!"

Then, I said, "I could be wrong, but people here in Hawaii are afraid to talk, especially in the legal profession. It's subtle but very deep. It is suffocating to the freedom of speech."

"If that's true, we would not call that happily living with freedom, but dismally existing with fear in Paradise. And America is the leader of freedom, it is indeed too sad."

And with a naughty smile, they said, "We can duplicate what happened to you and be instant millionaires. We could visit you more often. There are many Philippine companies in Manila, and we know people here who could start the suit. It would only take one Philippine company to countersue in Manila, that could result in tons of money judgment against a Hawaii lawyer."

"My experience is not typical. I hope it will never happen to anyone else."

They were kidding around, and I was pleased they were enjoying most of their short stay.

"You said that the judge in your indemnification case against the Price people, who call themselves Pohl, dismissed your case summarily without a trial, what was her basis?" Pete asked.

"The judge accepted the short unsigned and unsealed paper that suddenly surfaced. It looked like someone printed it from the computer in a rush for the hearing. Mr. Price's lawyers called it the Japan judgment. The paper said the Japan product was not defective and had a sales pitch. Judge Hifo, that's her name, concluded that therefore, the Price people are not liable to me."

"Erlinda, how could your courts leap to such a conclusion? An unsigned, unsealed piece of paper that quickly appeared from an unknown source, decided your huge contract with Mr. Price and his firm, and you were not even parties, nor knew of that? They made a case from straw."

Pete looked like he just heard something from fiction. He shook his head and added, "Wait till my friends find out about your case. It would certainly change our perception of American Justice and American Courts. In my modest opinion, you had no Day in Court, you had absolutely no due process. You are the victim of a word too ugly to mention! "

"Erlinda, it seems you are narrating a made-up legal nightmare. I never saw that happen in the Philippine courts and Philippines is quickly progressing. We thought we are following America's footseps. Do the Price people think you are dumb? We are repulsed and angry at the kind of justice you received and wish it is not racial," Pete continued.

"That's your prerogative to say, and it is your freedom of speech. You have no fears. You don't live here. But let's shift to a more pleasant topic instead of hurting everyone with my story."

"It's difficult to shift topics. Look at the beautiful ocean and it could be so treacherous as what happened to that girl in 2003 who lost her right arm to the sharks," they said.

"You mean Bethany Hamilton. And she never complained and was back surfing in one month, and my accuser testified under oath that even after almost fifteen years, she had ongoing pain in her entire arm and upper torso for mutilated fingers!"

"You should write a book to make something positive out of your experience," they said. "It's like knowing what actually happens in and out of a secluded monastery, interesting, and certainly a matter of public interest. You will speak for those who are afraid to talk, and only the truth."

"A book? I may be called a liar or a fool just like what my previous attorneys said. And I'm sure that the people who know what I went through would deny me. I don't blame them. They have families to feed."

"That's too bad if they are living in fear of power. There is no freedom that America is fighting for. But you have a duty to yourself and to others to write of your experience. The readers will be your jury. Your experience should not be ignored and forgotten. And a book has no funny accent."

Their last remark made them smile.

"What has accent got to do with anything?"

They again began to laugh—really, really hard.

"What we mean is, don't show that you are an Igorot, a head-hunter from the Cordillera Mountains of the Philippines."

Their jesting did not bother me. Their bottles of beer and wine did the talking. And their remark about the Igorot was a pleasant compliment in disguise.

I had to change the topic. We talked of the exotic culture of Hawaii, the beautiful beaches, the exciting volcanoes, the colorful rainbows, the many people of all races.

We didn't know what they were thinking. But they were there, with leis around their necks, frolicking under the sun. They came from all over the world to enjoy paradise. They did not know the prolems in paradise!

In three days, my friends said goodbye.

"As Evangelist Joel Osteen said, bloom where you are planted, and do the best you can there. The Philippines is not really far behind and could be much greater." Those were my parting words to them.

I looked up while their plane took off. The sun was out and the skies were clear.

One stagnant season after another—in beautiful Hawaii.

My Manila friends still called and I kept away from talking of my case.

"Erlinda, we think that you're now also afraid to talk, it's inhumane. That's what the problems caused you, and you are there in America. It's ironic!"

I preferred to say something of the beautiful Philippines. People are generally so poor there, but they are happy.

I waited for the appeal decision in my case against Pohl. I did not seek recusal or disqualification of any of the appeal judges or justices involved. I would get nowhere. Several of them voluntarily stepped aside, an admirable gesture.

The decision of the Hawaii Intermediate Court of Appeals arrived. It re-affirmed Judge Hifo's judgment in favor of Pohl without the need of a trial. The remaining Justices of the Hawaii Supreme Court refused a review. I did not expect they would.

Again, I was going to the United States Supreme Court even if my hopes were statistically close to zero. I was prepared for a strong dissent and contrary facts by Pohl's multitude of high-powered attorneys, their freedom of speech.

I would tell the Highest Court of this Nation how the Hawaii State Courts have disregarded the true issues, distorted the facts, violated fundamental U.S. laws, in favor of Pohl in Hawaii.

While preparing my petition, I came across a recent decision of the U.S. Supreme Court in regard to the Hawaiian ceded lands from the monarchy era. In its ultimate decision for the entire United States, this Highest Court said something I always knew but wanted to hear again- Courts have no judicial license to do what they want to do!

I felt some vindication. I was not wasting my time. I was not the Hawaii monarchy, but United States is my home. My Constitutional rights are as sovereign or more. After all is said and done, I was not crazy as my opponents described me.

I was not alone in Island Scandals, familiar words from the media. And one could say- just the isolated rambling or assessment of Erlinda Dominguez, a very small fry, a nobody!

Chapter Twenty

Shortly after my relocation in California, I watched the political conventions on TV. The speakers talked of lipstick on a pig, and it was bad, gross, rude or good, even funny, depending on who was talking. Yet, it could cost the candidates defining votes. The same thing may have happened to me. I was called uncivilized and invective instead of assertive; crazy and paranoid instead of a crusader for the rule of law. Indeed, everything could be subjective when it should not be.

Again, I remembered how Roy and Harvey used the words human, hate, feelings, friends, conduct, subjectivity and so on...

But there was something so morally uplifting. A Black man and a White man were opponents for the office of the President of the United States of America!

They were speaking to huge crowds of people. All races and colors. No one would know who was mighty and who was not, who was wealthy and who was poor. Everyone was equal at that moment. A single entity united, clamoring for change, change, change! Barack Obama's words were moving and powerful:

"This is our moment. The moment for change. America, we cannot turn back even if the path is uncertain. There is a better place around the bend...an American greatness that makes immigrants cross the oceans to join us regardless of color or creed...

You do not have to accept what you can't bear...*change, change, change!"*

The crowds were cheering. A few were in tears. Whites, Blacks, Browns—all colors were together. They were united.

People clamored for change, and the candidates repeated what leaders have said throughout the ages: the change begins with the individual—perhaps from atop the primitive mountains of a third world, who knows, then into a small crowd, a town, a city, a state, a nation, maybe the whole world!

I reflected on the words passionately spoken in the conventions. Nobody should accept the unbearable...and there is that American greatness that makes immigrants cross the ocean to join us.

The purpose of the malpractice case against me, the word used by Harvey, was not scientific. It is this manuscript that I started some months ago after I left Hawaii.

This book ends as a black gentleman whose roots are in Kenya, Africa, is now the President of the United States, the highest position in the whole world!

Barack Obama, our President, was born in the State of Hawaii, the 50th State of the United States, where all the events in this book happened. A fateful, inspiring, and hopeful coincidence!

Aloha, Mr. Obama. Your moment is everybody's moment. The U.S. Constitution belongs to all of us. Nobody can ever forget beautiful Hawaii!

For many a flower is born to blush unseen
And wastes its sweetness on the desert air.

—Poet, Thomas Gray, 1751

For many an evil lurks unseen
And emits its odor in the humid air.

To extract whatever truth comes from an
ugly story is beautiful, and in all those
things to think about.

—E.D., the author, 2010

Finally—whatever is true, whatever is
honorable, whatever is just, whatever is
pure, whatever is lovely, whatever is
gracious, if there is any excellence and
if there is anything worthy of praise,
think about these things.

—Philippians 4:8

To all who would be in Court for a serious problem:

- Your "awareness" is necessary;
- Your "gut feelings" should not be ignored;
- Don't be paranoid, shy, or over-trusting;
- You may need a second and "objective" opinion;
- Seek the law, not power. Power is fleeting. Truth is constant.
- Move forward legally and morally. The past is a lesson and the future is a promise. The present needs your commitment to your case. Nobody else would care as much.

—The author